THE EVERYTHING® FOUNDING FATHERS BOOK

Dear Reader,

We live in times when the phrase "Founding Fathers" is invoked almost daily. The Founding Fathers were great men who operated in a distant past but we often make the mistake of thinking about them as if they were a homogeneous collection of personalities who all thought alike and may as well be interchangeable. Nothing could be further from the truth.

They were an interesting collection of men; some of them ambitious politicians, some of them thoughtful statesmen. Some of them were philanderers, some of them were happily married, some of them eschewed the common man, and many of them were common men. They indulged in petty argument and published slanderous things about each other, but in the end—when it mattered—they guided the nation to its sovereignty. They were brave enough to stand up to British authority and military might, and they were daring enough to put aside their differences to create the government embodied in the Constitution of the United States.

We have assembled a collection of some of the more famous Founding Fathers and we hope you enjoy getting to know them.

Meg Greene, MA, MS and

Paula M. Stathakis, PhD

Welcome to the EVERYTHING® Series!

These handy, accessible books give you all you need to tackle a difficult project, gain a new hobby, comprehend a fascinating topic, prepare for an exam, or even brush up on something you learned back in school but have since forgotten.

You can choose to read an *Everything*® book from cover to cover or just pick out the information you want from our four useful boxes: e-questions, e-facts, e-quotes, and e-ssentials.

We give you everything you need to know on the subject, but throw in a lot of fun stuff along the way, too.

We now have more than 400 *Everything*® books in print, spanning such wide-ranging categories as weddings, pregnancy, cooking, music instruction, foreign language, crafts, pets, New Age, and so much more. When you're done reading them all, you can finally say you know *Everything*®!

QUESTION

Answers to common questions

FACT

Important snippets of information

QUOTE

Words of wisdom from experts in the field

ESSENTIAL

Quick handy tips

PUBLISHER Karen Cooper

DIRECTOR OF ACQUISITIONS AND INNOVATION Paula Munier

MANAGING EDITOR, EVERYTHING® SERIES Lisa Laing

COPY CHIEF Casey Ebert

ASSISTANT PRODUCTION EDITOR Jacob Erickson

ACQUISITIONS EDITOR Hillary Thompson

SENIOR DEVELOPMENT EDITOR Brett Palana-Shanahan

EDITORIAL ASSISTANT Ross Weisman

EVERYTHING® SERIES COVER DESIGNER Erin Alexander

LAYOUT DESIGNERS Colleen Cunningham, Elisabeth Lariviere, Ashley Vierra, Denise Wallace

THE EVERYTHING® FOUNDING FATHERS BOOK

All you need to know about the men who shaped America

Meg Greene, MA, MS and Paula M. Stathakis, PhD

Avon, Massachusetts

An Everything® Series Book.

Published by Adams Media, a division of F+W Media, Inc.
57 Littlefield Street, Avon, MA 02322 U.S.A.
www.adamsmedia.com

ISBN 10: 1-4405-2586-2
ISBN 13: 978-1-4405-2586-5
eISBN 10: 1-4405-2662-1
eISBN 13: 978-1-4405-2662-6

Printed in the United States of America.

10 9 8 7 6 5 4 3 2 1

Library of Congress Cataloging-in-Publication Data
Greene, Meg.
The everything Founding Fathers book / Meg Greene and Paula M. Stathakis.
p. cm. — (Everything)
Includes index.
ISBN-13: 978-1-4405-2586-5
ISBN-10: 1-4405-2586-2
ISBN-13: 978-1-4405-2662-6 (e)
ISBN-10: 1-4405-2662-1 (e)
1. Founding Fathers of the United States—Biography. 2. United States. Constitution—Signers—Biography. 3. United States—History—Revolution, 1775–1783. 4. United States—History—Confederation, 1783–1789. 5. United States—History—Constitutional period, 1789–1809. 6. United States—Politics and government—1775–1783. 7. United States—Politics and government—1783–1809. 8. Constitutional history—United States. I. Stathakis, Paula M. II. Title.
E302.5.G74 2011
973.3092'2—dc22
2011010218

Contents

The Top 10 Things You Might Not Know about the Founding Fathers

1. In 1916, at the Republican National Convention, Warren Harding, then a Republican senator from Ohio, first used the phrase "Founding Fathers" in his keynote address.
2. A number of Founding Fathers were slaveholders, including Benjamin Franklin. However, in 1784, Franklin freed his slaves. He was appointed as the head of the Pennsylvania Society for Promoting the Abolition of Slavery. The organization was one of the few public antislavery organizations in existence at that time.
3. Signing the Declaration of Independence was not just an act of rebellion by the Founding Fathers, it was also treason to the English Crown. If tried and found guilty, the punishment was hanging.
4. Not all of the Founding Fathers were college educated; in fact, George Washington did not go to college.
5. In one of the more interesting proposals put forth by the Founding Fathers, James Madison of Virginia proposed that congressional salaries be calculated based on the average price of wheat during a congressional member's time in office.
6. At least twenty-nine of the Founding Fathers served in the Continental army during the Revolutionary War.
7. Six of the Founding Fathers attending the Constitutional Convention were engaged in land speculation: William Blount, Jonathan Dayton, Thomas Fitzsimons, Nathaniel Gorham, Robert Morris, and James Wilson.
8. The average age at which the Founding Fathers died: sixty-seven years.
9. Four of the Founding Fathers attending the Constitutional Convention (Abraham Baldwin, Nicholas Gilman, Daniel of St. Thomas Jenifer, and Alexander Martin) were lifelong bachelors.
10. Nearly all of the fifty-five men who gathered at the Constitutional Convention had some kind of experience in colonial politics. By the time of the 1787 convention, four-fifths or forty-one of the framers had served or were currently serving in the Continental Congress.

Introduction

ELECTION YEARS COME AND go, and so do politicians. But one thing remains constant: invoking the names of the Founding Fathers when trying to score political points with voters. The practice of making comparisons to those men who helped establish the nation is not new, nor is associating the personalities and politics of the Founding Fathers with current political agendas.

In the rush to claim the Founding Fathers for a particular political issue or party, certain facts may be ignored or lost. Truth be told, commanding the legacy of the Founding Fathers is not as simple as it might appear. The Founding Fathers were not a unified, monolithic group. They were a curious mix of occupations and backgrounds: farmers, inventors, merchants, writers, politicians, judges, lawyers, scientists, doctors, and teachers. One was a college president. Three were retired. Twelve were slaveholders. Most were natives of the thirteen colonies. Nine had emigrated from a variety of countries and regions, including England, Ireland, Scotland, and the West Indies. Some were quite wealthy, others were well-to-do, and some struggled daily with financial problems.

They did not share exactly the same beliefs or principles, and they did not always agree with one another. They did not even have a common political agenda. Despite their many differences, these men agreed on one important point: freedom from tyranny was so vital and so precious it was worth risking their property, their reputations, and their lives to achieve it.

When people reference the Founding Fathers, they are often referring to a certain list of names: George Washington, Thomas Jefferson, Benjamin Franklin, John Adams, John Jay, James Madison, and Alexander Hamilton. While these men can be thought of as the primary group of Founding Fathers, in fact the number of men involved in the nation's founding was much greater. According to historian R. B. Bernstein, author of *The Founding Fathers Reconsidered*, most historians define the Founding Fathers as a larger group that includes individuals who were not present at the signing of the Declaration of Independence or who helped draft the Constitution, but whose contributions to the building of the United States are still valuable and helped those other Founding Fathers to achieve their goals.

The majority of Americans has likely never experienced a time when they could not think, say, and do what they pleased. Although they must, of course, obey the laws of the land, Americans are free to vote for the candidate of their choice. Americans are also free to criticize those elected to public office. Americans may speak their minds on a host of matters. They are free to work, live, and travel where they please. Americans are free to practice religion as they see fit, or not at all if they so choose. These freedoms that the present generation takes for granted can make it difficult to appreciate the struggles and risks that the Founding Fathers confronted.

That is where this book comes in. It is by no means intended as an exhaustive or definitive source on the Founding Fathers. Many of these men have assumed a larger-than-life status. In some respects, they were most remarkable men who were called on to carry out special duties, but every single one of them was also human. It is our hope that this book will not only show their great accomplishments but also their very human flaws.

The term "Founding Fathers" often refers to those who contributed to the establishment of American independence and the creation of a new nation. We have accepted that conventional definition because there is no compelling reason to change it, and have chosen to feature a number of individuals who played a key role in the fight for independence and/or the founding of the United States. The men chosen for this volume include those who wrote and those who signed the Declaration of Independence. These are the "Signers." We have also focused on those who crafted the Constitution. These are the "Framers." Finally, we have incorporated those who do not belong in either of the other categories but who nonetheless made valuable contributions to American independence and liberty.

PART I

★ THE WORLD OF THE FOUNDING FATHERS ★

The world of the Founding Fathers encompassed some of the most important events in American history. It was a road that started out as a desire for colonial autonomy from the British Crown that eventually led to a quest for freedom as a new nation. In the process, a war was fought, even as patriot leaders debated and argued over what this new free nation would be. No one had a map or a guide to what constituted this new country. Yet somehow, this seemingly disparate group of men from a wide variety of backgrounds and interests were able to craft a new nation bound by new documents that talked of freedom, equality, and government by and for the people. All very radical concepts made even more amazing in light of the gentlemen who dreamt, argued, and wrote of them.

Quiz: The World of the Founding Fathers, 1754–1789

1. **Where was the first shot fired in the Revolutionary War?**

   A. Boston Common
   B. Philadelphia
   C. Lexington
   D. Bunker Hill

2. **Who was King of England during the American Revolution?**

   A. Edward VI
   B. Charles II
   C. James I
   D. George III

3. **What was the name of the German mercenaries who fought in the American Revolution?**

   A. Hessians
   B. Alsatians
   C. Bavarians
   D. Silesians

4. **The Revolutionary War lasted from:**

   A. 1775–1777
   B. 1775–1783
   C. 1775–1789
   D. 1775–1792

5. **The last half of the war was fought in what area of the country?**

   A. The South
   B. The Northeast
   C. The West
   D. The Mid-Atlantic

6. **Which of the following were taxed by the British to raise money to pay their war debt?**

   A. Cloth and buttons
   B. Tea and newspapers
   C. Glass and china
   D. Roads and buildings

7. **Which of the following groups was most likely to approve the Articles of Confederation?**

   A. Those who believed in a strong central government
   B. Those who did not want any central government
   C. Those who feared a strong central government
   D. Those who wanted no state government

8. Which group dominated the American Constitutional Convention of 1787?

A. Former soldiers of the Continental Army
B. Men of property and wealthy business owners
C. Artisans and working men
D. Farmers and frontiersmen

9. Those who opposed the ratification of the Constitution were called:

A. Antifederalists
B. Federalists
C. Democrats
D. Jeffersonian Republicans

10. What was a major weakness of the Articles of Confederation?

A. It created a powerful executive branch.
B. It denied the Federal government mediation power over states.
C. It did not provide for a judicial or legislative branch.
D. It made it difficult for the government to raise money through taxes.

Answers

1.C 2.D 3.A 4.B 5.A 6.B 7.C 8.B 9.A 10.C

CHAPTER 1

The Road to Revolution

With the end of the French and Indian War in 1763, the English were at peace for the first time in more than fifty years, but new problems awaited the British Crown. It was clear to British statesmen that the previous decade had been fraught with a number of vexing problems in trying to manage their vast and growing empire. Saddled with a national debt of approximately £175 million, on which the annual interest alone amounted to £5 million, the English government desperately sought new sources of revenue. The colonies were the logical place to look for them. Yet, the experience of the French and Indian War made it clear that extracting money from the colonies would not be easy. The colonists were unwilling to allow Parliament to tax them, and were reluctant to levy taxes on themselves.

The Burdens of Empire

The problems of managing the Empire were compounded after the French and Indian War by a fundamental shift in imperial policy. In the past, the English government viewed the empire as a commercial venture and opposed the acquisition of territory for its own sake. After 1763, a number of English and colonial leaders argued that land itself was of value. Land could sustain a huge population, generate abundant revenue from taxes and other sources, and confer imperial splendor upon England itself.

The French and Indian War was a conflict between Great Britain and France in North America from 1754 to 1763. The name refers to the two main enemies of the British colonists: the French forces and the various Native American forces that allied with the French. The war was part of a much larger world conflict involving Austria, England, France, Great Britain, Prussia, and Sweden.

The territory added to the British Empire as a result of the French and Indian War in 1763 doubled its size. The difficulties of settling, administering, defending, and governing these holdings were immensely complex. Unfortunately, the expansion of the British Empire took place in the context of a worsening debt crisis in England itself. Landowners and merchants staggered under burdensome taxes, and objected to additional levies. Their resentment of the colonists deepened, for they believed that the colonists had contributed little to support a war fought largely for their benefit. They believed that only the imposition of taxes on the colonists could relieve the financial burdens of the empire.

Grenville's Crackdown

George Grenville, the prime minister of England, like many of his fellow Englishmen believed that the colonies had been coddled for far too long. They should now be compelled to pay some of the costs of defending and administering the Empire, and he quickly moved to increase the authority of Parliament in the colonies. In 1764, Grenville announced the Sugar Act, which was to eliminate the illegal sugar trade between the colonies and the French and Spanish West Indies. In addition, the act provided for the establishment of vice-admiralty courts in America that would try accused smugglers and also discourage the possibility of having cases heard before sympathetic jurors of their peers. The Sugar Act also placed duties on imported sugar, coffee, indigo, and wine.

In September, Parliament passed the Currency Act of 1764, which effectively gave the British Empire control over currency in the colonies. Until this point, colonists only had access to currency through trade with the British Empire. Suffering from a shortage of hard currency, the colonists had created their own paper currency in the form of Bills of Credit, the value of which differed from one colony to another. British merchants and creditors did not like being paid in a currency that wasn't based on any real value system and could easily depreciate in value. The Currency Act sought to protect them by making paper currency no longer valid for the payment of private debts.

In addition, colonial legislatures were ordered to withdraw all paper currency already in circulation within a reasonable period of time. The rationale for the Currency Act was to end inflation by reducing the money supply. Unfortunately, the colonies were in the midst of a severe depression, and limiting the amount of money available made a bad situation worse. Now colonists could not obtain the money needed to conduct business or to pay increased duties and taxes. In the colonists' eyes, the British government appeared unconcerned about their economic welfare.

The Stamp Act Crisis

If he had tried, Prime Minister Grenville could not have devised a better way of antagonizing the colonists than by introducing the Stamp Act of 1765, which placed a tax on almanacs, newspapers, pamphlets, legal documents, insurance policies, ship's papers, operating licenses for taverns and shops, and even dice and playing cards. The Sugar Act of 1764 had largely affected New England merchants, whose business it hampered. The Stamp Act, by contrast, affected all Americans, and as a result, evoked opposition from some of the wealthiest and most powerful groups in the colonies: lawyers, merchants, printers, tavern owners, and land speculators.

The colonists were not as upset about the costs of the Stamp Act as they were about the precedent it had apparently established. Prior to the Stamp Act, taxes were used to regulate trade and commerce, not to directly raise money for the British Empire. Colonists were almost unanimous in their opposition to a direct tax, fearing that if they did not resist, more burdensome taxes would follow. Moreover, Parliament had failed to obtain the consent of the colonial assemblies before imposing the tax. Some of the delegates to the Virginia House of Burgesses proceeded to challenge the legality of the Stamp Act and by implication, the right of Parliament to tax the colonies at all without first securing their consent.

FACT

As with the Sugar and Currency Acts, the economic burdens of the Stamp Act were comparatively insignificant. It was designed to raise £60,000 annually, which would generate about one-third of the estimated £300,000 needed to pay for the defense of the colonies.

Patrick Henry also introduced seven resolutions in which he asserted that Americans, as subjects of the Crown, had the same rights as Englishmen, and that only local representatives could levy taxes on the colonies. Virginians, Henry declared, should pay no taxes except those voted by the Virginia Assembly, and anyone who advocated the right of Parliament to tax Virginians should be deemed an enemy of the colony. The House of Burgesses defeated the most radical of Henry's proposals, but all of them were printed and circulated throughout the colonies as the "Virginia Resolves."

QUOTE

Foremost among the Virginia protestors was Patrick Henry. On May 29, 1765, Henry made a dramatic speech in the House of Burgesses in which he concluded that George III, like earlier tyrants, might lose his throne and perhaps his head if he did not reverse current policies. Henry is reputed to have ended his speech with the famous injunction: "Caesar had his Brutus; Charles the First, his Cromwell; and George the Third may profit by their example. If this be treason, make the most of it."

In Massachusetts, James Otis similarly persuaded his fellow legislators that the Stamp Act was illegitimate. He called for an intercolonial congress to act against it. In October 1765, the Stamp Act Congress met in New York, composed of delegates from nine colonies. They decided to petition the king and both houses of Parliament for redress. The petition conceded that Americans owned Parliament "all due subordination," but at the same time it denied that Parliament could tax the colonies.

Meanwhile, during the summer of 1765, serious riots had broken out in several cities along the Atlantic seaboard, the most serious of them in Boston. Men who belonged to the newly organized Sons of Liberty terrorized stamp agents and set the stamps ablaze. Many agents hastily resigned, and the sale of stamps in the colonies virtually ceased.

Certainly one of the most famous groups formed during this period was the Sons of Liberty, created in Boston during the early summer of 1765. The Sons of Liberty were initially a group of shopkeepers and artisans who called themselves the Loyal Nine and were against the Stamp Act. As that group grew, it came to be known as the Sons of Liberty. The group grew dramatically, attracting workers and tradesmen.

The violence in Boston continued to escalate when a mob attacked such pro-British aristocrats as the lieutenant governor, Thomas Hutchinson. Privately, Hutchinson opposed the Stamp Act, but as an officer of the Crown, he felt an obligation to uphold it. For his devotion to duty, Hutchinson paid a high price. An angry mob pillaged and destroyed his elegant home.

The Stamp Act thus provoked serious tension between the British government and the American colonies. The crisis subsided when Parliament backed down. It was not the colonial protests, speeches, resolutions, petitions, or even riots that deterred authorities in London; their attitude changed as the result of economic pressure. Beginning in 1764, many colonists boycotted English goods to protest the Sugar Act. By 1765, they had extended the boycott to include goods covered by the Stamp Act. The Sons of Liberty intimidated those colonists who refused to participate. Having lost their colonial markets, English merchants implored Parliament to repeal the Stamp Act.

The Townshend Acts

In July 1765, the Second Marquis of Rockingham, Charles Watson-Wentworth, succeeded Grenville as prime minister. Unlike his predeccesor, Watson-Wentworth was more concialatory toward the colonists while trying to maintain the goodwill of English merchants. On March 18, 1766, he engineered the repeal of the Stamp Act. On that same day, Rockingham issued the Declaratory Act, which asserted the authority of Parliament over the colonies "in all cases whatsoever." In their rejoicing about the repeal of the Stamp Act, most Americans ignored this new, sweeping declaration of parliamentary power.

The English response to Rockingham's policy of appeasement was less enthusiastic than the American response. English landowners contended that the government had sacrificed their interests to those of the merchants, and feared that the failure to tax the colonies would mean increased taxes on them. George III at last bowed to these protests and dismissed Rockingham in August 1766. To replace Rockingham, the king called on the capable but aging William Pitt, who was so plagued by illness that he turned the actual administrative duties to Charles Townshend, the chancellor of the exchequer.

Townshend was a brilliant but flamboyant, and at times reckless, politician. Among his initial responsibilities was to resolve the ongoing American grievances against Parliament. The most important of them, now that Parliament had repealed the Stamp Act, was the Quartering Act of 1765, also known as the Mutiny Act. This law required colonists to provide living quarters, food, and supplies to British troops stationed in the colonies at the homeowner's expense. British authorities considered this request reasonable. After all, the troops were in America to protect the colonists from attack and to police the frontiers. Lodging soldiers in private homes was simply a way to reduce the costs of maintaining them. To the colonists, the law was one more threat to their traditional liberties. They did not so much object to housing and feeding troops at their own expense as they resented that the government had made such contributions mandatory.

To enforce the Quartering Act, Townshend pushed two additional measures through Parliament in 1767. The first disbanded the New York Assembly until the colonists agreed to obey the law. The second levied new taxes, known collectively as the Townshend Duties, on goods, such as tea, lead, paint, glass, and paper, imported to the colonies from England.

Townshend made sure that the new duties conformed to the American definition of an external tax. Thus, he reasoned, the colonists could not logically or justly oppose them. Taxing imports was, even apparently in the opinion of most Americans, well within the authority of Parliament. Unfortunately, Townshend's efforts to resolve the grievances of the colonists were to no avail. The new duties on imports proved no more acceptable to Americans that the former Stamp Tax.

FACT

One outcome of Townshend's activities was the suspension of the New York Assembly. But that action did not have the effect that Townshend desired. Instead of isolating New York, Townshend's actions galvanized the colonists to support their besieged neighbors. The colonists now had begun to think of themselves as bound together by a common destiny in the face of a common enemy.

Opposing the Townshend Acts

Leading the colonies in their opposition to the Crown was the Massachusetts Assembly, which circulated a letter to all the colonial governments, asking for colonial resistance to every tax that was levied by Parliament. Written by Samuel Adams (1722–1803), the Massachusetts Circular Letter denounced the Townshend Duties as violating the principle of taxation without representation. Adams also asserted the impossibility of adequately representing colonial interests in Parliament, attacked the proposal to make colonial governors and judges independent of the people, and called for united opposition to British tyranny.

At first, the circular letter evoked little response in a number of colonial legislatures and even encountered strong opposition in Pennsylvania. Besides the Massachusetts legislature, only the assemblies of Virginia and New York favored the positions that Adams had outlined. But then the Secretary of State for the Colonies, Lord Hillsborough, finally responded in a letter in which he warned the colonial assemblies that if they endorsed the Massachusetts Circular, their governing bodies would be dissolved. The members of the Massachusetts legislature defiantly reaffirmed their views, voting ninety-two in favor to seventeen opposed to support the circular letter. This time every other colonial legislature, including the Pennsylvania Assembly, rallied to the support of Massachusetts.

A Board of Customs Commissioners

To complicate matters, Townshend strengthened the enforcement of commercial regulations in the colonies by creating a board of customs commissioners. It was Townshend's hope that this board, based in America, would finally end the corruption that existed in the colonial customs houses. Townshend's plan worked up to a point in that the new commission was able to almost completely halt smuggling activities in Boston, although smugglers continued to operate in other colonial seaports (and in fact, sometimes increased their activity to compensate for the crackdown in Boston).

Merchants in Boston, of course, were outraged. Like all colonists, they were long accustomed to the lax enforcement of the law. They were also aggravated that the new commission diverted lucrative smuggling to other coastal cities. As a consequence, they organized another colonial boycott of English goods. In 1768, the merchants of Philadelphia and New York joined them in what came to be known as the nonimportation agreement. Colonists boycotted all English goods subject to the Townshend Duties. Throughout the colonies, American homespun and other domestic products became suddenly fashionable, while English luxuries fell into disfavor. Relations between the Crown and her North American colonies continued to deteriorate, and for the Americans, solutions were becoming fewer and fewer. It was time for more drastic actions.

CHAPTER 2

The Fight for Freedom

With the death in late 1767 of Charles Townshend, the job of dealing with the increasingly difficult colonies fell to the new prime minister, Frederick North, the Second Earl of Guilford. In March 1770, Lord North repealed the Townshend Duties with the exception of the tax on tea. The prime minister's reasons were not wholly in favor of appeasing the colonists, but in the hopes of possibly driving a wedge between the colonies to stop any further attempts at causing more problems for the Crown. Lord North's actions offered too little and came too late. Events now began moving faster than English officials could respond to them.

The Boston Massacre

Before the news that Parliament had repealed the Townshend Duties reached the American colonists, an event that took place in Boston raised colonial resentment to a new level of intensity. The British government deployed four regiments of troops to Boston in an attempt to stop the harassment of customs agents. To many Bostonians, the presence of the soldiers was nothing less than an affront as well as a reminder of British oppression of the colonists. In addition, many British soldiers, poorly paid and poorly treated, sought other jobs in their off-duty hours and competed with local workers in an already tight labor market. As a result, there were a number of tense confrontations between the British regulars and civilian workers.

On the afternoon of March 5, 1770, a fistfight broke out between a worker and a soldier. By evening, the fight had escalated into a small riot. Angry bands of citizens and soldiers roamed the streets of Boston. At about nine o'clock, a mob began to pelt sentries at the customs house with snowballs and rocks. The British commander, Captain Thomas Preston, hastily assembled his men in front of the building to protect it. There was a scuffle during which someone knocked a soldier to the ground. In retaliation, the soldiers, on the orders of a person never identified, fired into the crowd. They killed three persons immediately and mortally wounded two others.

FACT

Local leaders transformed this unfortunate event, which was clearly the result of panic and confusion, into the "Boston Massacre"—a graphic symbol of British tyranny and brutality. The victims, including the mulatto sailor Crispus Attucks, became popular martyrs. A famous engraving done by Paul Revere, widely reproduced and circulated throughout the colonies, depicted the massacre as a carefully organized and calculated assault on a peaceful and unarmed crowd.

Only the timely actions of Lieutenant Governor Thomas Hutchinson averted a general uprising. Hutchinson bowed to the public's demand to withdraw British troops from Boston and relocate them to islands in the harbor. Colonial authorities, in the meantime, arrested Captain Preston and six of his men and charged them with murder. John Adams and Josiah Quincy agreed to undertake their defense. At the trial, which took place between October 24 and October 30, 1770, Preston and four soldiers won acquittal. Two soldiers were found guilty of manslaughter, branded on the hand, and released. Despite the verdict, colonial pamphlets and newspapers insisted that the soldiers were guilty of murder.

Considered to be the man most responsible for stirring up public outrage against the British was a distant cousin of John Adams, Samuel Adams. Samuel Adams had the inclination to view public events in strict moral terms. A failure in business, he had occupied several governmental positions, but his real importance to the emerging revolutionary cause was as a publicist. Adams has been considered to be the most effective radical of the colonial cause.

In 1772, Samuel Adams proposed the creation of a "committee of correspondence" in Boston to publicize throughout Massachusetts the grievances against England. Colonists elsewhere followed Adams's example, and there emerged a loose network of political organizations that sustained the spirit of dissent throughout the early 1770s.

The Tea Controversy

The apparent calm in the colonies in the aftermath of the Boston Massacre concealed a growing sense of resentment at British imperial policies. The customs officers who remained in the colonies despite the repeal of the Townshend Duties remained difficult to deal with. Many were corrupt and arrogant, using their office to harass local merchants and seaman about real or imagined transgressions over regulations. They also enriched themselves by accepting bribes and illegally seizing merchandise.

What at last revived the revolutionary fervor of the 1760s was a new act of Parliament, which the king and prime minister mistakenly expected not to be controversial. It involved the business of selling tea. In 1773, the British East India Company had accumulated a large stock of tea that it could not sell in the glutted English market; as a result, the company was on the verge of going bankrupt. In an attempt to save the company, Parliament passed the Tea Act of 1773 in which it gave the East India Company the right to export tea directly to the colonies. This allowed the company to bypass the taxes normally imposed on merchants. Although a boon to the company, it hurt American colonial merchants by underselling them and allowing the East India Company a monopoly on the tea trade, while further enraging the colonists.

As if that was not enough to increase colonial tempers, the company also decided to grant franchise rights to certain merchants. This meant they could sell tea in the colonies, but it also generated further resentment among those excluded from this lucrative business. Third, the law provided no new tax on tea, but the original Townshend Duty—the one tax that had not been repealed by Lord North—was still intact. Most important, the Tea Act revived American passions about the issue of taxation without representation.

Lord North mistakenly assumed that the colonists would welcome this new law because it promised a reduction in tea prices. Leaders of the anti-British movement argued that the Tea Act represented one more insidious example of illegal taxation. As a result, many colonists began boycotting tea, an important development in colonial resistance by this time, further linking all the colonies in a common cause.

The Boston Tea Party

During the last weeks of 1773, the leaders of several colonies planned to prevent the East India Company from unloading its cargos in various ports. In Philadelphia and New York, determined colonists prevented the tea from leaving the ships. In Charleston, colonists forced dockworkers to store the tea in a public warehouse. In Boston, after failing to prevent the entry of three ships carrying East India Company tea, local patriots staged a spectacular drama.

At two mass meetings held on November 29 and 30, 1773, the citizens of Boston resolved that the tea must not be sold in the colonies and must be returned to England. Lieutenant Governor Hutchinson, however, refused to allow the ships to return back to England. On the evening of December 16, 1773, a crowd of some 8,000 spectators assembled near the Old South Church to learn whether Hutchinson had stood by his decision not to allow the ships to return to England with their unsold cargo. (He did.) At a prearranged signal from Samuel Adams, three companies of fifty men each, disguised as Mohawk Indians, boarded the three ships, broke open the tea chests—342 in all—and heaved the tea into Boston Harbor. They damaged no other property on board. As news of the Boston "tea party" spread, the citizens of other port cities imitated the example of the disgruntled Bostonians.

The Coercive Acts

When the citizens of Boston refused to pay for the property damage they had caused, George III and Lord North adopted a policy of coercion to be applied only against Massachusetts, which they now regarded as the principal center of resistance in the colonies. In four acts passed between March 31 and June 2, 1774 and known collectively as the Coercive or the Intolerable Acts, Parliament set out to isolate and punish Massachusetts.

The Coercive Acts included the Boston Port Bill, which closed the port of Boston except to shipments of military supplies, food, and fuel. The Massachusetts Government Act virtually annulled the Massachusetts charter and drastically reduced the powers of self-government in Massachusetts. The Administration of Justice Act permitted royal officials accused of crimes to be tried in other colonies or in England. The Quartering Act required the quartering of British troops not only in barns, taverns, empty dwellings, and deserted buildings, but also in homes.

Parliament augmented the Coercive Acts with the Quebec Act, which was designed to provide a civil government for the French, Roman Catholic residents of Canada and the Illinios territory. The act also extended the boundaries of Quebec and granted political rights to Catholics as well as recognizing the Catholic Church.

Although the Quebec Act was intended to be an extension of religious and political tolerance, to many of the English colonists, the measure appeared threatening. The colonists were already alarmed by rumors that officials of the Church of England were scheming to impose Anglican authority on the various religious denominations. Furthermore, the extension of religious toleration and political rights to Catholics convinced many English colonists that a plot was afoot in Parliament to subject Americans to the tyranny of the Pope.

Sources of Resistance and Authority

Far from isolating and weakening the citizens of Massachusetts, the Coercive Acts made them martyrs in the eyes of many of their fellow colonists. In colony after colony, men and women began to resist British authority with determination and enthusiasm.

The most effective of these new groups were the Committees of Correspondence. Adams had organized the first in Massachusetts in 1772. A year later, in March 1773, the Virginia House of Burgesses appointed an eleven-man standing committee for intercolonial correspondence, the membership of which included Patrick Henry, Richard Henry Lee, and Thomas Jefferson. By July, the legislative assemblies of Rhode Island, Connecticut, New Hampshire, and South Carolina had also formed Committees of Correspondence, and by February 1774, the legislatures in all colonies except North Carolina and Pennsylvania had done so.

The Committees of Correspondence were an important development in the evolving colonial response to the British Crown. The committees were in effect shadow governments put together by American patriots. These groups met and coordinated organized responses to the Crown as well as sharing information among the colonies. Their power was formidable, and often superseded that of royal officials and recognized colonial legislatures.

The Virginians took the most important step in 1774 after the royal governor dissolved the House of Burgesses. A group of representatives met in Williamsburg where they declared the Coercive Acts a threat to colonial liberties and called for the establishment of a Continental Congress. In September

1774, the First Continental Congress convened in Carpenter's Hall in Philadelphia. Fifty-six delegates representing all the colonies save Georgia were present. They made five major decisions.

First, in a close vote, they rejected a plan of union under British authority that Joseph Galloway of Pennsylvania had proposed. Second, they endorsed a statement of grievances that conceded the right of Parliament to regulate colonial trade and acknowledged the sovereignty of the king, but also included a demand that all oppressive legislation passed since 1763 be repealed. Third, they approved the so-called Suffolk Resolutions, which a convention in Suffolk County, Massachusetts had passed.

The Suffolk Resolutions declared the Coercive Acts illegal, urged citizens to withhold the payment of taxes, and advised the people to arm themselves in defense against a possible British retaliatory attack.

Fourth, the congress agreed to halt all American commerce with Great Britain, by whatever means necessary. Last, the congress agreed to meet the following spring to attend to whatever business was necessary.

The Continental Congress, like the Committees of Correspondence, represented an important turning point for the colonies. With the congress, the colonists had in effect stated once more their autonomy to the Crown, while declaring an economic war.

The more optimistic Americans supposed that economic sanctions alone would win a quick, bloodless, and decisive victory. The more realistic had their doubts and feared that war was on the horizon.

During the winter of 1774–1775, Parliament debated proposals for conciliating the colonists, among them the withdrawal of British troops from America and the repeal of the Coercive Acts. But their efforts were fruitless for in early 1775, a series of measures known as the Conciliatory Proposals were passed. The proposals suggested that the colonists tax themselves instead of being taxed directly by Parliament. However, North underestimated the hostility of American public opinion. In any case, his offer came too late. It did not reach Americans before they had already fired the first shots of their war for independence.

CHAPTER 3

Independence!

For months, the farmers and townspeople of Massachusetts had been stockpiling arms, gathering ammunition, and preparing to fight. In Boston, British commander General Thomas Gage knew of the military preparations that were taking place, but considered his army too small to do anything to discourage them. He also resisted the advice of some officers who believed that the Americans would never fight and would in fact, retreat at the first show of British military power.

Lexington and Concord

At last, events compelled Gage to act. He learned that colonists had created a large supply depot in the town of Concord, twenty-one miles by road from Boston. He decided to strike quickly. On the night of April 18, 1775, he sent a detachment of 1,000 troops under the command of Lieutenant Colonel John Smith to Concord. Gage expected Smith and his men to surprise the colonists and seize the weapons, ammunition, and supplies without bloodshed.

FACT

Unbeknownst to Gage, the patriots in Boston were monitoring the movements of the British forces. During the night, two horsemen—William Dawes (1745–1799) and Paul Revere—rode out to warn the villagers and farmers of the impending arrival of British soldiers.

When the British troops arrived in the town of Lexington the next morning, April 19, seventy armed colonists under the command of Captain John Parker awaited them on the town common. The British regulars and the American minutemen exchanged fire; seven Americans died and ten more were wounded. As they approached the town of Concord, the British learned that the Americans had removed much of the gun powder and ammunition. Still, taking no chances, British troops burned all they could and moved on.

All along the road from Concord to Boston, farmers hiding behind trees, rocks, and stone fences harassed the British with relentless musket fire. Only the arrival of reinforcements from Lexington saved British forces from disaster. By the end of the day, British casualties numbered seventy-four men killed, 174 wounded, and twenty-six missing. Almost 4,000 American militiamen saw action at the battles of Lexington and Concord. Of these, ninety-three were killed, wounded, or missing.

It was not immediately clear that the skirmishes at Lexington and Concord were the first engagements of a war. Many on both sides saw them as simply another explosion of the tensions that had for years afflicted Anglo-American relations. Whether they recognized it at the time or not, the British and the Americans had altered their relations forever. The American War for Independence had begun.

American War Aims

On May 10, 1775, the Second Continental Congress met in Philadelphia, with delegates representing every state except Georgia. The members agreed to support the war, but disagreed sharply about its purpose.

At one extreme was a group of radicals, led by John and Samuel Adams of Massachusetts and Richard Henry Lee of Virginia, who favored immediate and complete independence from Great Britain. At the other extreme was a group of conservatives, led by John Dickinson of Pennsylvania, who hoped that modest reforms in imperial government would permit reconciliation with Great Britain. Most of the delegates tried to find some middle ground between these two positions. They demonstrated their uncertainty about which course to follow in two contradictory declarations that the Congress adopted in quick succession.

The two declarations adopted by the Continental Congress were the Olive Branch Petition of July 5, 1775, which offered one final, conciliatory appeal to the king. The second was the Declaration of the Causes and Necessity of Taking Up Arms, adopted on July 6, 1775, which proclaimed that the British government had left the American people with only two alternatives: unconditional submission to tyranny or resistance by force.

The attitude of the American people, for the most part, reflected that of the Congress. Initially, most Americans believed that they were fighting not for independence but for a redress of grievances within the British Empire. During the first year of the war, many Americans began to change their minds. First, as the human and material costs of war mounted, the original war aims seemed too modest to justify them. Second, whatever lingering affection that Americans felt toward the British greatly diminished when British soldiers began to kill their neighbors and when the British government recruited Native Americans, slaves, and mercenaries to fight against them. Third, and most important, Americans came to believe that the British government was forcing them to seek independence by rejecting the Olive Branch Petition in November 1775 and instead enacting the Prohibitory Act, which closed the colonies to all overseas trade and made no concessions to American demands except to pardon penitent rebels.

Common Sense

On January 10, 1776, a pamphlet appeared that galvanized American public opinion in favor of independence. It was called *Common Sense*, written by an English émigré by the name of Thomas Paine who had arrived in America in 1774. Paine had failed at every business venture to which he had turned his hand, but he proved a brilliant success as a revolutionary propagandist. His pamphlet attacked George III, whom he called the "Royal Brute," and exposed the folly of seeking reconciliation with Britain. Paine wanted to deflect colonial anger at Parliament and redirect it toward what he believed was the real problem: the English government itself. It was monarchy that was to blame for all the problems the colonists had experienced during the previous twelve years. Simple common sense, Paine asserted, suggested that Americans break free of a government that could elevate so corrupt and volatile a man as George III and permit him to inflict such brutality on his own people.

Common Sense is reputed to have sold 120,000 copies in the first three months after publication, and to have earned total sales of 500,000 copies. To many of its readers it came as a revelation; the pamphlet was instrumental in helping fan support for the American cause.

The Decision for Independence

After adjourning on August 2, 1775, the Continental Congress reconvened on September 12, and moved tentatively toward endorsing independence from Great Britain. On August 23, George III had proclaimed the colonies in open rebellion. On November 9, news arrived that he had rejected the Olive Branch Petition. On December 6, a little more than a month before the publication of *Common Sense*, the delegates to the Continental Congress denied any intention to reject the sovereignty of the king but disavowed allegiance to Parliament. Not until July 1776 did the Continental Congress at last opt for independence. On June 11, the Congress appointed a committee to prepare a declaration of independence.

The committee appointed to prepare the declaration of independence consisted of Benjamin Franklin of Pennsylvania, John Adams of Massachusetts, Thomas Jefferson of Virginia, Roger Sherman of Connecticut, and Robert Livingston of New York. Jefferson wrote most of it, with significant editorial assistance from Adams and Franklin. On July 4, 1776, Congress approved without dissent the Declaration of Independence the committee had written, although the New York delegation, advised by the New York Provincial Congress, abstained from voting.

The Declaration of Independence was divided into two sections. In the first, Jefferson restated the familiar theory, derived from John Locke and his work the *Second Treatise on Government*, that governments were formed to protect the natural rights of citizens to life, liberty, and property.

In the *Second Treatise on Government*, published in 1690, John Locke argued that when people gave consent to a government, it was with the expectation that the government would govern justly. When the government failed in carrying out the people's wishes, the citizens not only had the right but also the obligation to resist.

In the second section of the Declaration of Independence, Jefferson compiled a list of alleged grievances against George III, whom he stated had forfeited all claims to their loyalty and obedience. The American colonists had asserted their independence from Great Britain, but they would have to fight a war to keep it.

The First Phase of the War

On the surface, it seemed that all the military advantages in the contest between the colonies and Great Britain favored the British. By the time of the American Revolution, the British possessed the greatest army and navy in the world. They commanded a vast world empire with seemingly inexhaustible resources. The Americans were struggling to create a government, and had no standing army to speak of. Yet the colonists were not without their own advantages. They were conducting a war on their own home ground and were fighting for their very lives and livelihoods.

At crucial moments, they displayed remarkable exuberance, courage, and resourcefulness. They were deeply committed to the war. The British people, on the contrary, were unenthusiastic. Finally, beginning in 1777, the Americans were the beneficiaries of substantial aid from England's rivals abroad, especially France, as the American War for Independence became an international fight for imperial supremacy.

American victory came about in part because of a series of egregious blunders and miscalculations on the part of the British government and military officials in the early stages of the war, which the British army, for all its strength, could not overcome.

The war developed in three phases. The first extended from the spring of 1775 to the spring of 1776, when British military commanders in the colonies remained uncertain as to whether they were really fighting a war or a limited, localized uprising that would be contained by British troops. The British also believed that the majority of the conflict would be centered in and around the Boston area which appeared to be the hotbed of most of the conflict. However, over time, the colonials were able to take the offensive and force the war into the entire colonial region. Although the Americans lost the first major engagement of the war, the Battle of Bunker Hill (which was actually fought on nearby Breed's Hill) on June 17, 1776, by late winter American forces had surrounded Boston and occupied strategic positions on the heights. General William Howe, who had replaced General Thomas Gage as commander of British forces in the colonies on October 10, 1775, decided to evacuate.

Yet, the British evacuation of New England was not as much an American victory as it was a reflection of changing English assumptions about the war. By the spring of 1776, it had become clear to British military commanders and government officials that the war was not a local conflict that they could confine to Boston and its environs. The mounting evidence of colonial unity and determination suggested that the British had to fight a much larger and much longer war. The departure of the British from New England marked a change of strategy more than an admission of defeat.

ESSENTIAL

On March 17, 1776, the British departed Boston for Halifax, Nova Scotia. Less than one year after the war began, Massachusetts colonists had driven the British from American soil (at least temporarily). This date is still celebrated in the city as Evacuation Day.

The Second Phase

The second phase of the war lasted from 1776 until early 1778. During this period of nearly two years, the British army enjoyed its greatest prospects for victory. It is even possible that the British would have won the war had it not been for a series of disastrous mistakes made on the part of the British high command. During this phase, the war was conventional and the American military was woefully overmatched.

The British failure to win the war when they enjoyed such overwhelming advantages was, in large measure, the result of their own mistakes. William Howe abandoned his most important strategic initiative in the north and Canada, leaving the daring but inept John Burgoyne to fight alone. When he chose to engage the Americans, Howe refrained from going for the kill against a weakened Continental army, even though he had several opportunities to do so. Instead, Howe repeatedly permitted the American commander George Washington to retreat and reorganize. Howe, for example, allowed the Continental army to spend a long winter unmolested at Valley Forge, where Washington's men, weak, sick, and hungry, were easy prey for a British attack.

In the meantime, Burgoyne withdrew to Saratoga, New York, where the Americans forced the surrender of 5,700 men on October 17, 1777. The British surrender at Saratoga marked a major turning point in the war. It enhanced the possibility that the Americans could attract powerful foreign allies to aid their war effort. Just such an alliance was not long in coming. Soon after the British defeat in the New York campaign, the French government pledged to support the American cause.

The Third Phase

The third and final phase of the war was very different from the first two. The British government had never been fully united behind the war. The government had further reason to think again about their commitment to the war after the humiliating defeat of the British at Saratoga. Their old enemy, the French, lending the Americans support, seemed to heighten Parliament's determination to limit its involvement in the American conflict. Now it was time to try another tack, this time to mobilize those persons who still supported the Crown and were against the war. They tried, in effect, to undermine the Revolution from within. Since the British believed that Loyalist sentiment was strongest in the southern colonies, they concentrated their efforts there.

The new strategy was a dismal failure. British forces spent three years, between 1778 and 1781, fighting battles large and small throughout the South. All of their efforts ended in frustration and failure. There were many Loyalists in Georgia and the Carolinas, but there were many more American patriots than the British surmised. Even where their numbers were large, the Loyalists often refused to help the British because they feared reprisals from their anti-British neighbors.

The British also faced severe logistical problems in the South. American forces engaged in guerilla warfare. This allowed them to move freely throughout the countryside. More often than not, these soldiers found support within the local population, which also allowed them to blend in, making the task of recognizing the enemy even more difficult for the British. The British, try as they might, were fighting a war in a region that was for all intents, extremely hostile to them.

The war in the North settled into a stalemate; the decisive battles occurred in the South. Although British troops won conventional battles, guerrilla fighters under the leadership of such resourceful commanders as Thomas Sumter, Andrew Pickens, and Francis Marion harassed them as they moved through the southern countryside. At King's Mountain, located near the border separating North and South Carolina, a band of American backwoods sharpshooters, under the joint command of Colonel Isaac Shelby and Colonel William Campbell, killed, wounded, or captured the entire 1,100-man Loyalist force. Smaller, swifter American units then inflicted what British commander Lord Cornwallis described as "a very unexpected and severe blow" at Cowpens, South Carolina on January 17, 1781. Even when the British forces managed to drive the Americans from the field, as at Guilford Court House, North Carolina on March 15, 1781, the Americans inflicted such heavy losses that the British army was too decimated to continue the campaign.

The guerilla fighting was one aspect of the war that made it truly revolutionary. With the mobilizing of local citizens who might have been reluctant to engage in war activities, the patriots received an extra boost to help them. By tapping into support in communities that had been previously isolated from the war effort, the quest for independence did not diminish, as the British hoped it would, but increased.

Convinced that he could not restore British control in the Carolinas as long as Virginia remained a base of operations and supply for Americans, Cornwallis invaded Virginia with 1,500 men in late April 1781. Reinforcements brought his total strength to approximately 7,500 troops, vastly superior in number to the small American force under the Marquis de Lafayette of France and Baron von Steuben of Prussia.

With the help of the French expeditionary force and the French navy, Washington's next move was to trap Cornwallis at Yorktown, Virginia. Washington and his troops marched toward the town; on their way they joined forces with troops under Lafayette and von Steuben, while the French navy sailed up the York River. In the end, the Americans, aided by the French, trapped the British between land and sea. Cornwallis was pinned in and had nowhere to go.

Yorktown

On August 30, 1781, De Grasse arrived off the coast of Yorktown and set up a naval blockade. After he had driven off a British fleet on September 10, De Grasse sent vessels to transport the rest of Washington's and Rochambeau's army to Williamsburg. Meanwhile, Lafayette's and von Steuben's men joined them. From Williamsburg, a combined army of some 16,800 strong advanced on Yorktown.

Cornwallis now regarded his position as hopeless. A rainstorm ended his desperate thoughts of escaping with his army across the York River. After a feeble show of resistance, Cornwallis at last capitulated on October 17, 1781, four years to the day after Burgoyne had surrendered at Saratoga. Two days later, on October 19, Cornwallis formally surrendered his army of 7,500 men to George Washington. Although British forces still held Savannah, Charleston, Wilmington, and New York, except for a few minor skirmishes, the fighting was over.

While the fighting had come to an end, it wasn't until 1782 that the British government opened formal peace talks with an American delegation in Paris. The British and Americans signed a final treaty on September 3, 1783. Its terms, on the whole, were remarkably favorable to the United States. The British recognized American independence and established the boundaries, with some ambiguity, from the southern border of Canada to the northern boundary for Florida and from the Atlantic Ocean to the Mississippi River. Americans had every reason to celebrate as the last British soldiers left New York in the fall of 1783. General George Washington rode triumphantly into the city, which was to be the first capital of the new nation.

Articles of Confederation

Even as the fighting raged, the delegates to the Continental Congress were busy at work crafting what would be the nation's first attempt at a constitution. The Articles of Confederation, drafted in 1777, were written to bind together more closely the thirteen colonies. But the articles were much more than that. The document reflects the colonies concern against a strong national government that would ignore the needs of each colony/state. To avoid this potential conflict, the articles instead placed the largest share of power among the states.

As written, the Articles promised that the states would retain their "sovereignty, freedom and independence." There would be no executive or judicial branches of government; instead a committee of delegated representatives from the states would govern as a Confederation Congress.

Among the duties of the Congress would be the conducting of foreign policy, which included declarations of war or peace. What was more interesting about the Articles is what they did not authorize, which included the power to collect taxes, regulate interstate commerce, and enforce laws.

The state's wariness over a strong federal government meant that the new government under the Articles of Confederation would be very weak. The shortcomings of this new government would eventually force the states to meet again and write a new document—the United States Constitution.

The Articles of Confederation were adopted by Congress on November 15, 1777 and were finally ratified on March 1, 1781. At that point, the Continental Congress now became known as the Congress of the Confederation. Even though there were critics who believed that the document did not do enough to guarantee a strong and sound government, many more believed that the Articles were a step in the right direction. No one could see that there would yet be another meeting in Philadelphia to tackle the question of the new government quite so soon.

CHAPTER 4

Framing a New Government

By the late 1780s, the Continental Congress could no longer deal with the divisive nature and instability of politics, with the economic and commercial problems that beset the nation, and with popular uprisings such as Shays' Rebellion. A decade earlier, Americans had deliberately avoided creating a genuinely national government, fearing that it would encroach on the liberty and independence of the states. Now they began to reconsider that decision.

The Collapse of the Confederation

By the early 1780s, the Congress was so ineffectual that its members were like orphans, wandering from place to place in search of a permanent home. In 1783, they timidly withdrew from Philadelphia to escape the clamor of army veterans demanding back pay. They took refuge first in Princeton, New Jersey. Then, in 1785, the Congress moved to Annapolis, Maryland, and finally settled in New York City.

For the most part, the delegates were conspicuous by their absence. Only rarely, and with great difficulty, did Congress secure a legal majority so that it could conduct business, including ratifying the Treaty of Paris with Great Britain to end the Revolutionary War. Eighteen members representing only eight states voted on the most important piece of legislation that the Confederation government enacted: the Northwest Ordinance of 1787.

Toward Philadelphia

Weak, incompetent, and unpopular as it had become, the government under the Articles of Confederation had filled the need for a government for many Americans. Having fought a war for independence, the gentlemen who had crafted the Declaration of Independence and the Articles of Confederation wanted to make sure that political power stayed centered in the states, which they believed would fend off the possibility of a too-powerful federal government that might once again threaten their hard-fought and hard-won livelihoods.

ESSENTIAL

Veterans of the Revolutionary War were just one of many groups dissatisfied with how the Congress and new government was working. The group specifically was unhappy because the government had not yet paid back wages or tended to the issue of war pensions. Some of the disgruntled soldiers were officers, who at one point even entertained the idea of taking over the government with a military dictatorship in the so-called Newburgh Conspiracy of 1783.

But by the 1780s, some of the nation's more wealthy and powerful groups sought something different; a national government that would be more fully able to deal with the problems facing the new United States of America, especially the economic problems that most directly afflicted them. Now it seemed every group had some reason to complain about the Confederation government and its weaknesses.

In an address dated March 10, 1783, Major John Armstrong attacked the "coldness and severity" of Congress. He advised his fellow officers to challenge the authority of Congress and to abandon their posture of moderation and forbearance. He called on them to meet the next day, March 11, and draw up a "last remonstrance" that, if not adopted, could justify military defiance of Congress.

Armstrong had the support of such luminaries as General Horatio Gates and a man named Gouverneur Morris, who hoped to coerce the states into yielding more power to Congress. Many officers received Armstrong's address with enthusiasm. George Washington tactfully intervened to limit potential rebellion. On March 11, he issued an order forbidding the unauthorized meeting that Armstrong had proposed, but suggested that officers discuss their grievances at their regular meeting scheduled for March 15. After Washington withdrew, the officers adopted resolutions, without dissent, that affirmed their patriotism and asserted their confidence in Congress.

It was George Washington who helped quash the possibility of the army rebelling against the Congress. Addressing the March 15 meeting convened by Armstrong, Washington stressed that to take up arms against the government now would be an abomination. He expressed his confidence that Congress would treat the officers fairly, and counseled them to take no action that would sully the glory they had so recently won.

Army officers were not the only disgruntled Americans. Manufacturers were unhappy with tariffs imposed by the states and instead clamored for a national tariff. Businessmen and merchants also were unhappy with their respective state's commercial laws and wanted a uniform national commerce law. Then there was the question of western lands; speculators sensing the huge profits to be made from the sales of these lands wanted the government to do something about removing Native Americans from their area so white settlers could move in. Creditors, tired of dealing with the inflated paper currency issued by each state, wanted the government to step in. Investors wanted the government to honor their securities. Finally, the large land owners, fearful of mob violence from disgruntled farmers and former soldiers, looked to the government for protection, particularly in the aftermath of Shays' rebellion.

Shays' Rebellion

A rash of farm foreclosures in western Massachusetts set off a conflict that would reverberate throughout the nation. After the war, farmers in the area were hit particularly hard by taxes, an inflated state currency. Adding to that was the high salary paid to the state governor. In August 1786, a group of approximately 1,000 angry farmers and other citizens, led by Daniel Shays, a war veteran, marched on the city of Worcester where they proceeded to shut down the supreme court. Shays' "army" then marched on to Springfield where they broke into the local jail and freed several prisoners who were in jail because of debt.

FACT

Opinions over the rebellion among American political leaders varied. One of the leading proponents calling for the death penalty to the rebels was Samuel Adams, the strong patriot radical. However, Thomas Jefferson, then serving as minister to France saw the rebellion in a different light, writing, "The tree of liberty must be refreshed from time to time with the blood of patriots and tyrants. It is its natural manure."

In Boston, a number of wealthy individuals, fearful that the angry mob would march on the city next, raised monies to fund a private milita that would fend off the rebels if needed. Finally in February 1787, the militia defeated an attempt by the rebels to raid the Springfield Armory, and the rebellion was effectively crushed.

In the aftermath of the rebellion, a number of rebels were fined and imprisoned. Two were sentenced to death and hung. In 1788 a general amnesty was granted to the remaining protestors. Shays himself was pardoned and he returned to Massachusetts.

Shays' Rebellion, though a failure, did call attention to the fact that perhaps it was time for a stronger national government that would have the power to create uniform economic policies as well as being able to offer protection to property and land owners from those who might be tempted to threaten them. In effect, a strong federal government was the best chance for those who owned property to enjoy and keep their property without fear or threat from what was seen as the potentially explosive power in the hands of the common people.

Annapolis Convention

By 1786, the demands by the various factions clamoring for a stronger national government had grown to such a state that the Confederation Congress could no longer ignore their cries. The question now was not how the Confederation should be changed but in what way and how dramatic those changes would be. It was clear too, to those supporters of the Confederation, that the national government needed to be stronger, no matter their reluctance to what new dangers that might pose.

Taking the first action was James Madison, who persuaded the Virginia legislature to hold a conference for all the states in which the questions of national commerce would be discussed. Although only five states sent delegates to the conference that was held in Annapolis, Maryland, those that did not attend submitted their own proposal that called for a special convention to be convened in 1787 to revise the Articles of Confederation. By this time, Shays' Rebellion was underway and many state and national leaders who had earlier been indifferent to the Annapolis Convention now thought twice about attending the convention to be held in Philadelphia.

A Divided Convention

Between May and September 1787, fifty-five delegates representing all the states with the exception of Rhode Island made their way to the Philadelphia State House. It was an interesting group that convened during those months. Overall, the men were comparatively young. The average age of the delegates was forty-four; the oldest, Benjamin Franklin, was eighty-one. These men were well educated and had already made their marks in the various business and political circles of the states. Yet, even though they represented the more elite members of American society, these men were patriots, many of them having served the Revolutionary cause. They had all come to Philadelphia to put together a government.

Choosing George Washington to lead their sessions, the delegates, who had earlier decided to keep their sessions closed to the public, got to work. They had also decided that members of each state delegation would have a single vote. Major decisions did not require unanimity, as they did in Congress—only a simple majority.

Among the first order of business was a proposal put forth by the Virginia delegation represented by Edmund Randolph, George Mason, and James Madison. Calling their proposal the "Virginia Plan," the delegates outlined their ideas for a new national government.

The Virginia Plan provided for the organization of a new national legislature consisting of two houses. In the lower house, the states would be represented according to population. Members of the lower house were to be elected directly by the people. The plan also called for the election of members of the upper house by those delegates in the lower house; the candidates were to be nominated by the state legislatures. It was also suggested that not all states had to be represented in the upper house.

The Virginia Plan, crafted by James Madison, was an unusual document in that it called for the creation of a very different type of government than what had existed under the Articles of Confederation. The plan also aroused heated opposition from states with small populations such as Rhode Island and Delaware. Then too, there were some delegates who argued that the convention was to revise the Articles of Confederation only and that it was not necessary, nor desirable, to create an entirely new form of national government. Then there were some delegates who, while opposed to the Virginia Plan, offered alternatives to be considered by the convention delegates.

Other Plans

Another plan submitted to the convention was from Charles Pinckney of South Carolina. In Pinckney's plan, the new government would consist of a confederation of thirteen states with a bicameral, or two-house legislature consisting of a Senate and a House of Representatives. The number of representatives to the House would be based on population with 1 delegate for every 1,000 residents. Senators would be elected by the house and serve a term of four years. Congress would elect the president and would appoint the cabinet. Pinckney also provided for a supreme Federal Judicial Court. In the end however, the Pinckney plan was never under serious consideration.

Perhaps the most promising plan came from delegate William Paterson of New Jersey. In his "New Jersey Plan" Paterson suggested the idea of a federal government rather than a national government and to keep the existing unicameral, or one house, legislature in which each state had the same number of delegates. The plan also would grant Congress the right to tax and oversee commerce.

But, the delegates instead voted to table Paterson's recommendations, choosing instead to focus on the Virginia Plan for their debates and discussions. Clearly too, some resolution had to be reached with regard to the delegates from the smaller states if the Convention was to make any progress at all. It was then decided that members of the upper house would be elected directly by state legislatures rather than by the lower house of the national legislature. This way, each state would have at least one delegate in the upper house.

But other questions remained. For instance, how would states be equally represented; should there be equal representation or representation based on population? The issue of slavery also had to be considered; would slaves count as people or property? For members who represented the South, the solution seemed simple: count the slaves as people to determine the number of representatives, but for the sake of taxes, which were also to be based on population, count the slaves as property. For those delegates from nonslave-holding states, this was not an agreeable state of affairs. Instead, they argued, count slaves only as property when it came time to levy taxes, but not to count them for determining representation.

Hamilton Plan

Alexander Hamilton, not satisfied with either the New Jersey Plan or the Virginia Plan, also submitted his own plan for the new government. Known as the British Plan, because of its resemblance to the British system of a strong centralized government, Hamilton's proposal suggested the elimination of state autonomy and instead consolidating all thirteen states into a single nation.

The Hamilton Plan also included a two-house legislature, with the lower house elected by the votes for a term of three years. Electors who were chosen by the people would elect the upper house. Under the plan, governors were elected for lifetime service and would also have an absolute veto power over bills.

On June 18, 1787, Hamilton presented his plan to the convention and while the delegates thought it a well-conceived plan, in the end did not consider it because of the close similarities to the British system. The delegates were also unwilling to give up the idea of state sovereignty.

Compromise

All through June, battling heat and hot tempers, the delegates argued over the direction the new government would take. At times it seemed as if the convention were on the verge of disbanding without any hope of solving the political crisis. Benjamin Franklin strove to be the voice of reason, warning the delegates that if they failed at this task, they would "become a reproach and by-word to future ages. And what is worse, mankind may hereafter from this unfortunate instance, despair of establishing governments by human wisdom and leave it to chance, war, and conquest." The delegates continued to debate and discuss.

The Slavery Question

At last, on July 2, 1787, the convention established a committee consisting of a delegate from every state. Franklin would serve as chairman. Over the course of the next few weeks, several committees hammered out the details of the document that would become the United States Constitution, including the creation of yet another compromise over the issue of slavery. The delegates from the southern states feared that congressional power to regulate commerce might eventually enable Congress to interfere with the slave trade and with slavery itself.

One of the problems facing the delegates was the issue of population and taxation and how slaves were to be counted. Delegates debated over how to determine the value of a slave: whether it was a 4 to 3 ratio, a 1 to 2 ratio or even a 4 to 1 ratio. It would be James Madison who would suggest the ratio of 5 to 3.

Still, the northern delegates were not completely convinced. They argued that the South viewed their slaves as property; if they were to begin to count enslaved blacks as part of the population, then the North should be allowed to count livestock such as cattle and sheep as part of their population.

The committee finally came up with what would be called the "Great Compromise," in which, among other things, the thorny question of representation was addressed. The final proposal called for a legislature where in the lower house, the number of representatives would be chosen based on state population. Under this plan, enslaved blacks would be counted as three-fifths of a free person, which would also determine a state's representation and the amount of taxes it would pay. The upper house would be limited to two delegates. The committee's recommendations finally broke through the deadlock and on July 16, 1787, the convention voted to accept the compromise. Overall the compromise allowed for an even boundary between the North and the South wherein both sides accepted the Constitution and both had equal representation.

The convention also agreed that the new government could not impose a tax of more than ten dollars a head on imported slaves. Also, the government would have no authority to regulate the slave trade nor discontinue the international slave trade until 1808. To delegates from the northern states, and even a few from the southern states, who viewed the continued existence of slavery as an affront to the principles of the American republic, this concession was hard to make. They agreed to it because they feared, correctly, that without such a compromise, southerners would withhold their support from the new Constitution.

ESSENTIAL

The three-fifths compromise was based on the idea that slaves were only three-fifths as productive and free workers and so then contributed only 60 percent of the wealth to a state.

Other differences the convention could not resolve. The delegates disposed of them by evasion or omission, leaving crucial problems unattended that would resurface in the decades to come. The Constitution, for example, offered no definition of citizenship. More important, it contained no enumeration of individual rights that would define or restrain the powers of the national government. Madison, in fact, opposed the inclusion of such a bill of rights, insisting that to specify rights reserved to the people was unnecessary; however, others still harbored the fear of the potential danger of a government that might abuse its authority toward its citizens and become the enemy of liberty.

The Constitution of 1787

Many men contributed to the creation of the American Constitution. But none was more important than Virginian James Madison, certainly one of the most creative political thinkers of the revolutionary generation. It was Madison that designed the Virginia Plan from which the final document ultimately emerged. He also drafted most of the Constitution itself. But his most important contributions came in the resolution of two philosophical and troubling questions that plagued the delegates as they worked on the new Constitution. First was the question of sovereignty or self-government and the second was the issue of government powers.

The question of sovereignty had been among the principal sources of friction between the American colonists and the British government. It continued to perplex Americans as they attempted to fashion their own government. How could both the national government and the states exercise sovereignty? For Madison, the answer was quite simple: all the power ultimately derived from a third entity: the people. Neither the national nor the state governments were truly self-governing. Both derived their authority from the consent of the governed. The opening phrase of the Preamble to the Constitution—"We the people of the United States"—reflected the conviction that the new government derived its power from the citizens. Resolving the problem of sovereignty made possible one of the most distinctive attributes of the Constitution: the distribution of power between the national and state governments.

Unlike the Continental Congress, the national government would have extensive powers including the power to tax, regulate commerce and the currency. The government would also have the power to pass laws deemed "necessary and proper" that would allow it to carry out its duties. What was missing in the new document was the idea of state sovereignty as stated in the Articles of Confederation, which ordered that "each State shall retain every power, jurisdiction, and rights not expressly delegated to the United States in Congress assembled." Still, the Constitution did recognize the autonomy of the states.

In addition to the question of sovereignty, the Constitution produced a solution to the problem of concentrated governmental power, as nothing so frightened the leaders of the United States as the prospect of a tyrannical government. For many American leaders, the best and perhaps the only way to keep tyranny at bay was to maintain a government under the control of the people. This idea was based in part on the writings of the French political philospopher Charles Louis de Secondat, Baron de la Brede et de Montesquieu.

Montesquieu's ideas led Americans to the judgment that individual states must retain their autonomy; a strong centralized national government might lead them back down the road to tyranny that they recently escaped. Madison, however, pointed out that a large republic would be less likely to create tyranny as the possibility of creating many factions out of such a large group of people would make it almost impossible for one single group of people to ever dominate the government. Madison's idea that many diverse centers of power to balance each other and prevent the emergence of a single, despotic authority made it possible for Americans to approve of establishing a large republic. It also shaped the structure of the new government itself. One of the most distinctive characteristics of the Constitution was the separation of powers within the government and the system of checks and balances between the legislative, executive, and judicial branches.

According to Montesquieu, a republic should be a relatively small geographic area. Large nations, he believed, were more prone to the threats of corruption and despotism because rulers were so far away from the people that there was little in the way to control them from abusing their powers.

This new federal structure with clearly defined branches, each of which had distinct powers as well as the system of "checks and balances" which would divide power among the branches would hopefully protect the nation from any danger of corruption and tyranny whether it be one man, one group, or a majority.

The elder statesman Benjamin Franklin no doubt articulated sentiments that each of the delegates shared in one way or another when he said: "Thus I consent, Sir, to this Constitution, because I expect no better, and because I am not sure it is not the best."

Fears about the excesses of democracy were at least as important to the Founding Fathers as the fear of a single tyrant. To prevent the national government from being held hostage by the whims of public opinion, the Constitution provided that only members of the House could be elected directly by the people. As for senators, federal judges and even the president, there would be varying degrees for protection from undue public opinion and influence.

In late July, the convention appointed a Committee of Detail to draft a document based on the agreements that had been reached. After another month of discussion and refinement, a second committee, the Committee of Style and Arrangement, headed by Gouverneur Morris, and including Hamilton, William Samuel Johnson, Rufus King, and Madison, produced the final version, which was submitted for signing on September 17. Morris is credited, both now and then, as the chief draftsman of the final document, including the stirring preamble.

Not all the delegates were pleased with the results; some left before the ceremony, and three of those remaining refused to sign: Edmund Randolph, George Mason of Virginia, and Elbridge Gerry of Massachusetts. George Mason demanded a bill of rights if he was to support the Constitution. The bill of rights was not included in the Constitution submitted to the states for ratification, but many states ratified the Constitution with the understanding that a bill of rights would soon follow. Of the thirty-nine delegates who did sign, probably no one was completely satisfied. Their views were summed up by Benjamin Franklin, who said, "There are several parts of this Constitution which I do not at present approve, but I am not sure I shall never approve them. . . . I doubt too whether any other Convention we can obtain, may be able to make a better Constitution. . . . It therefore astonishes me, Sir, to find this system approaching so near to perfection as it does; and I think it will astonish our enemies. . . ." Finally, on September 17, 1787, thirty-nine delegates stepped up to sign the newly drafted Constitution. Now it was time to take the document to the states and enter the debates for ratification, pursuant to its own Article VII.

CHAPTER 5

The New American Republic

The delegates to the Philadelphia convention had greatly exceeded their instructions from Congress and the states. Instead of revising the Articles of Confederation, the delegates had created an entirely new form of government, one that could possibly be rejected by the states as, under the Articles, unanimous consent of all the states was needed for ratification. The Constitution, by contrast, stated that the new government could come into being when any nine of the thirteen adopted it. In addition, the delegates recommended that state conventions be held to debate and vote on whether or not to accept the Constitution as the new law of the land.

The Federalists

The Congress passively accepted the work of the Convention and submitted the Constitution to the states for approval or rejection. Legislatures in all the states with the exception of Rhode Island elected delegates to attend their state conventions. By early 1788, many of the conventions were under way. But that did not mean that others were not talking, debating, and arguing over the new document. State legislatures were also meeting to talk about the Constitution. Newspaper editorials, public meetings, and private conversations throughout the country were buzzing with what this document meant for the new nation. Those who advocated the Constitution enjoyed a number of important advantages over those who opposed it. First, the proponents of the Constitution had the support of the two most eminent and respected men in American society: Benjamin Franklin and George Washington. Second, they chose an appealing label for their movement. They called themselves "Federalists," which implied a commitment to maintaining the former system of autonomy and independence for the states even as they sought to establish a stronger national government. Third, the Federalists counted among their ranks the most able political philosophers in eighteenth-century America: Alexander Hamilton, John Jay, and James Madison.

Writing under the joint pseudonym "Publius," Hamilton, Jay, and Madison composed a series of eighty-five essays intended to explain the meaning, advantages, and virtues of the proposed Constitution. Published separately in newspapers throughout the United States during 1787 and 1788, these essays were later collected and issued as a book. They are known today as *The Federalist Papers*.

All advocates of nationalism, Hamilton, Jay, and Madison argued that the Constitution would preserve the American union, then in danger of breaking apart. They reminded Americans that Washington himself had declared that the American people faced a choice between the Constitution and disunion. The new Constitution, the Federalists asserted, would empower the government to act consistently and resolutely in the national interest. The Constitution would facilitate the resolution of economic and political conflicts because every state would be represented in the national legislature. Yet, at the same time, because the powers of the national government were few, limited, and defined, the Constitution did not threaten the traditional rights and liberties of the states. In short, from the Federalist point of view the new Constitution offered if not a perfect solution, then at least the best of all possible political options.

The Antifederalists

The Federalists labeled their critics "Antifederalists," implying that their rivals had nothing to offer except opposition and chaos. The label was a disaster for the Antifederalists, and has long caused confusion for students of American history. The Federalists controlled the debate over the Constitution and often badly distorted the issues. Their characterization of the Antifederalists, for example, was misleading. The Antifederalists were really federalists. The Federalists were not federalists at all, but nationalists.

In truth, the Antifederalists were not all negative in their criticism of the Constitution, but proposed serious and intelligent objections and alternatives. They presented themselves as the true defenders of liberty and independence for which Americans had fought the Revolution. Led by such principled statesmen as Patrick Henry of Virginia, George Clinton of New York, and Elbridge Gerry of Massachusetts, the Antifederalists believed that the Constitution betrayed those values by establishing a centralized and potentially tyrannical national government. This government, the Antifederalists contended, would increase taxes, obliterate the autonomy of the states, wield dictatorial power, initiate policies that favored the wealthy at the expense of ordinary citizens, and eventually restrict or eliminate individual liberty altogether.

The most serious complaint of the Antifederalists was that the Constitution lacked a bill of rights. The Antifederalists maintained that any government that centralized power would inevitably produce despotism. Their demand for a bill of rights issued from this conviction and the idea that human nature being what it was, there will always be the potential for an abuse of government power. Further, no government could be trusted entirely with the protection of the rights of its citizens. Only by carefully spelling out what those rights were would there be any guarantee that the people and their liberties would be protected. At its heart, the debate between the Federalists and the Antifederalists was a battle about two fears. The Federalists were afraid of the chaos that could result from a weak government. They dreaded the unrestrained power of the masses, and sought in the Constitution the guidelines to create a government that would function at some distance from the passions of the moment. The Antifederalists were not anarchists, as the Federalists alleged, but they were more concerned about the concentrated power of the government than about the dangers of the popular will. They opposed the Constitution for some of the same reasons that the Federalists supported it: it placed obstacles between the people and the exercise of power.

Ratification of the Constitution

Despite the Antifederalist efforts to prevent it, ratification of the Constitution proceeded quickly during the winter of 1787–1788. On September 20, 1787, the Constitutional Convention placed the final version of the Constitution before Congress. Congress then transmitted it to the states. By early 1788, the Constitution had been ratified either unanimously or by overwhelming majorities in Delaware (December 7, 1787), Pennsylvania (December 12, 1787), New Jersey (December 18, 1787), Georgia (January 2, 1788), Connecticut (January 9, 1788), and Massachusetts (February 7, 1788). The Massachusetts ratifying convention, however, attached a provision making ratification contingent on amendments being added to the Constitution to protect the rights of the states and individuals.

On March 24, 1788, the Federalists received their first setback when the Rhode Island convention rejected the Constitution. Angry Federalists boycotted the proceedings and thus ensured defeat, giving the Antifederalists a voting margin of 10 to 1. Only 237 out of the 2,945 who voted supported the Constitution. Federalist victories by large margins soon followed in Maryland on April 28, 1788 and South Carolina on May 23, 1788.

On June 21, 1788, New Hampshire became the ninth state to ratify the Constitution. The new Constitution was now theoretically in effect for those states that had accepted it, but two large, populous, and powerful states, Virginia and New York, had not yet acted. Much would depend on the decisions of their constitutional conventions. If either of these states decided against ratification, it would make the political waters of the nation much trickier.

Virginia and New York

In Virginia, prestigious statesmen stood on both sides of the debate. Patrick Henry, George Mason, and James Monroe opposed the Constitution. James Madison, Edmund Randolph, and most important, George Washington, supported it. Madison's logical arguments counteracted Henry's eloquent resistance. On June 25, the Virginia convention voted to ratify the Constitution by a vote of eighty-nine in favor and seventy-nine opposed. Yet, like the Massachusetts delegation, the Virginians insisted on the creation of a bill of rights.

The struggle now shifted to New York. For a while, much to the dismay of the Federalists, it seemed that New York would not enter the United States. The convention that assembled at Poughkeepsie was under the control of the fiercely Antifederalist governor, George Clinton. Organized against Clinton, the Federalists rallied to the leadership of John Jay and Alexander Hamilton.

Joined by James Madison, Jay, and Hamilton soon found themselves embroiled in a war of words with Clinton and other Antifederalists. Day after day the *Independent Gazeteer* published the short, insightful essays that Madison, Jay, and Hamilton wrote. These articles, which were later compiled and published as *The Federalist Papers*, helped to change the minds of the delegates to the New York convention.

Of equal importance to the ratification of the Constitution in New York was the pressure that merchants, artisans, and politicians from New York City exerted. They threatened that if the state of New York refused to join the Union, they would secede and join the Union on their own authority.

In addition to producing *The Federalist Papers*, Hamilton delayed the ratification vote until news of the decisions of the New Hampshire and Virginia conventions had an opportunity to influence the outcome of the vote in New

York. Hamilton's strategy worked. The New York convention yielded as even the most staunch Antifederalists feared that the commercial interests of New York would suffer if the state remained outside of the Union. On July 26, 1788, after an impassioned address by Hamilton, the New York delegates ratified the Constitution by a close vote of thirty to twenty-seven.

For all intents and purposes, the battle was over. The Federalists had won. Rhode Island and North Carolina were still outside the Union, though they were not as essential to it as were Virginia and New York. The North Carolina delegation, despite a strong Federalist presence, withheld ratification pending the incorporation of a bill of rights into the Constitution, eventually adopting the Constitution on November 21, 1789. Rhode Island, whose leaders had opposed the Constitution from the outset, did not even call a convention to consider ratification. Without fanfare, Rhode Island at last adopted the Constitution on May 29, 1790.

The New American State

The first elections under the Constitution took place in the early months of 1789. There was never any doubt about who would be the first president. George Washington had guided the Continental army to victory in the Revolutionary War. He had presided over the Constitutional Convention. Many Americans favored ratification only because they believed that Washington would also lead the new government. It is no exaggeration to say that Americans were willing to venture the experiment with a new national government only because of their unreserved trust in George Washington.

Washington won unanimous election to the presidency in 1789. Following a journey from his beloved Mount Vernon in Virginia to the temporary capital in New York City, which was marked by elaborate and enthusiastic celebrations all along the route, Washington took the oath of office and was sworn in as the first president of the United States on April 30, 1789.

The first Congress, which had assembled on March 4, 1789, served in many ways as a continuation of the Constitutional Convention. The most important task of the senators and representatives was to draft a bill of rights. On September 25, 1789, Congress approved twelve amendments to the Constitution, ten of which were ratified by the states. They became part of the Constitution on December 15, 1791.

These ten amendments constitute what is known today as the Bill of Rights. Nine of them place limitations on the government by forbidding it to infringe on certain fundamental rights and liberties that all citizens enjoy in common, such as the freedom of religion and speech, the immunity from arbitrary arrest, the guarantee of a speedy and public trial by jury, and the protection from cruel and unusual punishment. The Tenth Amendment granted to the states or the people all powers not specifically delegated to the national government. In other words, the amendment keeps the federal government from interfering with individual rights not granted in the Constitution to ensure that the government would not interfere with the daily lives of its citizens.

ESSENTIAL

On September 24, Congress enacted the Federal Judiciary Act, which provided for the organization of a supreme court that would consist of a chief justice and five associate justices. The Judiciary Act also authorized the creation of thirteen district courts and three circuit courts. John Jay became the first Supreme Court justice of the United States. Edmund Randolph became the first attorney general, the chief judicial officer in the land.

Meanwhile, while awaiting ratification, Congress established three executive departments: the Department of State, Department of War, and Department of the Treasury. Established on July 27, 1789, the Department of State fell under the leadership of Thomas Jefferson, whom Washington designated as his choice for Secretary of State. The Department of War was created on August 7, 1789. For Secretary of War, Washington chose Massachusetts Federalist Henry Knox. On September 2, 1789, Congress created the Department of the Treasury. Washington appointed Alexander Hamilton as Secretary of the Treasury because of his widely acknowledged expertise in public finance. In addition, Congress created the office of Postmaster General on September 22, and named Samuel Osgood to fill it.

There is no question that imagination and vision played vital roles in the creation of a new nation and government. Collaboration and compromise, guided by the belief that men should live free without fear of tyranny, forged the direction for thirteen colonies to grow from separate entities to a loose grouping and finally to a united group of states, dedicated to the proposition that freedom was essential and a government of the people was necessary for the creation of a republic.

PART II

★ THE TOP SEVEN FOUNDERS ★

In 1973, American historian Richard B. Morris wrote the book *Seven Who Shaped Our Destiny: The Founding Fathers as Revolutionaries*. In his work, Morris identified the following men as the seven key figures in the shaping of the new nation: John Adams, Benjamin Franklin, Alexander Hamilton, John Jay, Thomas Jefferson, James Madison, and George Washington. These men all played pivotal roles and served in a variety of capacities to help win American freedom and establish a new nation. While there are many other Founding Fathers in our nation's history, the story of our nation would be incomplete without noting the accomplishments of these seven.

Quiz: Astounding Accomplishments: Can You Name Them All?

1. The only president of the United States to be unanimously elected was:

A. Thomas Jefferson
B. James Madison
C. George Washington
D. John Adams

2. Alexander Hamilton was killed:

A. At the Battle of Long Island
B. At sea en route to his post as minister plenipotentiary to France
C. In a duel
D. In a riding accident

3. The Virginia Plan was:

A. A blueprint of a new national government
B. The demand of the delegates from Virginia that the Northern states recognize the legitimacy of slavery in exchange for no taxes on exports
C. The proposal that the government of the United States be modeled after the state government of Virginia
D. A method of scientific farming developed by George Washington and James Madison

4. Which of the Founding Fathers died within hours of each other on July 4, 1826?

A. Benjamin Franklin and George Washington
B. Alexander Hamilton and Aaron Burr
C. James Madison and George Washington
D. John Adams and Thomas Jefferson

5. The royal governor of New Jersey from 1763–1776 was the son of:

A. Alexander Hamilton
B. John Jay
C. James Madison
D. Benjamin Franklin

6. The first president to occupy the White House was:

A. George Washington
B. Thomas Jefferson
C. John Adams
D. James Madison

7. During The War of 1812:

A. Construction of the Washington Monument was suspended
B. Anglicans were forced to worship in secret
C. President Madison declared July 4 a national holiday
D. British troops burned the city of Washington

8. John Jay served as minister to:

A. France and England
B. Spain and France
C. England and France
D. Spain and England

9. Which of the following sold his books to restart the Library of Congress?

A. John Adams
B. John Jay
C. Thomas Jefferson
D. James Madison

10. Which president reduced the national debt by one-third?

A. John Adams
B. Thomas Jefferson
C. James Madison
D. George Washington

Answers

1.C 2.C 3.A 4.D 5.D 6.C 7.D 8.B 9.C 10.B

CHAPTER 6

George Washington

George Washington remains the most iconic of the Founding Fathers. He was the nation's first president, commander in chief of the Continental forces during the Revolutionary War, a statesman, and a planter. Washington's steady hand guided the country through war and the creation of a new republic.

Early Life

The early life of the man revered as the father of his country is remarkably obscure. He was born on February 22, 1732 on his father's tobacco plantation in Westmoreland County, Virginia. His father, Augustine Washington, had two sons and a daughter by his first marriage. George was the oldest of six children from Augustine's second marriage. In 1735, Augustine moved his family to another plantation, Little Hunting Creek, later called Mount Vernon. In 1738, the entire family moved again to another new plantation, Ferry Farm, near Fredericksburg.

When George was eleven years of age his father died, and in his will he left most of his property to his two eldest sons, Lawrence and Augustine. The remainder of his estate produced income to sustain his six younger children. Although Washington was born into Virginia's planter society, he did not enjoy a lavish upbringing. He was tutored at home. Many of his peers were educated abroad but there was no money for him to study in England, so his was a practical education, not the classical education that was the birthright of the upper classes of colonial America. He excelled in mathematics and learned surveying. He knew no foreign languages and never attended college.

Education was so important to Washington that he left money in his will to go toward the establishment of a free school in Alexandria, Virginia for the education of orphaned children. He also left fifty shares of his holdings in the Potomac Company toward the endowment of a university to be established in the District of Columbia. Columbian College was established in 1821, and in 1904 was renamed George Washington University.

After his father's death, Washington went to live with his older half-brother Lawrence at Mount Vernon. Lawrence became Washington's mentor, teaching him the rules of polite society and the details of plantation management. Washington continued his surveyor's training, and when he was sixteen he accompanied the surveyor of Prince William County on a trip to the Shenandoah Valley. He kept a diary of his experiences in which he describes the hardship of the trip, noting, for example, the experience of sleeping under "one Thread Bear blanket with double its Weight of Vermin such as Lice Fleas &c." The following year, when he was only seventeen years of age, Washington was appointed surveyor of Culpeper County. His surveying skills and travels into the frontier sparked his interest in the settlement of western lands.

In 1752, Lawrence died from tuberculosis and Washington inherited Mount Vernon, as well as his brother's place in the Virginia militia and his rank as major. Washington loved farming and excelled at the management of his estate. He was particularly proud of Mount Vernon and gradually increased the size of the plantation to more than 3,000 acres and enlarged and remodeled the plantation house.

When Washington inherited Mount Vernon the property came with eighteen slaves. By the time he died, more than 300 slaves lived on the property. Nearly half of them belonged to Washington and the rest were dower slaves (those his wife Martha brought to the marriage as her widow's share from the estate of her first husband). Washington's will stated that all slaves at Mount Vernon should be freed after Martha's death. However, Martha Washington freed all of the slaves shortly after his death.

Early Military Career

With the pleasure of owning Mount Vernon came civic and social responsibilities, and Washington was often called away from his home to tend to the security of the frontier. In 1753, Governor Dinwiddie sent Washington to the French fortifications in territory south of Lake Erie, the Ohio Country (what is now western Pennsylvania but was then claimed by Virginia), with a letter demanding they evacuate the area. (Possession of the Ohio Country was hotly contested by the British, the French, the Iroquois, and other native tribes residing in the area.) The French commander responded with a polite but firm refusal to leave the area. Such requests, he informed Washington, should be directed to the commander of French forces in North

America. When Washington returned to Williamsburg with the news, Dinwiddie decided to escalate his actions. He commissioned Washington a lieutenant colonel and charged him with organizing a militia to return to the Ohio Country to remove the French.

In 1754, Lieutenant Colonel Washington returned to the Ohio Country with a small contingent of volunteers and the promise of additional assistance from Mingo warriors. He led a successful surprise attack against the French, in which his men seized the French fort, killed nine soldiers, including the diplomatic emissary Joseph Coulon de Jumonville, and took the rest as prisoners. Washington retreated to Fort Necessity where he was subsequently surrounded by French forces and forced to surrender. The French allowed him to return to Virginia with his troops but the surrender document he signed accused him of assassinating Jumonville and the others. The document was in French, a language Washington did not know, and it is plausible he did not understand the terms he acknowledged by his signature. The attack and Washington's inadvertent confession of assassinating Jumonville by signing the surrender agreement sparked the rapid deterioration of relations between the French and the British in North America, which culminated in the French and Indian War.

Washington was promoted to colonel and served as an aide to General Edward Braddock, whose mission was to once and for all remove the French from the Ohio Country. Braddock's forces were routed at the Battle of Monongahela, where they were ambushed by the French and their Native American allies. Braddock was mortally wounded and it fell to Washington to organize a retreat, during which Washington had two horses shot out from under him and his coat was grazed by four bullets, although he was not hit. In August 1755 he was given command of the Virginia militia.

Washington's new role was difficult. He had to defend a frontier line that was 350 miles long with only 700 colonial troops. The Virginia legislature was stingy with money and provisions to supply the militia. Disheartened by the lack of government support and weakened by dysentery, Washington returned to Mount Vernon. In 1758 he was elected to the House of Burgesses and resigned his commission. By the age of twenty-seven he had considerable military experience to his credit, but he hoped to focus his life back on Mount Vernon and on domestic tranquility.

Marriage and Family

Washington married Martha Dandridge Custis on January 6, 1759. Martha was a wealthy widow and brought nearly a hundred slaves and considerable acreage to the marriage. Martha also had two young children who Washington adopted as his own. Relieved of his military responsibilities and surrounded with a new family, Washington settled contentedly into the life of a Virginia planter. He enjoyed supervising work on his land and was often observed rolling up his sleeves and doing some of the labor himself. He directed his plantations to be self-sufficient operations and purchased or imported as little as possible. Washington took his role of steward of the land seriously. He practiced crop rotation, experimented with breeding livestock, and maintained extensive fruit orchards.

Washington rarely attended church and enjoyed fox hunting and Madeira wine. He socialized with the other premier Virginia families, the Lees, Byrds, Carters, and Lewises. He liked to entertain, throw parties, play cards, and race horses. In the period between 1768 and 1775 he extended his hospitality to approximately 2,000 guests at Mount Vernon. This was the life Washington enjoyed and envisioned living for the rest of his days.

Revolutionary War

A peaceful life at Mount Vernon was, of course, not to be. While he was recognized by his peers as a man of high character, no one entertained the notion Washington possessed leadership qualities that would place him at the forefront of the coming war with Britain and the creation of a new nation.

However, Washington gradually came to resent Parliament's incursions into the economic affairs of the colonies. He was displeased by the Proclamation of 1763 that forbade settlement west of the proclamation line. He was interested in land companies that would have offered him the opportunity to speculate in western lands, but after 1763, that was no longer possible. The additional pressure of revenue taxes the British government imposed on the American colonists pushed him to protest imperial economic policies. Washington listened to Patrick Henry denounce the Stamp Act in 1765 and was inspired by the undercurrent of dissent against Britain. His opposition was gradual; it was not until the passage of the Townshend

Acts that Washington became active in the mounting protests against Britain. In 1769, he and George Mason drafted a proposal for Virginians to boycott British goods until the Townshend Acts were repealed. When the acts were suspended in 1770, Washington thought the worst was over. However, with the introduction of the Intolerable Acts in 1774, he realized Americans were not safe from commercial exploitation by Britain.

Washington supported the creation of a Continental Congress in 1774 and in May of that year was sent as one of Virginia's first representatives. Washington was not an especially vocal member of Congress, but by this time he had clearly drifted into the radical camp. He had grown weary of continually petitioning Parliament for relief from taxation only to have the requests summarily dismissed, and he concluded there was no longer a reason to nurture hope for reconciliation. It was clear to him that Parliament had no intention of adjusting colonial policy at the behest of the colonists or acknowledging the colonies' right to direct representation. He did not desire an armed conflict but saw no alternative considering the circumstances, and Washington was by no means alone in these sentiments. By 1775, Congress agreed the colonies needed to prepare for their own defense. When the Second Continental Congress met in Philadelphia in May 1775, Washington appeared in full uniform.

In March 1775, John Adams wrote, "Colonel Washington appears at Congress in his uniform, and by his great experience and abilities in military matters, is of much service to us."

Command of the Continental Army

No one knows whether Washington's decision to present himself in full uniform before the other congressional delegates was a calculated maneuver. He certainly had more military experience than most men in Congress but his record so far, while valorous, was not particularly distinguished. He had no formal military training and had no idea how to fight in large formations, manage cavalry or artillery, or organize massive supply logistics, but that was true of most of the men in Congress.

When the question of who should lead the colonial armed forces arose, John Adams immediately proposed Washington. It was difficult for anyone to find fault with the suggestion. Washington was widely regarded as a virtuous, sober, calm, modest, capable man. He was clearly ready to rise to the challenge, and although he missed his home and his family, he was cognizant of the destiny that was set out for him. There are other considerations that played into Washington's appointment as the commander in chief of the Continental army. Up to this point, the Massachusetts radicals had steered most of the course of the action. John Adams recognized the utility of appointing a Virginian, a southerner, to lead the Massachusetts volunteers against the British. Washington's appointment was a way to bring the colonial armed effort under the aegis of a national army.

There was another reason John Adams supported George Washington as commander in chief. The other man obviously interested in the job was John Hancock. Hancock and Adams were former friends and political allies, but by 1775 were politically at odds. John and Samuel Adams were alarmed at Hancock's rapid ascension to power and were determined to rein him in. Blocking Hancock's chances of acquiring the one position he coveted more than anything else, commander in chief, was a political coup for the Adamses and a slight to Hancock that he never forgot.

At War with Britain

Washington's first military encounters went deceptively well. He removed the British from Boston, largely because the British position there was unsustainable, largely owing to choked supply points. In June 1776 the British returned under the command of General William Howe, who was ordered to seize New York City. Howe was in command of the largest expeditionary forces Britain had sent abroad.

Washington's first test came at the Battle of Long Island, a disastrous encounter in which Washington was outmatched and outmanned. He managed to direct his retreating forces to safety across the East River without casualties. His ability to save his men and supplies was laudable, but his subsequent encounters with the British were similarly calamitous. Washington suffered a series of humiliating defeats in 1776. His luck changed on December 25, 1776 at the Battle of Trenton, which was followed by another victory at the Battle of Princeton in January 1777. These victories forced the British back to New York City, which they held until 1783.

Nevertheless, these victories were not enough to end the war in favor of the Americans. The Continental army fought against monumental challenges, the worst of which were the lack of adequate supplies, uniforms, food, and pay. Congress could requisition money from the colonies, but had no authority to collect it. The colonies most likely to contribute were those in the path of imminent danger from the war; those on the periphery were less likely to contribute much if anything. The continental currency was worthless, and local suppliers were less inclined to sell provisions to the American forces when the British army was prepared to pay in pounds sterling. Hence, the Continental army was starved, bedraggled, and ill-equipped.

Washington had to contend with this crisis as well as rumblings to relieve him of his duties. He knew he was pitted against British superiority in numbers and resources. General Howe believed if the British captured major American cities, the colonists would surrender. In 1777, he moved against Philadelphia. Washington tried to stop him but was defeated at the Battle of Brandywine and the road to Philadelphia lay open to the British. Although Philadelphia fell, the Americans kept fighting. The Congress was evacuated to Baltimore and the war continued. Washington's inconsistent record on the battlefield left some to wonder if he should remain in charge of the Continental forces. His inability to protect Philadelphia in 1777 increased chatter among his detractors in Congress that Washington should be relieved of his command. In addition to grumblings in Congress, Washington had to defuse a plot hatched by some of his officers to promote themselves by removing Washington from his responsibilities. When Washington became aware of the plot to remove him, he confronted the parties involved and with the support of heavyweights such as the Marquis de Lafayette and Alexander Hamilton, Washington survived the conspiracy.

The crucial moment of the war was Cornwallis's defeat at Yorktown. Washington's management of the Battle of Yorktown was his finest hour, and the British surrender at Yorktown signaled the last phases of the war. The British still had troops in New York, Charleston, and Savannah, and the British navy still lurked off the cost. The Treaty of Paris was not signed until 1783, and on December 23 of that year, Washington officially resigned his commission and returned to Mount Vernon.

Benjamin Franklin wrote to an English friend in 1784, "An American planter was chosen by us to command our troops, and continued during the whole war. The man sent home to you, one after another, five of your best generals, baffled, their heads bare of laurels, disgraced even in the opinion of their employers."

The Road to the Presidency

Again, Washington's retirement to Mount Vernon was brief. Although he enjoyed his relaxation into private life, he was a keen observer of the post-war world. The news of Shays' Rebellion disturbed him, and seemed to be symptomatic of a general state of disarray and chaos. The government under the Articles of Confederation was clumsy and ineffective. The condition of the economy was dire. The increasing dominance of state interests over national ones, in his opinion, compromised an already unstable national government. By 1785 it was obvious to anyone concerned for the fate of the new nation that reform was essential. He wrote to James Madison that the country needed a robust constitution if they ever hoped to survive.

Washington was in favor of reform but when he was chosen as a delegate to the Constitutional Convention in 1787, he went reluctantly. He was unanimously selected to preside over the convention but he was mostly a silent observer to the proceedings. He was, nevertheless, a crucial and ardent supporter for the document's ratification. When the Constitution was adopted, he returned to Mount Vernon intending to enjoy life worrying about his crops and his trees, and not worrying so much about the new government.

Presidency

The Electoral College unanimously elected Washington to be the nation's first president in 1789, a position he accepted with honor and some reluctance. He remains the only president in America to be unanimously elected. He took the presidential oath of office at Federal Hall in New York City on April 30, 1789. As the first president he was acutely aware that his actions and his administration would establish precedent that would define the office, a concern he expressed to James Madison, "As the first of everything in our situation will serve to establish a precedent it is devoutly wished on my part that these precedents be fixed on true principles." Washington also took pains to establish a republican style that would in no way resemble the aristocratic trappings associated with European heads of state.

Washington delivered his first State of the Union address modestly attired in a "crow colored suit of clothes, of American manufacture...This elegant fabric was from the manufactory in Hartford." —*The Virginia Herald and Fredericksburg Advertiser*, January 21, 1790

Domestic Affairs

In his first term, Washington was primarily preoccupied with establishing the role of the executive branch. He immediately surrounded himself with talented men, appointing Alexander Hamilton as Secretary of the Treasury, Thomas Jefferson as Secretary of State, Henry Knox as Secretary of War, and Edmund Randolph as Attorney General. This inner circle of experts developed into the presidential cabinet. By the end of his first term, much of Washington's time was spent managing the egos of the personalities he had chosen to help him, notably dealing with the inevitable quarrels between Hamilton and Jefferson.

Perhaps the most important matter Washington had to deal with was the fragile state of the economy. America was burdened by staggering foreign and domestic debts accrued during the war. At issue was how to raise money to pay them. Secretary of the Treasury Alexander Hamilton proposed levying tariffs on imports and a tax on liquor. He also favored the creation of a national bank. All of these proposals immediately put Washington and Hamilton at loggerheads with Thomas Jefferson who disapproved of granting the federal government such overarching authority. Hamilton and Jefferson were able to arrive at a compromise in which Jefferson assented to Hamilton's policy to address the debt and the national economy and Hamilton acquiesced to Jefferson's request that the new and permanent capital for the nation be relocated to a site on the Potomac near Virginia.

This was the last episode of amity between the two and by the end of Washington's first term the ideological split that divided them coalesced into two clearly defined rival factions. Jefferson emerged as the head of the Democratic-Republican Party and Hamilton as the leader of the Federalists. The collapse into partisanship that Washington had feared and tried to prevent happened anyway and it occurred early in the life of the new government.

During his tenure as president, Washington was also required to make the decision to use military force to suppress an internal uprising, the Whiskey Rebellion, and to quell Indian attacks on the northwestern frontier. He sent troops under the command of General Anthony Wayne to fortify the Northwest Territory (later to become Ohio) against marauding Indians. By the summer of 1794, General Wayne and his forces defeated a coalition of seven Indian tribes at the Battle of Fallen Timbers, forcing the Indians to move westward and acquiring substantial parcels of Indian lands for the United States.

Disputes with Indians were hardly Washington's only problem in the interior. Frontier districts in western Pennsylvania and Virginia erupted in protest over the excise tax on distilled liquors. Washington ordered state militias to restore order, and he personally led the troops to the disruptive districts. As the militias marched into western Pennsylvania the rebellion collapsed, and Washington proudly claimed the situation was settled without a drop of bloodshed. In the end, twenty men were arrested but all were eventually acquitted or pardoned. Washington's willingness to bring federal power to bear on a violent uprising against the laws of the government was viewed as a success and as proof of the new constitution's effectiveness.

Foreign Affairs

The year 1789 not only marked the date of Washington's first inauguration but also the beginning of the French Revolution. Although many Americans supported the French revolutionaries in a gesture of solidarity from the days the French supported the American war for independence from Britain, Washington intended to remain neutral on the matter. His position of neutrality became more difficult to defend as the British provoked Indians to attack American settlers moving westward, and the historic parallels between a deserving France and a hostile Britain seemed very clear to many Americans. Washington grew concerned over mounting American popular support for military assistance to France in the event France became entangled in a war with Great Britain, and was convinced the last thing America needed was to jeopardize its future by wedging itself between two great European powers at war. Washington's decision to remain neutral set the precedent for future presidents to determine when or if America should become involved in disputes between foreign powers.

Shortly after Washington's second inauguration, the revolutionary government of France declared war on most of Western Europe, including Great Britain. In these circumstances, Washington found the task of enforcing neutrality all the more difficult in the tide of growing anti-British sentiment. By 1793 the British declared they would seize American ships trading with France. The British also fortified parts of Ohio in an effort to destabilize the northwest frontier.

Determined to keep America out of war, Washington sent John Jay as an envoy to Britain to negotiate a diplomatic solution to the tensions between Britain and America. The Jay Treaty kept America out of war with Britain until 1812. According to the treaty, the British agreed to abandon their western forts and to compensate American ship owners, but Jay was unable to secure an agreement that ended the impressments of American sailors, and this was the point of contention that would later reignite tensions between the United States and Great Britain in the early nineteenth century.

Washington also concluded two other treaties during his second term. The United States was forced to make a treaty with Algiers in 1796 to protect American shipping from pirates along the Barbary Coast in Northern Africa. The treaty was more on the order of formalizing protection money for the safe passage of American commercial shipping in the region than it was a diplomatic arrangement. In exchange for payments to the Regency of Algiers, American ships could pass unmolested along the Barbary Coast.

Other nations were also plagued by the Barbary pirates and either had to pay tribute to ensure the safety of their merchant shipping, or they maintained naval squadrons in the area. By the time of Washington's presidency, the United States navy consisted of 700 men, and the scarce military appropriations that were available were designated toward the maintenance of an army. There were disputes whether or not a navy was necessary. Thomas Jefferson and James Madison both believed a foreign naval force would never pose a serious threat to American liberty. The situation in the Mediterranean was proving otherwise. Washington's belief that a navy was essential to the security of the new republic gained credence with the conclusion of the treaty with the Regency of Algeria. Washington's petitions to congress for appropriations to organize a navy eventually culminated in the Act to Provide Naval Armament, which Washington signed on March 27, 1794. The act provided for the construction of six frigates of a quality that surpassed anything in service in the navies of Europe. Instead of using private contractors, government employees would build the ships and the government authorized the establishment of six shipyards located along the coast to geographically distribute the economic benefits of the naval build up. The shipyards were located in Portsmouth, Boston, New York, Philadelphia, Baltimore, and Norfolk.

ESSENTIAL

Washington personally selected the names for five of the new frigates: *Congress, Constitution, President, United States, and Constellation.* The sixth frigate, *Chesapeake*, was named later.

Washington's administration also reached a formal agreement with Spain in the Treaty of San Lorenzo (1796). The treaty defined the boundaries between American territory and Spanish Colonial holdings in North America. As a result of this treaty, the Spanish agreed to allow unrestricted access to the Mississippi River and the Ohio River Valley to American trade and settlement. Spain also ceded the Philippines, Guam, Puerto Rico, and other islands under Spanish control on the West Indies to the United States.

Life after the Presidency

In 1797 Washington finally returned to Mount Vernon, where he was able to enjoy a few years of life as a country gentleman. He focused on his family, the operations of his plantation, and the care of his slaves. His tranquility was temporarily interrupted by his appointment as commander in chief of the Provisional army when it appeared as though America would go to war with France, but that prospect passed and much to his relief he never had to fulfill this responsibility.

Washington died at home on December 12, 1799 at sixty-seven years of age. He was buried at Mount Vernon.

Upon Washington's death, Congress chose Henry "Lighthorse Harry" Lee, a fellow Virginian, Continental army officer, and a longtime friend of Washington's, to deliver a eulogy on behalf of the country. The following section is legendary: "First in war, first in peace, and first in the hearts of his countrymen, he was second to none in humble and endearing scenes of private life. Pious, just, humane, temperate, and sincere; uniform, dignified, and commanding, his example was as edifying to all around him as were the effects of that example lasting."

Legacy

Washington is forever memorialized as the father of his country, a capable leader of the Continental army, the first president of the United States of America, and the man for whom the national capital is named. No matter how many times his country called on him, he always maintained he was "dispensable." In his farewell address from the presidency, Washington invoked a sentiment that embodied the total of what his career as a soldier and as a politician had been about, the fruits born from the struggle to create the American republic, ". . . I anticipate with pleasing expectation that retreat, in which I promise myself to realize, without alloy, the sweet enjoyment of partaking, in the midst of my fellow Citizens, the benign influence of good Laws under a free Government—the ever favourite object of my heart, and the happy reward, as I trust, of our mutual cares, labours and dangers."

CHAPTER 7

John Adams

John Adams rose from obscurity as a country lawyer to become one of the most influential figures of the American Revolution and the early national period. He was an early advocate of independence and the creation of a republic. He was a member of the Continental Congress and a signer of the Declaration of Independence. Adams also served extensive diplomatic tours in France, Holland, and Britain, posts that kept him abroad during the Constitutional Convention. He was Washington's vice president and the second president of the United States. He was also the father of a future president, John Quincy Adams.

Early Life

John Adams was born October 30, 1735 in Braintree, Massachusetts, the eldest of three sons, to John Adams Sr. and Susanna Boylston Adams. His branch of the Adams family traced their history in America to the first Puritan settlers in New England. John Adams Sr. was a farmer and rose to the position of deacon in the Congregational church and was a selectman for the village. He wanted John to become a minister and sent his son to Harvard to prepare for a career in the ministry. John graduated in 1755, but by then was not sure he was suited for the clergy. He became a schoolmaster until he decided what he should be doing with his life. After three years of searching, he was confident his true calling was the law. Adams began his legal studies in the law offices of John Putnam and was admitted to the bar in 1758.

John Adams and John Hancock were both born in Braintree and were boyhood friends. Adams recalled that the two were sent to Dame Belcher's school in their early days, as soon "as we were out of petticoats."

Adams married Abigail Smith in 1764. Abigail was a bright young woman who had taken great pains to educate herself, and she proved to be a worthy intellectual companion as well as an affectionate and devoted spouse. Abigail came from distinguished stock. Her father, William Smith, was a minister and her grandfather, Colonel John Quincy, was a Harvard graduate and a speaker of the Massachusetts House of Representatives. Although Abigail had little formal education, she immersed herself in her father's library and she developed a sophisticated view of the world from the varied guests that visited her grandfather's home. John and Abigail had five children, one of whom, John Quincy, would become the sixth president of the United States. Their marriage was as much a political partnership as a partnership of the heart.

Adams moved his family to his father's farmstead in Braintree and built his law practice from the modest farmhouse he called home as a boy. His clients included many wealthy local landowners and businessmen, among them his boyhood friend John Hancock. The right of law was his guiding principle when he entered politics.

Revolutionary War

Adams rapidly became a prominent figure in the American resistance to taxation. His opposition to the Stamp Act is outlined in his "Dissertation on the Canon and Feudal Law," in which he argued that Parliament's attempts to tax the colonists was a blatant example of the corruption within English politics. In this document he reinforced the concepts that the Stamp Act was a violation of the colonists' rights as Englishmen and free men should only be taxed by their consent.

In 1770, his devotion to the principle of law was further illustrated when he was asked to defend the British soldiers in the aftermath of the Boston Massacre. Serving as defense counsel for British soldiers did not make him very popular at the moment, but most had to admit that it proved him to be a man of character. Adams was satisfied with the outcome of the trial because he believed the trial was conducted fairly and justice was served. It was important to prove to Britain that legal proceedings in Massachusetts could be done without further resorting to mob violence.

QUOTE

Adams's sentiments regarding the trial were recorded in his diary. "It was, however, the most gallant, generous, manly and disinterested actions of my whole life, and one of the best pieces of service I ever rendered my country. Judgment of death against these soldiers would have been as foul a stain upon this country as the executions of the Quakers or witches, anciently."

Early Career in Revolutionary Politics

Along with his second cousin Samuel, Adams was a delegate to the First Continental Congress. They both quickly emerged as leaders of the radical faction. Prepared to move for independence, they rejected any idea of a compromise or reconciliation with Britain. John Adams was a member of the secret

Committee on Foreign Correspondence to secure foreign aid, the War and Ordnance Board, and the committee to draft the Declaration of Independence.

A powerful orator with a formidable style, Adams advanced persuasive arguments calculated to win over reluctant delegates who may have favored the concept of liberty but who were cautious about severing relations with Britain. Adams threw himself passionately into the proceedings. Thomas Jefferson described him as "our Colossus on the floor" who may not have been the most elegant or tactful of speakers, but who "came out with a power . . . which moved us from our seats."

Adams was pleased with the Declaration of Independence and sobered by the thoughts of what lay ahead and what future generations would make of July 4, 1776. He wrote to Abigail, "I am well aware of the toil and blood and treasure that it will cost us to maintain this Declaration, and support and defend these States. Yet through all the gloom I can see the rays of ravishing light and glory. I can see that the end is more than worth all the means. And that posterity will tryumph in that day's transaction, even altho we should rue it, which I trust in God we shall not."

During the Second Continental Congress, Adams nominated George Washington to serve as commander in chief of the Continental army and proposed Thomas Jefferson should write the draft of the Declaration of Independence. Adams deeply admired both men, but he had motives for making the selections he did. Drawing on two talented and capable Virginians was a calculated move to link the fates of the northern colonies and the southern colonies in a common cause.

Political Career

Adams's primary contributions during the Revolutionary War were in diplomacy. In 1777, he was selected by the Continental Congress to join Benjamin Franklin in France to assist with the negotiation of an alliance with France. He left for France in February 1778, with his son John Quincy. The voyage was dangerous; they had to navigate their way through violent storms and around British warships and by the time they arrived, Franklin had already completed the treaty. Adams returned to Massachusetts in 1779 in time to attend the Massachusetts Constitutional Convention. Adams was the principal author of the constitution for the state of Massachusetts.

After his work on the Massachusetts Constitution, he again went abroad to work on a variety of missions. He assisted Benjamin Franklin as part of the American delegation to negotiate the peace treaty with Britain. Subsequently he was sent as ambassador to the Dutch Republic, where he was instrumental in the negotiation of a Treaty of Amity and Commerce and a loan of 5 million guilders to help America pay its European creditors.

In 1784 Thomas Jefferson was sent to Paris to replace Franklin as the American minister and to work with Adams. During this period they came to know each other well and became close friends. In 1785, Adams was sent to London as minister to the Court of St. James, where he was finally reunited with his family after a separation of five years. As Americans, John and Abigail were regarded with suspicion and received a frosty reception at the Royal Court. The family returned to Massachusetts in 1788. By the time they returned, a new Constitution for the United States was complete and the country was in the process of forming its new government.

In 1786 Thomas Jefferson was sent to England on diplomatic business. When there he and Adams took time to tour much of the country including visiting Shakespeare's home. While there the pair chipped off a bit of Shakespeare's chair and took it with them as a souvenir.

The Vice Presidency

Adams was elected vice president in the election of 1789, receiving thirty-four electoral votes to Washington's sixty-nine electoral votes. Adams's role as vice president was confined to presiding over the senate and little else. Washington rarely consulted him on legal or political matters and Adams's talents were neglected. Adams served Washington dutifully for two terms but he would have preferred to have been the chief justice of the Supreme Court.

QUOTE

Adams described the office of vice president as "the most insignificant office that ever the Invention of man contrived or his Imagination conceived."

Presidency

When Washington indicated he would not run for a third term, Adams appeared to be his natural successor. He won a narrow victory over Thomas Jefferson, who became his vice president. Adams retained Washington's cabinet, a decision that turned out to be a mistake. The cabinet was geared to working with Washington and it was dominated by Alexander Hamilton, who did not take Adams seriously. Adams's intent in keeping the cabinet was largely motivated by his desire to offer a smooth transition from Washington's administration to his and he claimed he foresaw no difficulties in the prospect of working with them. He also intended to continue Washington's programs, so retaining the original cabinet made sense. Adams offered Jefferson a seat in his cabinet, but Jefferson preferred to remain independent. Their friendship was challenged by the political factions that divided them. Adams remained a Federalist and Jefferson staunchly sided with the Democratic-Republicans. They would vehemently disagree over many issues and, unfortunately, politics overrode their friendship during their presidencies.

FACT

John Adams was the first president to live in the White House. In a letter he wrote to Abigail on his second night there, he said, "Before I end my letter, I pray Heaven to bestow the best of Blessings on this House and all that shall hereafter inhabit it. May none but honest and wise Men ever rule under this roof."

The Quasi-War

The Quasi-War was an undeclared war between the United States and France. The French Revolution had become a European affair and Britain and France were at war. As president, Washington had insisted on American neutrality in the conflict, and through the Jay Treaty the United States had defined a diplomatic and commercial relationship with Britain. In retaliation for American trade with England, France embarked on a policy of seizing American ships en route to Britain and rejected the American minister sent to France in 1796. Opinions on how to handle this situation diverged along party lines. This was a test of the new nation to see how it handled itself on the international stage. Should America take a side and go to war or try to remain neutral?

The Federalists thought war with France was a viable option if the alternative meant estrangement from Britain. The Democratic-Republicans asserted France was America's only European ally—why provoke a war with them? Adams tried to take the middle road.

In 1797 he sent a delegation to Paris to negotiate terms to end hostilities, but the French Directory (the French Revolutionary government) demanded a bribe before they would meet. Adams recalled the delegates and appeared before Congress to request funds to build up the navy in the eventuality of an outright war with France. Hawkish Federalists in Congress called for raising an army of 30,000 and finally got Adams to agree to it. Before he had to go to war, Adams tried diplomacy once more, which worked. By the time Adams sent this second diplomatic delegation, the French Directory had fallen to Napoleon Bonaparte. War with the United States was not on Napoleon's agenda and he was therefore willing to negotiate with the American envoys. France signed the Treat of Mortefontaine in 1800, which effectively ended the Quasi-War. Adams's insistence on diplomacy in this matter is regarded as his wisest presidential action. By pressing forward with negotiations, he spared the country a war it had no resources to fight.

The Alien and Sedition Acts

Adams signed the Alien and Sedition Acts into law in 1798, when America was on the verge of war with France. Their purported intention was to defend the country from enemy aliens and to suppress opposition to and criticism of the government. Individuals could be arrested for making derogatory remarks about government officials. These laws were more indicative of the divisiveness between the Federalists, who wrote the bills, and the Democratic-Republicans, who did not support them. The Federalists wanted to curtail the power of the Democratic-Republicans who were openly sympathetic to the French revolutionary cause. The laws were also directed against immigrants, who tended to vote Democratic-Republican.

The Alien and Sedition Acts are four laws that: changed residency requirements for citizenship from five years to fourteen years, gave the president the authority to imprison or deport aliens thought to be "dangerous to the peace and safety of the United States," and made it illegal for American citizens to "print, utter, or publish . . . any false, scandalous, and malicious writing" about the government.

Thomas Jefferson was an outspoken critic of the acts and harshly criticized Adams for signing them into law. Adams was not a proponent of any of these acts although he reluctantly signed them. The Alien and Sedition Acts caused considerable damage to their friendship.

Election of 1800

1800 was an inauspicious year for John Adams and his family. His son Charles died, and Adams ran on the Federalist ticket with Charles Cotesworth Pinckney and lost the election to Thomas Jefferson and Aaron Burr. Adams was politically wounded by the Alien and Sedition Acts, and by the deep fractures within the Federalist Party. Adams did not stay to attend Jefferson's inauguration because he wanted to be home with his family following the death of his son. He was the first president to absent himself from his successor's inauguration.

Life after the Presidency

Adams retired to his farm in Massachusetts and lived another twenty-five years, long enough to see his son John Quincy become the sixth president of the United States. He occupied his time by corresponding with old friends, working on his autobiography, and publishing a meticulous refutation of Alexander Hamilton's scathing pamphlet regarding his political abilities and acumen. The pamphlet, written in 1800, and titled *A Letter from Alexander Hamilton Concerning the Public Conduct and Character of John Adams, ESQ, President of the United States*, was intended for circulation among other Federalists, but a copy of it was leaked to the Democratic-Republican Party. When the letter became public fodder it was highly damaging to Adams's reputation and to the Federalists' image. It is likely Adams was caught in the middle of a war of personalities between Hamilton and Burr, as many suspected it was Burr who obtained a copy of the letter and made it public in his intention to damage Hamilton's integrity. Adams smarted from the criticism in this letter and in 1809 began his campaign to redeem his reputation even though Hamilton was long dead.

Perhaps the best aspect of Adams's retirement was his reconciliation with Jefferson. Their reunion was facilitated by their mutual friend Benjamin Rush, who suggested they should write to each other. In 1812 Adams decided it was time to mend fences with Thomas Jefferson, and Jefferson agreed. The renewal of their friendship and their voluminous correspondence lasted for the remainder of their lives.

"You and I ought not to die before We have explained ourselves to each other." **—John Adams to Thomas Jefferson**

Adams and Jefferson died within hours of each other on July 4, 1826, fifty years after they signed the Declaration of Independence together. Thomas Jefferson passed away at Monticello hours before Adams, who did not know his friend was also on his deathbed. Adams's final words are purported to be "Thomas Jefferson survives."

Legacy

Adams spoke out early in favor of independence from Britain, at a time when no one was certain how events would unfold. It was a dangerous proposition, but he persevered in his steadfast belief in the Enlightenment principles of the rights of man. He was a member of the Continental Congress and a signer of the Declaration of Independence and the Constitution. He willingly applied himself to diplomatic missions that were crucial to foreign recognition of an independent America and to the procurement of foreign credit and capital to fund the revolutionary effort.

CHAPTER 8

Thomas Jefferson

His power lay in his command of the pen and in fact, he found public speaking difficult. For Thomas Jefferson, writing allowed him to "verbalize" some of the most important ideas that helped shape the new nation of America. He not only helped guide a loose confederation of colonies into a cohesive group of states seeking their freedom, he helped bring to life many of the ideals that Americans cherish today. He was a writer, philosopher, architect, teacher, visionary, and Founding Father. He served his country for more than fifty years and left a legacy that continues to enrich and educate countless numbers of Americans today.

Early Life and Education

Thomas Jefferson was born on April 13, 1743 in Shadwell, Virginia, the third of ten children. Shadwell was located in Albemarle County, near the Blue Ridge Mountains. His parents, through marriage and blood, came from some of the more prominent families of colonial Virginia. His mother, Jane Randolph Jefferson, was the daughter of a ship's captain and planter and was descended from one of the more renowned families of Virginia, the Randolphs. His father Peter Jefferson was a prosperous planter and surveyor who owned sixty slaves. According to family lore, Jefferson's earliest memory was as a three-year-old boy being carried on a pillow by a mounted slave when the family moved from Shadwell to the plantation of Tuckahoe.

In 1752, Jefferson began attending a local school, run by a Scottish Presbyterian minister, where he undertook the study of Latin, Greek, and French. He also learned to ride and was particularly interested in learning about the natural world. In 1757, when Jefferson was fourteen, his father died. As a result, Jefferson inherited about 7,000 acres in western Virginia, as well as a large number of slaves. Unfortunately, his father's death led to increasingly strained relations between Jefferson and his mother; from that point on, Jefferson did whatever he could to get away from his mother's grasp.

His father's death did not stop Jefferson from continuing his education. From 1758 to 1760 he attended the school of a minister by the name of James Maury, near Gordonsville, Virginia, where he boarded with the minister's family. In addition to continuing his studies of Greek and Latin, Jefferson also studied history and science. In 1760, at the age of sixteen, Jefferson enrolled at the College of William and Mary in Williamsburg, then the capital of colonial Virginia. His course of studies included mathematics, metaphysics, and philosophy.

In addition to his interest in philosophy, Jefferson continued to study French and read the classics in Latin and Greek; he could often be seen around the campus with his Greek grammar book. He also enjoyed playing the violin, which he would often practice three hours a day. He became so adept at the instrument that he often would play at parties held by the royal governor. Jefferson soon earned a reputation as a diligent and intelligent pupil who, it was said, often studied up to fifteen hours a day. Still, Jefferson found time to indulge in a growing love for wine and spend time with family and friends. Jefferson's experience with his mentors stayed with him for the rest of his life and he would later incorporate that concept of mentoring at the University of Virginia.

Monticello

In 1762, Jefferson graduated from William and Mary, earning high honors, and decided to study law. Jefferson began his legal studies under law professor and noted colonial jurist George Wythe. Five years later, in 1767, Jefferson was admitted to the Virginia bar. For Jefferson, the study of law was more than a means to earn a living—the law enabled one to study society, including its history, culture, and institutions, as well as evaluate the conscience of a people. Between 1768 and 1773, Jefferson took on more than a hundred cases a year in the general court, in addition to balancing a host of other legal duties in the colony. Jefferson mostly represented small planters in cases involving land claims and titles. Although he handled no landmark cases and was often a nervous speaker in the court, he soon earned a reputation for his keen legal mind.

Monticello is one of the great American examples of a Roman neoclassical building with influences from then-contemporary French architecture. Jefferson was greatly influenced by the designs of the Italian Renaissance architect Antonio Palladio. Much of Monticello's interior decoration reflects the ideas and ideals of Jefferson himself.

In 1768, Jefferson's life began to take two distinct directions. The first was initiated when he undertook construction of his own home situated on top of an 867-foot-high mountain near Shadwell that he eventually named Monticello, which in Italian means "little mountain." The construction of Monticello fulfilled Jefferson's childhood dream of building a home within sight of Shadwell, where he was born. Jefferson went greatly into debt by spending lavishly to create both the house and grounds of Monticello. In 1772, Jefferson married Martha Wayles Skelton, a wealthy widow and daughter of a prominent Virginia lawyer and landowner. Jefferson and his bride then moved to a small one-room brick house at Monticello.

Monticello was also a working plantation. Over the course of his life at Monticello, Jefferson owned more than 600 slaves who not only helped with the building of the house and grounds, but who were also essential to the day-to-day running of the plantation. The majority of slaves lived in an area known as "Mulberry Row," in cabins that Jefferson had designed.

Early Political Life

The second event that shaped the direction of Jefferson's life was the decision to enter local Virginia politics. In 1769, Jefferson decided to run as a candidate to represent Albemarle County for the Virginia House of Burgesses. Jefferson's political timing could not have been better, for he won the election and entered the House just as tensions were rising between the American colonies and the British Crown. Although Jefferson made few speeches and tended to follow the lead of the more privileged and influential leaders from the Tidewater area, he also cast his support for measures that opposed the authority of Parliament's over the colonies.

In 1774, following the passage of the Coercive Acts, Jefferson wrote a set of resolutions that became the basis for his first written work, *A Summary View of the Rights of British America*. Unlike other written criticisms of the Coercive Acts that focused on the legal and constitutional issues of the legislation, Jefferson took a more philosophical tack in that he argued that the colonists had the natural right to govern themselves, which was a very radical idea for the time.

In June 1775, not long after the outbreak of war between the American colonies and Great Britain, Jefferson was appointed to serve as a delegate to the Second Continental Congress. However, his terrible shyness prevented Jefferson from playing any significant role in the heated debates that were taking place. John Adams later wrote about how Jefferson would sit silently through the talks, though it was clear in private conversations that Jefferson was staunchly in favor of American independence.

It also was clear to other members that Jefferson's strong suit was as a writer, and many of his initial convention duties were taken up with the writing of resolutions. It was in that capacity in June 1776 that Jefferson, along with Adams and Benjamin Franklin, was appointed as a member of a five-man committee whose job it was to draft the resolution of independence from Britain. At the time, Congress simply viewed the writing of the resolution as no more important than any of the other writing and drafting of legislation that had been taken up. Adams asked Jefferson to prepare the first draft, which he did, drawing on his own proposed draft for the Virginia Constitution and another document drawn up by George Mason for the Virginia Declaration of Rights.

Jefferson later claimed that in writing the Declaration of Independence he was not striving for "originality of principle or sentiment," but only seeking to describe "an expression of the American mind," which was expressed in the longest section of the document that lists the colonial grievances against King George III.

These fifty-five words are often considered to be the birth of America's political culture: "We hold these truths to be self-evident, that all men are created equal, that they are endowed by their Creator with certain inalienable rights, that among these are life, liberty and the pursuit of happiness. That to secure these rights, governments are instituted among men, deriving their just powers from the consent of the governed." **—Thomas Jefferson, Declaration of Independence**

On June 26, 1776, Jefferson presented his completed draft to Congress. On July 2, Congress voted in favor of the resolution for independence and next turned their attention to fine-tuning the document. During the days of July 3 and 4, Congress debated and edited Jefferson's draft. Jefferson did not take the editing of his work lightly and was quite upset that the delegates found it necessary to make any changes at all to the document. Notably, one of the passages that was taken out from the Declaration of Independence was a passage critical of the slave trade because of protests from delegates from South Carolina and Georgia, who were slave owners as well as some Northerners who were either involved directly or peripherally in the slave trade.

Finally, on July 4, 1776, the document was approved. The Declaration of Independence would, in the end, be Jefferson's most recognizable writing and although at the time the work was deemed a collaborative effort, in years to come, Jefferson would be acknowledged as the document's true author.

The following is a portion of the passage removed from the Declaration of Independence regarding slavery: "He has waged cruel war against human nature itself, violating its most sacred rights of life and liberty in the persons of a distant people who never offended him, captivating & carrying them into slavery in another hemisphere or to incur miserable death in their transportation thither. . . . Determined to keep open a market where Men should be bought & sold, he has prostituted his negative for suppressing every legislative attempt to prohibit or restrain this execrable commerce."

Return to Virginia

In October 1776, Jefferson returned to Virginia where he was elected to the newly created Virginia House of Delegates. He was prodigious in his legislative output, drafting almost 126 bills in the three years he served. With all of his legislative writings, Jefferson sought to reform the state's legal code to make it more relevant and in tune with the principles of the American Revolution. Three areas of keen interest for Jefferson were the abolition of primogeniture, the establishment of an educational plan that would provide education for all citizens (as well as state support for the creation of institutions for higher learning), and the passage of a law that promoted religious freedom and the complete separation of church and state. The last two proposals were bitterly debated, but eventually passed. Jefferson also sought to eliminate the death penalty but was roundly defeated.

In 1779, Jefferson was elected governor of Virginia. During this period, Jefferson oversaw the transfer of the state capital from Williamsburg to Richmond, the creation of the nation's first honor code for the College of William and Mary, and the appointment of his mentor George Wythe as the first professor of law at an American university.

Unfortunately, two personal misfortunes marred Jefferson's time in office. In June 1781, a surprise invasion by the British caught Jefferson and the state off guard. Jefferson, along with Patrick Henry and other leaders of the state were minutes away from being caught. Jefferson fled from the British troops at Monticello and managed to escape. However, his escape was portrayed in the local press as being cowardly and public disapproval of his actions hurt Jefferson's political career in Virginia. He would never again hold public office in the state. Then, in September 1782, his wife died after complications from the difficult delivery in May of their third daughter. Jefferson swore never again to forsake family for politics.

Jefferson and National Politics

Thomas Jefferson's career in state politics may have been finished, but he was now poised to make his mark on the national stage. On June 6, 1783, the Virginia legislature appointed Jefferson as a delegate to the Confederation Congress. While meeting in Philadelphia, Jefferson was a member of the committee that set foreign exchange rates. He also recommended that a Committee of the States be established that would function as an executive branch of Congress when that body was not in session.

From 1785 to 1789, Jefferson served as the United States minister to France. Although he was unable to attend the Constitutional Convention in 1789, Jefferson kept abreast of the convention's goings on through his letters to James Madison. In general, Jefferson was in favor of the new United States Constitution, though he was bothered by the lack of a bill of rights that he believed necessary for the protection of the nation's citizens.

During his five years in Paris, Jefferson was not able to accomplish much in large part because of the relatively weak position of the new United States government. Heavily in debt because of the war, it was difficult to broker treaties with reigning world powers such as France. Great Britain still had a stranglehold on American commerce, making it challenging to negotiate commercial treaties with other nations. Compounding the problems faced by the new American government was the precarious position of the French monarchy, which made any kind of diplomatic business almost impossible to carry out. Jefferson was able to negotiate a large loan from Dutch bankers that allowed the American government to consolidate its European debts, but primarily John Adams conducted even that piece of diplomacy.

However, in spite of his failure to make great diplomatic strides, Jefferson was able to make the most of his time in Paris. He maintained a home on the Champs-Élysées and took in the architectural sights of the city while enjoying the social swirl of Parisian high society. He was a frequent dinner guest at the homes of the Paris elite; he also entertained many of the city's intellectuals at his own dinner parties. Despite his friendships with the social and noble elite, when the French Revolution swept through the country, Jefferson's sympathies were with the revolutionaries.

Jefferson was accompanied to Paris by two slaves, James Hemings and his sister Sally. Jefferson paid for James Hemings to be trained as a French chef. Some historians speculate that it was in Paris that Jefferson began a long-term relationship with Sally Hemings. Jefferson also brought his two daughters to Paris, but he eventually placed both his daughters in a French convent for their education.

Service Under Washington

In 1790, Jefferson reluctantly agreed to serve as Washington's secretary of state in the nation's first administration. As secretary, Jefferson had a budget of only $10,000 and a small number of employees. Despite these limitations, he was able to organize and efficiently run his department. As secretary of state, Jefferson supported closer relations with France while advocating a close watch on England. However, Jefferson's attempts at maintaining improved relations with France were often blunted in favor of Washington's policy of strict neutrality.

Jefferson increasingly ran into resistance from Alexander Hamilton over matters of fiscal policy, particularly in the area of paying the war debt. Hamilton wanted all the states to pay an equal share of the debt, while Jefferson wanted each state to pay its own debts. Because Virginia did not have much in the way of war debt, Jefferson believed that the state would be carrying an unfair tax burden. As a result, Jefferson increasingly viewed Hamilton, along with the other Federalists, as having more in common with the English Tory party and monarchists, who he believed were a constant threat to the ideals of democracy and republicanism. As a result, he and James Madison created the Democratic-Republican Party and worked tirelessly to build a nationwide network of Republican allies to combat Federalists across the country. When his term ended in 1793, Jefferson retired to Monticello, where he continued to orchestrate opposition to Hamilton and Washington. From 1794 to 1797, he operated as the informal leader of what would become the nation's first opposition political party, the Democratic-Republicans.

In 1796, Jefferson ran as a reluctant candidate for president and came within three votes of being elected. Because of a flaw in the Constitution, Jefferson became vice president under his opponent and political enemy, President John Adams. According to the Constitution, each elector would cast one ballot with two names. Adams, a Federalist received the most votes. Jefferson, a Democrat-Republican received the next largest number of votes. The problem arose because the delegates to the Constitutional Convention did not favor political parties and did not take them into account when framing the document. As a result, the election saw a president and vice president from two different parties and who personally differed on a number of important issues.

Although Jefferson chafed within the largely ceremonial duties of the vice president, he fulfilled his responsibilities as presiding officer of the Senate and wrote *A Manual of Parliamentary Practice*, which remained the guiding text for congressional meetings for years to come.

Perhaps most importantly, Jefferson, even though he was vice president, did little to stop the growing Democrat-Republican opposition to the Adams administration. This was particularly evident when Adams signed the Alien and Sedition Acts, designed to curb Democrat-Republican opposition to his foreign policy.

In response to the Alien and Sedition Acts, Jefferson wrote the Kentucky Resolution of 1798. In this document Jefferson offered a summary of the theory of the Constitution and challenged the federal laws created by the Adams administration as unconstitutional. James Madison joined Jefferson by writing a similar resolution adopted by Virginia, known as the Virginia Resolution.

President Jefferson

In 1800 the defect that earned Jefferson the vice presidency caused a more serious problem. The Democrat-Republicans, in the hopes of electing both a president and vice president, cast a tie vote between Jefferson and his opponent Aaron Burr. The House of Representatives settled the election, with Jefferson winning the presidency. Ironically, it was Alexander Hamilton, one of Jefferson's staunchest critics, who urged the House to cast its votes for Jefferson over Burr.

Clearly there were many who were nervous at the thought of Jefferson as president. His actions during the Adams administration suggested that Jefferson rejected the very powers of the executive branch that he now swore to uphold. The Federalists wondered how Jefferson would protect the very government that on occasion he had sworn to dismantle with his talk of the primacy of the rights of states. However, in his inaugural address, Jefferson struck a note of conciliation as he stated, "We are all Republicans—we are all Federalists." Time would tell whether he was serious.

In Jefferson's first term, he cut the budget, slashed army and navy expenditures, and reduced the national debt by one-third. He succeeded in sending an American naval squadron to fight the Barbary pirates, who were disrupting American commerce in the Mediterranean. In one of his most daring uses of his executive power, and perhaps one of the boldest moves by any president in American history, Jefferson acquired the Louisiana Territory from Napoleon in 1803.

In 1807 explorer Captain Zebulon Pike sent Jefferson a gift of two grizzly bear cubs. The bears grew quickly and soon were too big for their cages, so Jefferson kept them in an enclosure on the White House lawn. Jefferson quickly realized the bears were not suited to life at the White House and sent them to his friend Charles Willson Peale for his Philadelphia museum.

Jefferson was re-elected to the presidency in 1804. Much of his second term was spent monitoring American foreign policy, particularly with France and England. During this period, the Napoleonic Wars were taking place in Europe and Jefferson worked to make sure that the United States was not pulled into the conflict or forced to choose between supporting England or France. Compounding the problem was the fact that both the English and the French kept interfering with American neutrality at sea. Jefferson's attempted solution was an embargo upon American shipping, which meant that American ships could only engage in coastal trade and were not allowed to sail for foreign ports. Jefferson hoped that the embargo would stop the harassment by the French and the English.

Unfortunately, the embargo worked badly and was unpopular, particularly in New England which depended heavily on the shipping industry. Throughout the region, ships floated idly in the waters while sailors roamed the streets looking for work. Merchants, dockworkers, bankers, anyone at all connected with shipping felt the pinch of the embargo.

As president, Jefferson adopted a more relaxed atmosphere at the White House. He was known to greet visitors in his slippers; he also discontinued the practice of delivering the State of the Union address, instead sending his written remarks to Congress. During the course of his presidency, Jefferson would give only two public speeches.

Retirement

After leaving the presidency, Jefferson returned to Virginia and his beloved Monticello. During the last seventeen years of his life he maintained an active schedule, rising at dawn every day and then bathing his feet in cold water. Mornings were spent on correspondence and then he worked in his garden. He spent his afternoons riding the grounds. Dinner, served in the late afternoon, was usually spent with family or any number of guests who would come to Monticello to visit.

In spite of his many successes, Jefferson faced a perennial specter: debt. Debt followed Jefferson throughout his life in part because of his obligations, lavish lifestyle, and despite his carefully ordered ledger books, an unwillingness to look closely at where his money was going. By the 1820s the interest on Jefferson's debt was staggering, as he was more than $100,000—in today's terms, several million dollars—in debt. The crushing amount of debt would mean that after Jefferson's death, Monticello, including land, mansion, furnishings, and the vast bulk of the slave population, would be auctioned off.

On July 4, 1826, Thomas Jefferson died. It was the fiftieth anniversary of the adoption of the Declaration of Independence. He died a few hours before John Adams, with whom he had reconciled in his later years.

FACT

Jefferson never lost his zeal for education and in 1819, one of his biggest dreams came to fruition when he founded the University of Virginia in Charlottesville. Upon its opening in 1825, it was the first university in the United States to offer a large number of elective courses to its students. The school was also notable for being centered around a library rather than a church. No campus chapel was included in Jefferson's original plans. Until his death, students and faculty often came to call at Monticello.

Legacy

As John Adams lay dying, his last words were purported to be "Thomas Jefferson still survives." Although his old enemy and friend had passed away hours earlier, Adams's words are a fitting tribute to the man who many consider if not the greatest, certainly the most contradictory, possibly the most intelligent, and among the most controversial of Founding Fathers.

Through the Declaration of Independence he articulated the American dream of freedom and equality, while at the same time standing as one of the larger slave owners in the South. He was a critic of a strong and powerful federal government, yet when president he pushed the limits of that power to purchase the largest piece of real estate in American history. In doing so, he set in motion the dream of westward expansion and the promise of freedom and land for Americans.

CHAPTER 9

James Madison

James Madison served in the Virginia House of Delegates and the Continental Congress. Dissatisfied with the Articles of Confederation, he was one of the early voices calling for a new constitution. One of his main contributions at the Constitutional Convention was the Virginia Plan. Together with Alexander Hamilton and John Jay, he wrote a series of essays under the name *Publius*, in favor of ratification. He was secretary of state under Thomas Jefferson and was the fourth president of the United States.

Early Life

James Madison was born on March 16, 1751 in Orange County, Virginia, the oldest of twelve children born to James Madison Sr. and Nellie Conway Madison. Madison's father was the largest land owner in Orange County, with holdings in excess of 5,000 acres. Madison inherited his father's home, Montpelier, and called this estate at the foot of the Blue Ridge Mountains home for his eighty-five years. Madison suffered from poor health when he was a young child and was tutored at home. When he was eleven he was sent to Reverend Donald Robinson's boarding school, where he was in the company of the sons of other local planters. In the three years after Reverend Robinson's school, Madison studied with Reverend Thomas Martin, the rector of his parish church. Martin received his degree from the College of New Jersey (now Princeton University) and encouraged Madison to go there.

Madison entered the College of New Jersey when he was eighteen years of age and completed a four-year curriculum in two years, graduating in 1771. He stayed an additional year after graduation to study Hebrew, ethics, and theology with President John Witherspoon. Madison planned to return to Virginia and pursue a career in the ministry, but the frantic pace of his college days nearly pushed him to a nervous collapse and he was forced to return to Virginia to rest. While he was recuperating at home he studied law. He abandoned the idea of becoming a minister and turned his attentions to his other passion: political philosophy. By the time Madison returned to Montpelier from college, he identified with Whig principles and those sentiments strengthened as tensions between America and Britain increased in the 1770s.

Early Political Career

Madison was elected to the Virginia Committee of Safety in 1774. In 1776 he was sent to Virginia's Revolutionary Convention, where he was a primary contributor to the Virginia Constitution (he was responsible for inserting the guarantee of the free exercise of religion). In October 1776 Madison was elected to the Virginia House of Delegates, where he met and befriended Thomas Jefferson. He stood for re-election in 1777 but lost because he refused to provide free whiskey to the voters.

Although he was not re-elected to return to the Virginia House of Delegates, Madison was elected to the eight-member Council of State in 1777, and was sent to the Continental Congress in 1779. His ongoing health problems kept him from active service during the Revolutionary War, but Madison remained politically active during the conflict. He was a congressional delegate until 1783. Initially reticent, he did not speak on the floor for six months. It was as a member of the Congress that Madison attained political maturity and adopted a national perspective in his thinking. He was adept with such weighty and diverse issues as trade, defense, debt, foreign relations, fiscal policy, and the administration of western territories.

Providing liquor for the electors, or "Swilling the Planters with Bumbo," was once a common practice. (Bumbo is a rum punch that originated in the Caribbean.) If a candidate did not offer liquor or if he did not have enough, the results could be disastrous. Madison was not the only politician to lose an election by running afoul of this tradition. George Washington believed he lost his first bid to the Virginia House of Burgesses because he did not provide enough whiskey for the voters.

In 1784 Madison was re-elected to the Virginia House of Delegates. One of his accomplishments was to create the framework for a complete separation of church and state through the Statute for Establishing Religious Freedom (1785). He also immersed himself in the complex and difficult issue of state finance. The issue that was at the forefront of his thoughts, however, was a national one: the weakness of the Articles of Confederation. He was a principle figure behind the organization of the Mount Vernon Conference (1785) and the Annapolis Convention (1786), the meetings that set in motion the plans for a general convention to revise the Articles of Confederation.

Political Career

Madison was convinced the Articles of Confederation were not strong enough to keep the new country together. When Shays' Rebellion broke out in Massachusetts, General Henry Knox was sent to investigate, and he was alarmed at what he saw. Knox wrote to George Washington, "This dreadful situation has alarmed every man of principle and property in New England . . . What is to afford us security against the violence of lawless men? Our government must be braced, changed or altered to secure our lives and property." Washington forwarded Knox's letter to Madison, posing the question "How could Americans expect to enjoy secure lives if the government could not defend them, their property, and their liberty from people who took the law into their own hands?" Madison did not need convincing. He had long maintained the Articles of Confederation needed to be discarded and a new constitution that provided for a strong central government should take their place.

The Constitutional Convention was called for May 14, 1787 and Madison arrived in Philadelphia on May 3. He was the first out-of-town delegate to get there and he promptly checked into the accommodations he always used, the boarding house run by Mrs. Mary House. He arrived prepared to do business or battle, depending on the circumstances. Prior to the meeting he prepared a considerable amount of research on the history of governments and compiled his work in a manuscript titled "Of Ancient and Modern Confederacies." Thorough to the last, he also prepared a manuscript titled "Vices of the Political System of the United States," a treatise of American political experiments starting from the time of the Declaration of Independence. If this were not enough, he was also armed with a plan for the structure of a new government. What he really had in mind was to scrap the Articles of Confederation completely. This idea needed to be introduced gradually as most of the delegates in attendance believed they were there solely to make revisions, and many of the delegates would immediately chafe at the idea of a strong federal government that had the potential to override states' interests.

ESSENTIAL

In brief, the Virginia Plan provided for a national legislature with two branches in which all states would have representation, based either on the number of their free inhabitants or in proportion to their contributions to the national government.

The Virginia Plan

The Virginia Plan was the blueprint Madison laid out for the Virginia delegates in the preliminary meetings before the convention began. Virginia governor Edmund Randolph presented the plan, which Madison explained as being the right decision, Randolph "being the Governor of the state, of distinguished talents, and in the habit of public speaking." The Virginia Plan provided a starting point for what would become a rigorous debate.

Ratification

Once the Constitution was prepared, the next challenge was the process of ratification. Madison joined forces with Alexander Hamilton and John Jay as an author of a series of published essays in favor of the Constitution. Although they were written by different men, the essays appeared under the pseudonym *Publius*, and are known collectively as *The Federalist Papers*. Most of Madison's essays emphasize what the government could not do rather than what it could. Madison wrote twenty-six essays and collaborated with Alexander Hamilton on two.

Madison did not initially believe a bill of rights was necessary, but in conversations with men who were not entirely happy with the final draft of the document, he understood they were required to make the Constitution palatable to all. He was particularly influenced by Thomas Jefferson, who frankly told him the main thing he did not like about the Constitution was the absence of a bill of rights. As a member of the first House of Representatives, Madison was a significant force in the passage of the first ten amendments to the Constitution, which form the Bill of Rights.

Madison's Shift from Federalism

During his tenure in Congress, Madison's approach to government was that it should exercise limited power. His strict constructionist interpretation of the Constitution put him at odds with old friends and allies, particularly with George Washington and Alexander Hamilton. He was particularly alienated by Hamilton's assertive approach to financial affairs. Madison and Thomas Jefferson emerged as leading voices against Hamilton's vision of an active government. By the end of Washington's second term, these ideological differences fractured into distinct political camps, Federalists and Democratic-Republicans, with Madison and Jefferson more comfortable in the latter.

Madison decided to retire from politics when his term in the House of Representatives expired in 1797. He was weary of factional disputes, and matters at home demanded his attention. His elderly parents were in frail health, his brother Ambrose had died, and in 1794 he married. He looked forward to enjoying a quieter life at Montpelier with his new wife.

In 1794, forty-three-year-old Madison married twenty-six-year-old Dolley Payne Todd. She is credited with defining the role of the First Lady, not only as a political partner of the president, but also as an elegant and cultured hostess of the White House. Dolley Madison was an unpretentious woman endowed with a generous and amiable personality, and was very popular with the public.

Despite his resolution to retire at the end of his term, Madison had invested too much of himself in the politics of the past decade to completely ignore the developments in the Adams administration. He and Jefferson were especially concerned with the passage of the Alien and Sedition Acts (1798). Madison drafted the Virginia Resolutions the same year, calling for a national protest against the Acts and against the growth of federal power that occurred in the past five years. Madison returned to public life in 1800 upon his election to the Virginia Assembly, where his first action was the Report of 1800 that assailed the Alien and Sedition Acts as unconstitutional.

Secretary of State

Laws such as the Alien and Sedition Acts undermined the Federalist Party and helped the Democratic-Republican party gain the presidency in 1801, when Thomas Jefferson was elected president. The first order of business was to eradicate the Federalist structure imposed in government during Adams's tenure. Jefferson's vision of a new America included eliminating internal taxes and stripping the military to the smallest possible size. He appointed Madison as his secretary of state, a role in which Madison was also Jefferson's trusted confidante and his heir apparent. Madison was selected by the party to run for president in 1808. He handily defeated Federalist candidate Charles Cotesworth Pinckney, who only carried five states and 32.4 percent of the popular vote.

"I was beaten by Mr. and Mrs. Madison. I might have had a better chance had I faced Mr. Madison alone." —**Charles Cotesworth Pinckney**

Presidency

Madison's first term was consumed with the details of disputes with France, Spain, and Britain. Jefferson and Madison struggled with the question of how to secure American neutrality and commercial rights in a hostile Atlantic, where American vessels were alternatively harassed by British or French ships. The Embargo Act and Non-Intercourse Act were attempts to resolve the problem by restricting foreign trade from 1807 to 1812. These laws were unpopular at home and were broken as a matter of course.

Madison seized western Florida from Spain, fortifying American control of the Gulf Coast. He also allowed the charter for the National Bank to expire. The National Bank, one of Hamilton's accomplishments, had troubled Madison from the beginning. Madison objected to what he believed to be Hamilton's tendency to endow the federal government, and in this case, national institutions, with too much authority. He furthermore did not believe there was a constitutional basis for a National Bank. He had been unable to stop its creation, but he finally found himself in a position to oversee its demise.

Madison was re-elected for a second term in 1812, and was immediately plunged into the consequences of the escalating tensions between Britain and the United States. The British continued to capture American merchant vessels and impress the crew into service in the British navy. With all negotiations at an impasse, Madison extracted a declaration of war from Congress on the eve of his re-election, launching the War of 1812. Madison hoped an American invasion of British Canada would forestall a larger-scale conflict. This plan went awry and the British and their allies marched into the United States, reaching the capital city of Washington on August 24, 1814 where they burned many public buildings, including the White House. The war ended after the Battle of New Orleans, where American forces led by Major General Andrew Jackson defeated the British on January 8, 1815.

The loss of the National Bank proved to be a liability during the War of 1812. Without the bank, financing the war was a hardship. Secretary of the Treasury Alexander Dallas petitioned for a new bank in 1814, but Madison vetoed the bill in 1815. Later that year, he had time to reflect on domestic matters and changed his mind and proposed a recharter of a national bank, as well as limited protective tariffs, and the authority of the government to assume internal improvements. He signed the Second National Bank into law in 1816.

Life after the Presidency

Madison left the White House for retirement at Montpelier. He happily returned to the life of managing his plantation and became a student of scientific farming. In 1816 he was selected for the Board of Visitors, a body responsible for planning the establishment of the University of Virginia, and became the university's second rector in 1826. His final political contribution was as a delegate to the Virginia convention to write a new state constitution. Madison died at Montpelier on June 28, 1836.

Legacy

Madison's long political career took him from the state assemblies of Virginia to the Continental Congress and the Constitutional Convention, where he was instrumental in shaping the framework of the federal government. His introduction of the Virginia Plan provided a foundation for the debate that resulted in the United States Constitution and earned him the sobriquet Father of the Constitution. He was elected to the first class of congressmen under the new Constitution and had a principal role in the creation of the Bill of Rights. Later, he served as secretary of state under Thomas Jefferson and became the nation's fourth president in 1808, serving two terms in the office. He was no less busy during his nineteen years of retirement. He served on the Board of Visitors with Thomas Jefferson in the creation of the University of Virginia, and after Jefferson's death he became the university's second rector. Although no longer directly active on the political stage, Madison penned several essays and letters in favor of abolition and against the principles of states' rights and nullification.

CHAPTER 10

Benjamin Franklin

Benjamin Franklin was an eighteenth-century celebrity. His was a classic American rags to riches story—he came from a humble background in Boston and rose to prominence as one of America's wealthiest men. An astute businessman, publisher, inventor, writer, diplomat, political theorist, and a bit of a rogue, Franklin contributed to nearly every facet of American life and culture.

Early Life

Benjamin Franklin came from a large family, the tenth son out of seventeen children. He was born on January 17, 1706 in Boston. His father was a chandler and a soap maker and the circumstances of his household were modest. However, Franklin was able to attend school for a year and was tutored privately for a year. He was a quick and voracious learner, and made the most from his limited education. By the time he was ten years of age, his education was over.

When he was twelve, Franklin was apprenticed to his brother, James, who owned a print shop. Franklin learned the business of printing during his five-year apprenticeship. Surrounded by print all day, he applied himself to the craft of writing in his spare time. He realized that a person who knew how to write and how to write well was in possession of a valuable asset and could take advantage of many opportunities to make a good living.

Franklin became a published author at the age of fifteen when he wrote a series of satirical essays that appeared in *The New England Courant*, a weekly newspaper published by his brother. Franklin wrote under the pseudonym Silence Dogood. No segment of society or social institution was safe from the parodies Franklin wrote under the guise of a middle-aged woman. To his great delight, Franklin's identity was never suspected, initially not even by his brother.

Franklin Moves to Philadelphia

After a rift with his brother, Franklin left Boston and settled in Philadelphia, where he found work as a printer and a room in the boarding house owned by his future in-laws. In 1724 Franklin was approached by Governor Sir William Keith to travel to London to buy printing equipment and to make contacts with London booksellers. Keith promised to give Franklin letters of credit and letters of introduction to finance the venture. Franklin gladly took advantage of the opportunity, but discovered when he was halfway across the Atlantic that Keith never delivered the letters.

Franklin traveled with his friend James Ralph, and when they arrived in London, Franklin quickly found work in a printing shop. They were young and poor but managed to make the most of their time in London. They went out on the town, enjoyed going to the theater, and met as many women as they possibly could. They had so much fun that Franklin was inspired to write "A Dissertation on Liberty and Necessity, Pleasure and Pain," in which he asserts since humans do not have freedom of choice, they are not responsible for their actions. In his maturity, Franklin regretted this publication and destroyed all but one of the copies remaining in his possession.

"If the Creature is thus limited in his Actions, being able to do only such things as God would have him to do, and not being able to refuse doing what God would have done; then he can have no such thing as Liberty, Free-will or Power to do or refrain an Action."
—Benjamin Franklin, "A Dissertation on Liberty and Necessity, Pleasure and Pain," 1725

Return to Philadelphia

By 1726 Franklin had tired of London and took advantage of a good offer to return to Philadelphia. A Quaker merchant offered him a position in his Philadelphia office, but the arrangement fell through when the merchant died within a few months of Franklin taking the job. Thrown back on his own resources, Franklin returned to the world of printing and by 1730 he had a shop of his own.

1730 was the year Franklin determined to settle down both in business and in his private life. He reunited with Deborah Read, the daughter of his former landlord, to whom he had made vague promises of marriage before he left for London in 1726. In the intervening years and in the absence of any communication from Franklin, Deborah married John Rodgers, who absconded with her dowry and abandoned her. Because she was not divorced, she and Franklin lived in a common law marriage. Adding to the complexity of the situation, Franklin had an illegitimate son, William, who lived with him and was part of the package Franklin brought to the relationship. William traveled with his father on Franklin's various diplomatic assignments and was educated in England. William's political allegiances were different from his father's. He became the royal governor of New Jersey and remained loyal to the crown during the Revolutionary War. William's choice resulted in estrangement from his father.

Franklin's printing business did well. He printed currency for Pennsylvania and also acquired contracts to print currency for New Jersey, Delaware, and Maryland. In addition to currency he also wrote and published *The Pennsylvania Gazette* and *Poor Richard's Almanack* (1732–1757). His flourishing printing business allowed him to invest in rental properties in Philadelphia and in printing shops in the Carolinas, New York, and the West Indies. By the 1740s he had become a very wealthy man.

Franklin published *Poor Richard's Almanack* under the name of Richard Saunders. In addition to a calendar, weather, and astronomical information, the almanac was famous for its proverbs, many of which are familiar even today, for example: "Early to bed, and early to rise, makes a man healthy, wealthy, and wise."

In 1727 Franklin organized a club devoted to politics and debate called the Junto, also known as The Leather Apron Club. The group met every week to discuss "Morals, Politics, or Natural Philosophy." To stimulate and facilitate discussion, members were encouraged to read in these topics and since books were scarce, Franklin solicited members to donate their books to form a lending library for the group. This led to the creation of the Library Company of Philadelphia (1731), the first lending library in the colonies. Discussions in the Junto resulted in practical solutions to everyday social problems such as the creation of a city patrol, whose functions were similar to that of a police force, and a volunteer fire department. In 1743 Franklin decided to extend the reach of the Junto to other colonies, resulting in the creation of the American Philosophical Society.

By the age of forty-two, Franklin was privileged to call himself a man of great wealth. He decided to take advantage of his good fortune and retire from actively running a business. He maintained a silent partnership in a printing company for another eighteen years, from which he derived more profit to finance his new passions, scientific inquiry and politics.

Franklin is renowned for his pioneering work in electricity. He published *Experiments and Observations on Electricity* in 1751. His development of the lightening rod is a practical application of his research. In addition to his study of electricity and conductivity, Franklin also charted the Gulf Stream and invented the Franklin stove, bifocals, and the urinary catheter.

Political Career

As much as he enjoyed the intellectual pursuit of science, Franklin's genuine ambitions lay in public service. His political career began in 1737, when he became the clerk for the Pennsylvania legislature. In 1748 he was selected to sit on the Philadelphia city council, and in 1749, he was made a justice of the peace. In 1751 he served as a city alderman and in the Pennsylvania Assembly. The plum position he had been waiting for was that of deputy postmaster general, a royal appointment he received in 1753. He was responsible for the oversight of mail delivery in the northern colonies. The political offices he held prior to this were entirely provincial; as deputy postmaster general, he enjoyed an appointment from the Crown and one in which he could exert influence beyond Pennsylvania.

In 1757 Franklin departed for eighteen years of diplomatic service in London as the colonial agent for Pennsylvania. Unlike his previous trip to London, Franklin did not have to worry about how he was going to feed and lodge himself. He was an affluent American abroad with government credentials. He had money, power, and within a short time, he had fame. Franklin presented himself well, with an interesting personality and a quick wit. He traveled in high society with other famous people. In 1759 he was awarded an honorary Doctor of Laws degree from the University of St. Andrews, after which everyone called him Dr. Franklin. Benjamin Franklin became all the rage in London in record time.

The political climate in America changed rapidly after Franklin returned to England. Within a year, Parliament passed the Stamp Act and the colonies rebelled against the tax. Franklin had a difficult time finding his bearings in this crisis. As a colonial agent, he knew he should also oppose the tax, but he saw no way to stop it or have it repealed. In what was viewed as his complicity with the tax, Franklin ordered stamps for his printing firm in Philadelphia, which caused outrage at home. Franklin was sufficiently detached from the prevailing mood of the colonies that he did not realize how unpopular this action would be, and he was surprised to learn of the mob action incited by the Stamp Tax.

Franklin returned to Philadelphia only once during his eighteen-year stint in London. He visited from 1762 to 1764 to tend to post office business and visit his family. His wife was reluctant to travel with him, and he returned to England without her. It was the last time they saw each other—she died in 1774.

His instincts led him to try to repair the divisions that were forming between the colonies and Britain. He wrote in excess of 100 newspaper articles in which he attempted to explain the American protest to the British and the British position to the Americans. Despite the volume of his writing, he was not successful in convincing either side how much they still had in common; in fact, it seemed that neither side appreciated his efforts.

Franklin fell from grace in London by an ill-conceived attempt to repair the rift between the colonies and Parliament. In 1772 an anonymous source sent him a package of letters written by the royal governor of Massachusetts, Thomas Hutchinson. In these letters, which were never intended for public consumption, Hutchinson encouraged Parliament to send more troops to Boston to suppress the unruly colonists, and recommended Parliament consider a program in which the colonists were gradually stripped of their rights. Franklin thought if Hutchinson's intentions were known, the ire of Boston would focus on Hutchinson and not on the British government, and perhaps the problem would diffuse. Franklin counted on the discretion of the recipients of these letters, but they were leaked to the *Boston Gazette*. Hutchinson was run out of Boston and Parliament began inquiries to determine who had breached the security of the letters. When Franklin's role became apparent, he was publicly chastised, stripped of his postmaster appointment, returned to Philadelphia a chastened man.

Revolutionary War

Upon his return, Franklin was elected to the Continental Congress. In June 1776 he was appointed to the committee to draft the Declaration of Independence. Although Thomas Jefferson is the principal author of the Declaration, Franklin worked with him to refine the final draft. While Franklin labored over the details of the document, his estranged son William, royal governor of New Jersey, was imprisoned in Connecticut.

After signing the Declaration of Independence, Franklin allegedly quipped, "Gentlemen, we must now all hang together, or we shall most assuredly all hang separately."

Much to Franklin's delight, he was posted overseas again in 1776, this time in France; he far preferred to sparkle in European capitals. His mission was to get the French government to recognize America as independent from Britain and to secure loans for the war. Franklin reveled in his task. He was warmly received by the French and happily exploited his image as the homespun American revolutionary to the French aristocracy, who were seduced by his rustic charm. He played a crucial role in getting the French to love the idea of America.

Much to his dismay, Franklin was not in France alone. Congress also sent John Adams and Arthur Lee to assist him. Neither of these men possessed the diplomatic talent nor the social grace that Franklin effortlessly used to penetrate the aristocratic culture of the French court. He often came to blows with them over what he considered their bungling efforts, and in the end did not endear himself to either one of them.

Franklin's work, combined with play, began to pay dividends. In 1778 France agreed to military and diplomatic alliances with America. After the conclusion of the war, Franklin was a central figure in the treaty negotiations with the British.

After the War

Franklin reluctantly returned to America in 1785. He was seventy-nine years old and it was time to go home. He did not arrive to a hero's welcome. John Adams and Arthur Lee still held a grudge for their chilly relationship in France, and they maligned Franklin at every opportunity. For example, they suggested Franklin liked France much better than America, that he was far more content in the company of aristocrats than plain Americans, and that he had been a bit of a playboy while he was away from home. Nevertheless, when Franklin returned to Philadelphia he was elected president of the Supreme Executive Council of Pennsylvania, a political office similar to a governor.

Franklin was elected as a delegate to the Constitutional Convention at eighty-one years of age. He was more of a presence than an influence, but his diplomatic talents served him well as he was often the voice of reason and compromise. Otherwise Franklin did what he did best—he gave dinner parties and treated the delegates to quality English porter, creating a convivial atmosphere that was often lacking on the convention floor. When the Constitution was complete, Franklin was the only delegate present who had signed the Declaration of Independence, the Treaty of Paris, the Treaty of Alliance with France, and the United States Constitution.

Franklin spent his last years finishing his autobiography, a project he began in 1771. He died on April 17, 1790 at eighty-four years of age.

Legacy

Franklin's career spanned a long life and covered an extraordinary list of interests and accomplishments. He left lasting impressions on society and culture through the establishment of the American Philosophical Society and the Junto, which produced the concepts of police and fire departments, and a public lending library. His most widely used inventions, such as the Franklin stove and bifocals, had an immediate and long-lasting impact on everyday life. He was a signer of the Declaration of Independence and the Constitution, and performed valuable diplomatic service on behalf of his country during the Revolutionary War and in the early years of the new republic.

CHAPTER 11

Alexander Hamilton

The "bastard brat of a Scotch pedlar"—this is how John Adams described Alexander Hamilton. It is true, Hamilton was born out of wedlock, but he overcame the stain of illegitimacy and lived a rich life as a poet and essayist, an aide to George Washington, a battlefield hero, a congressman, abolitionist, founder of the Bank of New York, delegate to the Constitutional Convention, Federalist, lawyer, and the first secretary of the treasury. Brash, outspoken, and often confrontational, Hamilton often made enemies, but such was the price of doing business or politics.

Early Life

Alexander Hamilton was born in 1757 on Nevis Island in the British West Indies. His maternal grandfather, John Faucett, owned a small but prospering sugar plantation. Faucett married Mary Uppington in 1718, a few months after the birth of their second child. Hamilton's mother, Rachel Faucette, was born in 1729 and in some accounts is referenced as a mixed race child although she was always counted as white on the island tax rolls. The Faucettes separated when Rachel was sixteen years of age. Shortly after the separation, Mary Faucette arranged the marriage of her daughter to Johann Michael Lavien. The marriage was dreadfully unhappy and produced only one child, Peter. Rachel left Lavien and her son in 1750. Lavien had her imprisoned for adultery, a charge for which there was no evidence, and once she was free from jail, Rachel fled Nevis for St. Kitts, leaving her estranged husband and son behind.

Nevis Island was initially colonized by criminals and other members of the underclass. The white population of the island was uncharitably described by an Anglican minister in 1727 as "whole shiploads of pick-pockets, whores, rogues, vagrants, thieves, sodomites, and other filth and cutthroats of society."

While in St. Kitts, Rachel met James Hamilton, the fourth child of Alexander Hamilton, a Scottish nobleman. Although James Hamilton was of noble ancestry, as the fourth son he could expect to inherit nothing. With no formal education or actual ambition to recommend him, James Hamilton made his way to the Caribbean hoping to get rich quickly, despite his lack of a plan or capital. By the time he met Rachel he had failed at many schemes, and was working as a merchant. They had two sons, Alexander and James, and eventually returned to Nevis, where Rachel inherited a house from her father. Rachel had not obtained a divorce from Lavien and lived in a common law marriage with James Hamilton for several years.

In 1766, James Hamilton moved his family to St. Croix and abandoned them there, leaving Rachel to raise their sons on her own. She opened a small shop where she sold staple goods to local planters and earned a meager living for her small sons. She also somehow managed to provide them with a small personal library of thirty-four books. Hamilton would not see his father again, but he kept in touch with him for the rest of his life.

QUOTE

"The truth is that, on the question who my parents were, I have better pretensions than most of those who in this country plume themselves on ancestry." **—Alexander Hamilton**

Rachel and Alexander contracted a fever in 1767. Gravely ill, mother and son lay next to each other in her bed and endured the same primitive course of treatments—enemas, emetics, and bloodletting. Rachel Faucette Lavien died on February 19, 1768, leaving Alexander and James in the care of her older cousin Peter Lytton, who would commit suicide within the year.

ESSENTIAL

After Rachel's death, Lavien claimed her estate and did not distribute any of it to Alexander or James. A family friend is purported to have purchased the thirty-four books and given them back to young Alexander, who was devoted to reading.

Hamilton on His Own

Between 1765 and 1769 Hamilton suffered a series of sobering setbacks. He was abandoned by his father, his mother died, his guardian died, and his aunt, uncle, and grandmother died. Not only was he left bereft of family, he was without financial support, as none of his family members included provisions for him or his brother in their estates. The brothers went different ways at this point. James was apprenticed to a carpenter and Alexander found refuge in the home of his close boyhood friend, Edward Stevens. He was apprenticed to clerk in the firm of Beekman and Cruger, the New York traders who supplied his mother's shop.

Hamilton was not able to have a formal education, but his time with Beekman and Cruger (later known as Kortright and Cruger) served as a real time business school. There he learned proper penmanship, how to handle money, how to keep track of inventory, and how to convert money from one currency to another. He impressed his employers with his quick mind and his enthusiasm for work. When poor health forced Nicolas Cruger to return to New York in October 1771, he left the fourteen-year-old Hamilton in charge of the St. Croix office for several months. Hamilton's facility for financial affairs was evident even at this young age and he proved to be particularly adept at managing the firm's finances and collecting bills.

When the sloop *Thunderbolt*—owned in part by the firm for which Hamilton worked—arrived in St. Croix with forty-one emaciated mules, young Hamilton promptly reprimanded the captain to "Reflect continually on the unfortunate voyage you have just made and endeavor to make up for the considerable loss therefrom accruing to your owners."

Young Hamilton's Luck Begins to Change

Through his apprenticeship Hamilton learned the inner workings of the business world. He witnessed how traders and smugglers behaved, how the lack of credit or cash could impair business development, and how the Caribbean economy balanced precariously on a single cash crop. Hamilton also witnessed the inhumane and terrifying punishments meted out to the island slave population. Renegade slaves were routinely mutilated and tortured. All white males over the age of sixteen were expected to serve in the local militia as a defense against potential slave rebellion. Hamilton came to detest the oppressive and autocratic rule imposed by the planters and their culture, and he resented the constant threat of chaos and instability and the lack of a well-ordered system to manage it.

Hamilton's fortunes took another turn for the better when the *Royal Danish Gazette* began publication in 1770. Hamilton began to write poetry and submitted it for publication. His poems became regular features. Hamilton was also taken under the intellectual wing of the Presbyterian minister Henry Knox. Knox invited Hamilton to use his library and encouraged his scholarship. After a ferocious hurricane devastated the island on August 31,

1772 Hamilton wrote an eloquent letter to his father begging him to send any assistance he could spare. The letter was masterful in its description of the storm, the destruction of most of the island, and the destitution that would soon become a reality for the majority of the inhabitants. Knox was so impressed with the letter he had it published in the *Royal Dutch Gazette*. Once it was made public, the letter made Hamilton an overnight sensation. Local businessmen organized a collection to send such a bright mind to North America for a proper education. In late 1772, Hamilton sailed for Boston, never to return to his island home. His new life was beginning.

Knox studied divinity at the College of New Jersey (now Princeton) under the college president Aaron Burr, Sr., the father of Aaron Burr, Hamilton's future political nemesis and the man who would ultimately kill him.

Education

From Boston, Hamilton traveled to New York City to the main offices of Kortright and Cruger, the custodians of his scholarship funds. At first the only person he knew in New York was his childhood friend Edward Stevens, who was at King's College. Some of Hamilton's biographers believe he briefly boarded at the home of Hercules Mulligan, a tailor whose brother was a junior partner at Kortright and Cruger. Mulligan was a member of the Liberty Boys and Hamilton would have received a practical education on the growing sentiments of colonial resistance to taxation while in Mulligan's household.

Hamilton was largely self-taught and though he had some degree of formal instruction with Henry Knox, he was by no means ready to matriculate to college, even though he was of an age to do so. He began preparatory studies at Elizabethtown Academy, a school that sent most of its graduates to the College of New Jersey (now Princeton University). At Elizabethtown Academy, Hamilton was introduced to a classical curriculum, and he continued to write poetry and also wrote the prologue and epilogue for a play performed by local British soldiers.

Knox's letter of introduction opened doors into a world Hamilton might have otherwise only dreamt of. Through Knox he became acquainted with William Livingston and Elias Boudinot, prominent New York lawyers, Presbyterians, and Whigs. Livingston was fond of young Hamilton and made him a member of his household. There Hamilton came under the spell of Livingston's beautiful daughters, Sally and Kitty. Sally Livingston was successfully courted by John Jay. Hamilton briefly enjoyed Kitty's flattering attentions, winning her favor over his friend and rival for her affections, Gouverneur Morris.

"We will even make excursions in the flowery walks and roseate bowers of Cupid. You know I am renowned for gallantry and shall always be able to entertain you with a choice collection of the prettiest things imaginable . . . You shall be one of the graces, or Diana, or Venus, or something surpassing them all." **—Alexander Hamilton to Kitty Livingston**

Hamilton applied to the College of New Jersey, asking for special consideration to complete the curriculum at a faster pace than the other students and finish his degree before the rest of his graduating class. By the time he applied to college he was already eighteen years of age, far older than the other students. The Board of Trustees refused his request, but King's College (now Columbia University) agreed to his terms and he began his studies there in late 1773. Hamilton began college at an age when most young men were graduating from it. He was often seen pacing along the bank of the Hudson River, muttering to himself as he practiced his lessons.

Revolutionary War

When news of the Boston Tea Party reached New York, Hamilton published his first political piece, which was firmly in favor of the destruction of the tea. As the political activity intensified, Hamilton was increasingly distracted by it and soon identified with the agenda favored by the Liberty Boys. On July 6, 1774 he made an impromptu speech on the King's College Commons at a Sons of Liberty meeting, in which he applauded the Boston Tea Party, condemned the closing of the harbor, and urged colonists to unite against unjust taxation and support the boycott of British goods. If the colonists were apathetic they could expect that "fraud, power, and the most odious oppression will rise triumphant over right, justice, social happiness, and freedom."

That summer the Continental Congress was formed. The body hoped to pursue reconciliation with Britain, but also formed the Continental Association to implement a broad-based trade embargo. Local committees were established to attend to the details of enforcement. Hercules Mulligan, with whom Hamilton is purported to have boarded, sat on the New York committee. Prohibitions on British trade and colonial action against Britain divided Americans.

Hamilton's political involvement became firmly entrenched in this period. Clearly allied with the liberal faction of New York politics, Hamilton published a pamphlet titled *A Full Vindication of the Measures of Congress*, a response to a Loyalist tract titled "A Westchester Farmer." Hamilton argued in favor of the natural rights of man and government based on the consent of the governed. Hamilton wrote enthusiastically in favor of the liberal cause that steered the revolution and engaged in a pamphlet war. In the pamphlet *The Farmer Refuted* he predicted the colonies were capable of securing their independence from Britain and foreign powers would come to their aid. Also present in his thoughts was a cautious optimism regarding ongoing relations with Great Britain.

QUOTE

"The origin of all civil government, justly established, must be a voluntary compact between the rulers and the ruled, and must be liable to such limitations as are necessary for the security of the absolute rights of the latter; for what original title can any man, or set of men, have to govern others except their own consent?" **—Alexander Hamilton, *The Farmer Refuted*, 1775**

Military Career

Hamilton joined a volunteer militia club at King's College and was quickly promoted to the rank of lieutenant. The company saw action at the Battle of Long Island (August 1776) and at Chatterton's Hill at the Battle of

White Plains (October 1776). His leadership abilities drew the attention of General Nathaniel Greene when Hamilton led his company in a raid that captured British cannon installed in the Battery. General Greene introduced Hamilton to George Washington and Hamilton served as an aide-de-camp on Washington's staff as a lieutenant colonel, a position he held from March 1777 to February 1781. Hamilton was present at Valley Forge, where 9,000 men camped, starving and freezing because the government was incapable of providing for its most basic needs.

As a result of an inept government, Hamilton seethed, the army "is now a mob without cloathing, without pay, without provision, without morals, without discipline. We begin to hate the country for its neglect of us; the country begins to hate us."

Hamilton's duties expanded and he essentially functioned as Washington's chief of staff. His responsibilities ranged from intelligence to diplomacy. Washington praised him as the man who could "think for me, as well as execute my orders." As a result of this position, Hamilton developed relationships with several New York congressmen. In them he found an audience to air his dissatisfaction with the inefficiency of a decentralized government, a dissatisfaction based largely on congressional inability to finance the war. In 1780 he wrote a treatise on the failings of the existing system and offered ideas on "the changes necessary to save us from ruin." He called for a convention of all the states to form a new government. He outlined a fiscal policy for the new nation, which he would later implement as the first secretary of the treasury, such as securing a foreign loan, taxing businesses and farmers, and creating a national bank.

By 1780, Hamilton was anxious to get out from under Washington's shadow and to command in active combat. His hopes for this prestige grew dimmer as the war neared its end. He and Washington parted ways in February 1781, and although Hamilton left a prominent position, he was anxious to move forward with a career in politics. He was well-positioned to take this course. He had established a network of influential persons in New York and he had recently married into one of the pre-eminent New York families.

Hamilton's marriage to Elizabeth Schuyler occurred on December 14, 1780. She was the daughter of General Philip Schuyler. Hamilton came to the marriage with nothing but his good name and reputation. His father-in-law believed Hamilton had great potential and welcomed him into the family. He and Elizabeth had eight children and by all accounts had an affectionate and happy marriage.

After leaving Washington's command, Hamilton spent much of his time honing his political philosophy. He communicated extensively with Robert Morris, America's new superintendant of finance, and published the initial installments of his first official essays on American government, a six-part series titled "The Continentalist." These activities were interrupted in July 1781, when Washington gave Hamilton command of the New York Light Infantry to fight alongside French troops at Yorktown where Hamilton successfully led his battalions. Cornwallis subsequently surrendered to Washington on October 19, 1781. After the Battle of Yorktown, Hamilton resigned his commission and returned to New York.

Political Career

After the war, Hamilton was busier than ever. Superintendant of Finance Robert Morris appointed him continental receiver of taxes for New York, and although he was authorized to receive taxes, he had no authority to collect them. He began law studies in Albany and completed a three-year course in six months, and was admitted to the New York state bar. He was also elected to the Continental Congress in 1782. There he met and befriended James Madison, who was as impatient with the weak Confederation government as he was. He and Madison would become confederates in the mission to reform the government as it was under the Articles of Confederation to become a strong, central government.

Hamilton resigned from the Continental Congress in 1783 and returned to New York to practice law from his office on Wall Street. He remained detached from politics for several years, but continued to be devoted to public service. He wrote the charter for the Bank of New York in 1784, and with John Jay he formed the Society for the Manumission of Slaves. In May of 1786 he was elected to the state legislature, and shortly after that was sent as a delegate to the Annapolis Convention.

The Annapolis Convention

The convention was poorly attended. Only twelve delegates from five states were present and only Delaware, Virginia, and New Jersey had voting quorums. In these circumstances there was no chance of accomplishing anything, and this represented the state of affairs Hamilton viewed as symptomatic of the greater problems plaguing the country. Hamilton revived the idea he had in 1780 of the need to convene a national meeting to transform the government from decentralized ineffectiveness to his vision of an efficient centralized body. Under Hamilton's leadership, the Annapolis delegates decided to organize another convention to meet in Philadelphia in May 1787 for the purpose of revising the Articles of Confederation. In Hamilton's mind, this meant increasing the power of the federal government.

The Constitutional Convention

New York reluctantly sent delegates to the convention, and Hamilton was one of them. New York was a particularly independent-minded state and was suspicious of any intent to create a strong national government. As Governor George Clinton came to understand the scope of Hamilton's Federalist sentiments, he directed the selection of the other delegates to counteract Hamilton's influence in the proceedings and his vote. Instead of choosing the five delegates that Hamilton requested, Clinton's bloc in the senate chose to send three: Hamilton the troublemaker and two others who would be reliably compliant with Clinton's purposes—Robert Yates and John Lansing.

In a five-hour speech, Hamilton laid out a plan that included a national legislature with two houses—the lower house elected by the people and the Senate elected for life by electors chosen by the people—a judiciary of twelve justices with jurisdiction over all lawsuits, and a national executive elected by electors chosen by the people to serve a life term and with absolute veto power.

Without Lansing's and Yates's cooperation at the convention, Hamilton's involvement was limited. When they abandoned the convention in protest,

Hamilton was left without a vote, as the rules required a state to have at least two delegates present to vote. Despite these setbacks, Hamilton was not completely obscure. On June 18, he offered his own plan as an alternative to the Virginia Plan and the New Jersey Plan, both of which he considered inadequate.

Ratification

Hamilton was the only delegate from New York to sign the Constitution and his principal contribution to it was his zealous devotion to its ratification. Hamilton's efforts to secure ratification were consistently blocked by delays and conditional approval of amendments. However, as one state after another approved the document, Hamilton and other Federalists argued that New York was in danger of isolating itself from a popularly accepted new government. Once Virginia ratified the document, New York followed suit, and the Federalist faction in New York achieved what was once regarded as impossible.

Secretary of the Treasury

During Washington's presidency, Hamilton was appointed first secretary of the treasury. Under his direction, the United States was able to secure credit, create the United States Mint and the First National Bank. His "Report on Manufactures" laid the groundwork for a commercial policy that promoted national interests and protective duties. He also managed to get congressional approval for an excise tax on distilled liquors as an additional source of revenue.

FACT

Sections of western Pennsylvania and western Virginia erupted in a popular uprising over the tax on whiskey. George Washington resolved to use military force to suppress the Whiskey Rebellion and he rode to the scene with federal forces accompanied by Alexander Hamilton. The insurgents begged for clemency and the incident was resolved without bloodshed.

As the new government was established, political factions invariably emerged in response to the remaining tensions between those who supported a strong, central government and those who did not. Hamilton was recognized as a leading voice within the emerging Federalist Party. After the death of George Washington, acrimonious disputes surfaced between Hamilton and John Adams and the Federalist Party fractured into those who agreed with Hamilton and those who agreed with Adams. The opposition, under the leadership of William Giles, Thomas Jefferson, and Hamilton's former political ally James Madison became known as the Democratic-Republican Party.

Hamilton left public office in January 1795 and returned to New York to practice law. Although he held no formal appointment, he remained active in the Federalist Party. His brash, opinionated style alienated him from many of the leading political figures of the day. The death of Washington left him adrift. Washington appreciated Hamilton's intellect and talents and was able to overlook the intemperate facets of Hamilton's personality that estranged him from others. Hamilton described Washington as "an Aegis very essential to me."

Indeed, Hamilton's later years were filled with acerbic wrangling largely with members of his own party. Most particularly he distrusted John Adams and nursed a fifteen-year grievance with Aaron Burr. During the election of 1800, Hamilton actively campaigned against the Democratic-Republican nominee, as well as against the Federalist candidate, John Adams. He printed a pamphlet titled *A Letter From Alexander Hamilton Concerning the Public Conduct and Character of John Adams, ESQ, President of the United States*. The pamphlet was only intended for circulation among other Federalists, but a copy found its way into the hands of the Democratic-Republican Party, some say thanks to Aaron Burr who was determined to destroy Hamilton politically. The letter was critical of Adams's economic and foreign policies and accused him of being unfit to be president.

The Duel

The duel between Alexander Hamilton and Aaron Burr is one of the most famous encounters in American history. As young men, the two served together in the Continental army and practiced law. Over time, Hamilton viewed Burr as a political opportunist who was generally unsuited to high public office. Most of their association was marked with a caustic disregard for each other, sentiments that worsened as they grew older and relations between the two men reached the breaking point in 1804. Charles D.

Cooper, a New York lawyer and Democratic-Republican politician was at a dinner party where he claimed to have heard Hamilton make disparaging remarks about the Federalist's intention to nominate Burr as their candidate for governor of New York. Cooper wrote a letter to Hamilton's father-in-law Philip Schuyler complaining of Hamilton's "despicable opinion" of Burr. The letter was also published in the *Albany Register* where everyone, including Burr could see it. The letter appeared shortly after Burr was defeated in the gubernatorial election, and as far as Burr was concerned, this represented the final outrage in his relationship with Hamilton. Burr demanded an explanation from Hamilton. Hamilton responded that although he remembered being at a dinner at which Cooper was also present he was unable to recollect exactly what he may have said regarding Burr's candidacy for governor, but he was certain he would not have made reference "to any particular instance of past conduct or private character." Burr did not accept Hamilton's explanation as satisfactory and challenged him to a duel.

The dueling site Burr and Hamilton selected at Weehawken was a favorite locale for duelists as dueling was illegal in New York and the site was isolated. It is cruel irony that Hamilton's eldest son Philip was also killed at this same location in 1801 using the same pistols, in a duel defending his father's honor.

Both men reviewed their wills the night before the duel and Hamilton prepared a statement in which he said he felt "no ill-will to Colonel Burr" and that he decided to "reserve and throw away my first fire, and I have thoughts of even reserving my second fire." The two met at a secluded ledge near Weehawken, New Jersey. Accounts vary as to who shot first; Hamilton's shot missed Burr but Burr's shot hit Hamilton. It is clear Burr was unaware of Hamilton's intention to throw away his first shot, a common practice in dueling which allowed the parties to discharge their weapons without actually aiming for each other. When each side had their turn they could determine if they wished to fire again or agree the dispute had been addressed. Why Hamilton did not apprise Burr of his intention is unknown. Had Burr been aware of Hamilton's plan, the rules of dueling would have compelled him to behave similarly.

As Hamilton accepted the challenge, he had the prerogative to select the weapons. He chose custom-made pistols with smoothbore barrels loaded with .54 caliber balls, and he directed his seconds to disable the hair-triggers, making the weapons less sensitive to pressure from the trigger finger, and requiring the shots to be deliberate. Fired at extremely close range they could be fatal, but at the distance used in dueling, their aim would be inaccurate and it was likely no one would be hit, or at least not seriously.

Much to his horror, Burr's shot hit Hamilton just above the right hip, mortally wounding him. The bullet fractured his rib cage, traveled though his liver and diaphragm, and lodged in his second lumbar vertebra. Hamilton survived long enough to be carried back to his home where he died the following day, July 12, 1804, surrounded by his grief-stricken wife and children. Aaron Burr faced charges of multiple crimes, including murder, but all charges were eventually dropped. There was a massive outpouring of sympathy and outrage at Hamilton's death. His friend Gouverneur Morris gave the eulogy at Hamilton's funeral.

Legacy

Hamilton rose above the limitations of his background to become a proponent for American independence. He was a member of the Continental Congress and served in the Continental army. Following the war, he was appointed assistant superintendant of finance, and was later appointed the first secretary of the treasury under George Washington. Of all of the Founding Fathers, Hamilton was most modern in his approach to the issues surrounding the creation of a nation, a government, and the financial structure on which it would all rest, as is evidenced in his promotion of a strong central government, a national banking system, and his use of the press and propaganda to promote his ideas. He was a framer of the Constitution, and wrote prolifically in favor of its ratification. He helped create two banks, the Bank of New York and the Bank of the United States, and was a founder of the New York Manumission Society. In spite of the impressive list of his achievements, he is most famous for dying in a duel with Aaron Burr.

CHAPTER 12

John Jay

John Jay's long and eventful life saw numerous key events in the building of the American nation, including the break from the British Crown, the Revolutionary War, the contentious events leading up to the making of a new government, and the creation of a new nation. Jay played many roles, including those of lawyer, politician, court justice, diplomat, and Founding Father.

Early Life and Education

John Jay was born on December 12, 1745 in New York City, the sixth son of ten children born to Peter Jay and his wife Mary Van Cortlandt Jay. His paternal grandfather, Augustus, came to America from France in 1685, when the Edict of Nantes, which abolished the rights of French Protestants, was passed. Augustus Jay eventually settled in New York where, blessed with both an advantageous marriage and a thriving business as a merchant, he was able to establish a life of prosperity for his family.

Shortly after Jay's birth, Peter Jay moved his growing family from the island of Manhattan to the city of Rye, New York, because two of his children were blind and two others suffered from mental handicaps. It was hoped that the quieter and more healthy environment of fresh air and countryside would benefit all the children.

Education

John Jay's childhood was spent in Rye. By all accounts he was a child who showed extraordinary promise and possessed a keen mind. His education consisted of private tutoring until he was eight years old, at which time he was sent to the city of New Rochelle, where he studied under an Anglican pastor by the name of Pierre Stoupe. After completing three years of study with Stoupe, Jay returned to Rye in 1756, where he resumed his education with private tutors. In 1760, at the age of fourteen, Jay traveled to New York City, where he enrolled in King's College.

King's College would eventually become Columbia College. The school was founded in 1754 as King's College by royal charter of King George II of England. Columbia is the oldest institution of higher learning in the state of New York and the fifth oldest in the United States. In July 1754, Samuel Johnson held the first class in a new schoolhouse; there were eight students in the class.

In 1764, Jay graduated from King's College with high honors. He had by this time decided to study law, so he then became a law clerk. In 1768, Jay was admitted to the bar of New York, after which he entered into private practice with Robert Livingston until 1771, when Jay decided to go out on his own.

Entry Into Public Life

Jay's first appearance in the public arena came in 1774 when he served as secretary for the New York Committee of Fifty One. Like his father, John Jay was a Whig, though he tended to be moderate in his political views. His political stance no doubt helped as he represented the conservative faction of the New York delegation. The committee was primarily interested in preserving property rights and the existing law. However, the group also recognized that the British Crown had violated American rights and wished to have those redressed.

The Whigs were originally an English political party that emerged during the 1680s and supported the idea of a constitutional monarchy while opposing the idea of an absolute monarchy (in which the monarch has complete control over everything). In the American colonies, Whigs in the beginning sided with their British counterparts. However, by the time of the Revolution, American Whigs began adopting the term Patriots.

Initially, as a delegate to the First Continental Congress in 1774, Jay supported the notion that the British tax measures were unfair and the American resistance was justified. But he also wished to see some kind of reconciliation with Parliament and did not advocate revolution. Jay continued to stress reconciliation up until 1776 when restoring good relations with Britain appeared impossible. Jay pushed for a break with England and also attempted to sway his New York delegates to support the cause of independence.

Service During the American Revolution

With the outbreak of the American Revolution, Jay worked unceasingly for the cause of the Patriots. Among his many roles was as a delegate to the third New York Provincial Congress, where he drafted the New York Constitution in 1777. Unfortunately, his duties in Congress prevented Jay from voting on or signing the Declaration of Independence. Jay also served on a committee that kept watch on Loyalist activity and sought out any sign of conspiracies that might threaten the American cause. On May 8, 1777, Jay was elected the chief justice of the New York Supreme Court, where he would serve for two years.

In 1778, Jay was elected as a delegate to the Continental Congress. After only three days, the delegates decided to hold elections for a new president of the Congress. Jay defeated then-president Henry Laurens of South Carolina and served as president of the Continental Congress from December 10, 1778 to September 28, 1779.

Diplomat

On September 27, 1779, President George Washington appointed Jay to the position of minister to Spain. Among Jay's duties was to seek financial aid, negotiate commercial treaties, and seek recognition of American independence by the Spanish government. Unfortunately for Jay, the royal court refused to receive him, as Spain still did not recognize the United States as a newly formed nation. Jay also found the Spanish too arrogant in his dealings and made arrangements to journey to Paris in June 1782.

Spain refused to recognize American independence until 1783, for fear that to do so would inspire their own colonies to seek independence. Jay, however, was successful in asking Spain for a loan of $170,000 for the United States government.

Jay left Spain in May 1782 and by June had made his way to Paris, where negotiations were under way to end the American Revolutionary War.

While in Paris, Jay stayed near the quarters of Benjamin Franklin, who was also there to help with negotiations. It was Jay's wish to learn as much as possible from the elder statesman and diplomat. In July 1782, the British offered the Americans their independence, but Jay refused the terms on the grounds that the British refused to recognize American independence during the earlier talks between the two nations, in which the British asked to meet with representatives of the American "colonies" and not the United States of America. Jay was also supported by Franklin. But as a result of Jay's dissatisfaction with the talks, negotiations stalled until the Fall, with the British awaiting instructions from London on how to proceed with the Americans.

Taking this position also put the Americans in a tricky place with the French, who were pushing for a speedy end to the treaty talks. Jay became increasingly suspicious that the French were up to negotiating a separate treaty on their own with England. Without consulting Franklin, Jay contacted an official in Britain to stop the French, which led to the Americans negotiating a separate peace with England.

In the end, the final treaty granted the United States its independence and stated that the British would withdraw their troops in exchange for the United States ending the seizure of property belonging to Loyalists. Although the treaty gave the United States its freedom, many of the provisions would not be enforced.

Secretary of Foreign Affairs

In 1784, John Jay was appointed as the second secretary of foreign affairs, a position he would hold until 1789. That year Congress passed a law that gave additional domestic responsibilities to the Department of Foreign Affairs and also changed its name to the Department of State.

The United States Department of State (often referred to as the State Department) is responsible for overseeing the international relations of the United States. The department is equivalent to the foreign ministry departments of other nations. The Department of State was the first executive department established.

During his time as secretary of state, Jay sought to create a strong and viable foreign policy for the United States. Among his aims were to achieve recognition of the new nation by other foreign countries, to establish a stable American currency, and to secure credit based on loans from European banks. He also wished to pay back America's creditors and wipe away the heavy war debt from the revolution. Jay was also concerned about establishing secure territorial boundaries against possible foreign invasions and Native American groups, and the protection of American ships against piracy. Finally, Jay was also worried about the ability of the new government to survive under the Articles of Confederation.

John Jay, Federalist

As secretary of state, Jay grew increasingly concerned over his perceived lack of authority as a member of the new federal government. Along with fellow Federalists Alexander Hamilton and James Madison, Jay began lobbying for the creation of a stronger central government than the one currently in place under the Articles of Confederation.

Although Jay did not attend the Constitutional Convention in Philadelphia, he did join with Hamilton and Madison in writing *The Federalist Papers* to argue in favor of a more powerful central government that was also balanced in how it used its powers.

The *Federalist Papers* consisted of a series of eighty-five articles written to persuade American citizens to support and ratify the newly proposed Constitution of the United States. Jay wrote the second, third, fourth, fifth, and sixty-fourth articles of *The Federalist Papers*.

John Jay, Supreme Court Justice

In September 1789, Jay was again offered the position of secretary of state by President George Washington. In essence, Jay would have carried out the same duties as before but with a new title, but Jay declined to serve. Wanting to keep Jay in service to the new government, Washington then offered him the position of the first chief justice of the United States Supreme Court. Jay gladly accepted.

Jay was officially nominated to the post of Supreme Court justice on September 24, 1789. This same day, Washington signed into law the Judiciary Act of 1789 that created Jay's position. Jay was unanimously confirmed by the United States Senate two days later, on September 26, 1789.

For the first three years, the Court under Jay's direction, was primarily concerned with creating a system of rules and procedures for the Court's operations. The Court also regulated the admission of attorneys to the bar. In addition, the justices traveled to preside over cases in the circuit courts of the new judicial districts established by the federal government. Jay made the most of a relatively light work load to become more involved in the affairs of Washington's administration, talking to people about the government's stand on neutrality and publishing reports by the French minister to win American support for the French.

During Jay's tenure as chief justice, the Supreme Court heard only four cases. Perhaps one of the more important cases was *Chisholm v. Georgia*, which allowed the Court to establish judicial review, or the idea that legislative and executive actions are subject to review, and possible invalidation, by the judicial branch.

No matter how involved Jay was in the political affairs of Washington's administration, he was extremely protective of the Supreme Court's independence as a separate branch of the federal government. In 1790, Jay demonstrated this when Secretary of the Treasury Alexander Hamilton wrote to Jay, requesting the Court's endorsement of legislation that would assume the debts of the states. Jay's response was that the business of the court was in ruling on the constitutionality of the cases being tried before it, and the Court would not take a position one way or the other on matters of legislation. It was an important stand to take—one that ensured that the judicial branch would remain apart from potentially contentious and divisive political issues.

Jay Treaty

By the 1790s, relations with Great Britain were rapidly deteriorating. As far as Americans were concerned, the behavior of Great Britain—including British treatment of American ships (which they raided for cargo) and the impressments of American seamen into the British navy—was growing increasingly more intolerable. The British had also continued to occupy western outposts within the boundaries of the United States, which they had previously pledged to honor during Jay's talks with them in Paris in 1789.

Finally, in 1794, President Washington sent Jay to England to seek some kind of a solution to the escalating tensions between the two nations. As a result of his talks with the British, an agreement was reached known as the Jay Treaty or Jay's Treaty. Among the most important provisions of the treaty was the withdrawal of British troops from the western outposts, with the creation of a commission to settle outstanding border issues between the U.S. and Canada. Another commission was to be created that would resolve American losses in British ship seizures and Loyalist losses during the American Revolution. However, missing from the treaty was any kind of provision for the British to stop seizing American ships, cargo, and seamen.

Opposition to Jay's Treaty ran high. Alexander Hamilton was supportive of the treaty, while Thomas Jefferson was highly critical of it. Many Americans were not happy with Jay's Treaty either. For one thing, the treaty did nothing to address the problem of impressments of American sailors by the British navy. Among Southerners the treaty was denounced because of the British refusal to pay restitution for slaves who were taken by the British. Despite public opposition, the treaty was ratified by the Senate.

Jay's Treaty was still a significant diplomatic effort in part because of the hostile reactions from the American public. For one of the few times in his political career, Washington was heavily criticized for signing the treaty. Jay resigned from the Supreme Court and later remarked that he could have traveled the length of the country by the light of bonfires burning his effigy.

Although historians today acknowledge that Jay's Treaty had many flaws, it is generally acknowledged that given the fact that America, as a new nation, had little political power on the international stage, it was the best that Jay could do.

Governor of New York

In 1795, while staying in Britain, Jay was elected as the second governor of New York. He resigned from the Supreme Court on June 29, 1795, and served as governor until 1801. While governor, President John Adams nominated Jay again for a seat on the Supreme Court, but Jay refused, citing his increasingly poor health. Jay was also disturbed by what he believed was a lack of dignity and power in the Supreme Court.

While governor, Jay ran as a candidate in the 1796 presidential election. He won five electoral votes, but lost to John Adams. Jay ran again in the 1800 election, winning one electoral vote, but lost to Thomas Jefferson.

In 1801, Jay stepped down from the office of governor, refusing to run again for the position. He instead retired to Westchester County, New York where his next role was that of a gentleman farmer. He would never again enter the political arena.

End of Life

On the night of May 14, 1829, Jay was stricken with palsy that may have been caused by a stroke. He lived on for three days and then died on May 17, 1829. Jay had requested that he be buried in Rye, his childhood home, at his family's private cemetery. Today, the Jay Cemetery is an integral part of the Boston Post Road Historic District, adjacent to the historic Jay Property. Today, the cemetery is taken care of by Jay's descendants and remains the oldest active cemetery associated with a figure from the American Revolution.

Legacy

Next to many of his contemporaries, John Jay would not be considered a genius. Rather, Jay's importance lies in his keen legal mind, his discipline, and his moral vigor. His contributions to the founding of the nation are many: as patriot, diplomat, secretary of state, and as the nation's first chief justice of the Supreme Court. As diplomat, his insistence on the recognition of the United States as a new nation and not as a group of colonies, helped the country take its first tentative steps onto the world stage of diplomacy. His subsequent efforts, while not popular, also underscored a keen understanding of world affairs and probably kept America from entering a war. In his capacity as chief justice of the Supreme Court, Jay helped forge an indelible legacy of national supremacy of the federal government. In all these efforts, Jay worked tirelessly to promote the idea of freedom while helping to shape the responsibilities that come with it.

PART III

★ THE SIGNERS ★

Drafted by Thomas Jefferson between June 11 and June 28, 1776, the Declaration of Independence is probably the most recognized document of American history. In signing their names, fifty-six men effectively pledged their lives and livelihoods to the pursuit of freedom, while knowingly committing treason. Yet on a hot July day in 1776, there seemed little recourse but in declaring, once and for all, the intention of the thirteen American colonies to break free from the British Crown. It was a difficult time: War had erupted a year earlier and the future seemed uncertain for the colonies. There was no clear indication that the colonies would even win their struggle. Still, the signers prevailed. Their legacy not only included a blueprint for democracy and a free nation, but a reminder of how precious that ideal truly is.

Quiz: Decoding the Declaration of Independence

1. **What is the first word of the Declaration of Independence?**

    A. We
    B. Our
    C. The
    D. When

2. **Which of the following men did not help draft the Declaration of Independence?**

    A. John Adams
    B. James Monroe
    C. Roger Sherman
    D. George Washington

3. **Which colony had the most signatories of the Declaration of Independence?**

    A. Massachusetts
    B. New York
    C. Pennsylvania
    D. Virginia

4. **According to the Declaration of Independence, the government gets its power from:**

    A. The Constitution
    B. The governed
    C. The Senate
    D. The Supreme Court

5. **Where did Thomas Jefferson write the Declaration of Independence?**

    A. Declaration/Graff House
    B. Independence Hall
    C. Monticello
    D. Philadelphia Tavern

6. **Where was the first public reading of the Declaration of Independence held?**

    A. Boston
    B. New York City
    C. Philadelphia
    D. Washington D.C.

7. **Which two future presidents signed the Declaration of Independence?**

    A. John Adams and Thomas Jefferson
    B. Thomas Jefferson and James Madison
    C. John Adams and George Washington
    D. Thomas Jefferson and George Washington

8. **The oldest delegate who signed the Declaration of Independence was:**

    A. John Adams
    B. Robert Morris
    C. Benjamin Franklin
    D. Edward Rutledge

9. Which signer of the Declaration of Independence first proposed a resolution that the colonies break free from the Crown?

A. Samuel Adams
B. Richard Henry Lee
C. Thomas Paine
D. John Hancock

10. Where can you see the Declaration of Independence today?

A. Library of Congress
B. National Archives
C. Smithsonian
D. White House

Answers

1. D 2. D 3. C 4. B 5. A 6. C 7. A 8. C 9. B 10. B

CHAPTER 13

John Hancock

John Hancock is a Founding Father nearly everyone can name. His large signature on the Declaration of Independence is perhaps his most famous attribute. Despite his role as a major player in the colonies' bid for independence, as a member of the Continental Congress, as a signer of the Articles of Confederation, and as a nine-term governor of Massachusetts, he was not initially interested in politics. He was a successful Boston merchant and spent his early career developing his lucrative family business. His political career was as much a result of his grievances against Parliament's revenue acts as his desire for power. History has not always judged him favorably, casting him as an opportunist, a tool of Samuel Adams, and an egomaniac whose rise to fame and power was predicated on his self-serving interests.

Early Life

John Hancock was born on January 12, 1737 in Braintree, Massachusetts, and was the fifth generation of his family born in the Massachusetts Bay Colony. His ancestors were of humble origins, but the Hancock family rose to prominence in New England, first as clergymen and later as wealthy merchants. Hancock was the first son of a Congregational minister, the nephew of three Congregational ministers, and the grandson of the locally influential Bishop Hancock of Lexington, Massachusetts. It was his uncle Thomas Hancock, a Boston merchant, who exerted the most influence over the man who would take his place in history as a patriot and Founding Father.

John Hancock's ancestors in the Massachusetts Bay Colony were farmers and cobblers. When Harvard College was established, his grandfather was sent there to study for the ministry. From that point forward, the family's fortunes turned from obscure laborers to respected and influential members of the community. Hancock was expected to follow in the family tradition of the ministry.

Young Hancock's pastoral life in Braintree changed irrevocably in 1744 when his father died suddenly at the age of forty-two. John was only seven years old. In the months following his father's death, Hancock watched all other physical vestiges of him disappear as his mother distributed his clerical robes, clothes, and books to the friends and colleagues named in his will. Within a year, Hancock's mother placed him in the custody of Uncle Thomas and Aunt Lydia.

Education

Thomas and Lydia Hancock owned a luxurious mansion on Beacon Hill in Boston, the likes of which their nephew John was quite unaccustomed. They were childless and took him in as one of their own, lavishing him with affection, gifts, fine clothes, a formal education, and the expectation that he would one day be a prosperous merchant like his uncle. Thomas hired a tutor to prepare John for the prestigious Boston Latin School, run by the autocratic John Lovell.

Hancock graduated from Boston Latin School in five years and entered Harvard with the class of 1754. At Harvard he was an average student and graduated without scholastic distinction. He was good at repetitive work and he was tenacious, but he did not distinguish himself as a creative thinker. Nevertheless, college was not necessarily dull for him. He and his classmates were not above the occasional prank: they tormented their professors and spent a wild night in town contributing to the intoxication of a slave. Hancock's mediocrity as a student did not extend to his dress, as he was purported to be the campus dandy, outfitted in the latest continental fashions, such as a lavender suit with fine lace cuffs, a gift from his doting aunt and uncle. After his graduation from Harvard in 1754, he entered into a six-year apprenticeship with his uncle's retail and shipping business.

Career

Thomas Hancock made most of his money in shipping. He owned three ships that carried local rum to Newfoundland in exchange for skins, fish, and whale oil, which he sent to England in return for manufactured goods such as cloth, haberdashery items, and tea, which he sold in his Boston shops. When John Hancock came to work for his uncle, fresh from Harvard, he started in the eighteenth-century equivalent of the mailroom. John may have been heir to all his uncle had, but Thomas was shrewd enough to make John earn his place as a partner and successor.

In the background of Hancock's early business career was the increasing tension between the British and the French in North America. Parliament awarded lucrative wartime contracts and Thomas Hancock was first in line to acquire such contracts to supply and outfit British military operations against the French forces in Canada. Thomas Hancock's military contracts were so profitable that he was able to suspend his shipping activities during the war.

By the late 1750s Thomas Hancock was increasingly sidelined by gout and more of the responsibility of managing the business was shouldered by his nephew. Thomas sent John Hancock to London to make business contacts and to determine the new trends in post-war commerce. Armed with a letter of introduction from his uncle and the promise of contacts in the highest commercial circles, John Hancock set forth to prove he was finally ready to help direct the future of the Hancock family business.

Thomas Hancock was paid in British pounds sterling, and this supply of cash allowed him to function not only as a provisioner, but also as a banker. He loaned money to farmers and used their land as collateral. He increased his real estate holdings both through foreclosed farmland and by being in a position to purchase choice parcels on Hancock Wharf and Long Wharf in Boston along with several shares in the Kennebec Land Company, a real estate speculation to develop lands along the Kennebec and Androscoggin Rivers in Maine.

Hancock had never been away from home and from the overwhelming influence of his aunt and uncle, and it comes as no surprise once he settled into life as a young gentleman abroad, he was determined to make the most of it. Ostensibly he was supposed to be social for the sake of business and when he was not doing that he was to call on Thomas's old business contacts, particularly those who owed him money, and try to collect from them. Hancock enthusiastically plunged into the London social scene, bought new clothes, and did not write home very often. Thomas fumed from Boston, "be frugal of Expenses, do Honor to your Country & furnish your mind with all wise improvements." Hancock's whirlwind life only slowed because of the death of King George II. The nation went into a period of mourning and Hancock had to adjust his life accordingly and complained in a letter, "Everything here now is very dull." He was only supposed to stay in London for a few months, but was star struck with the impending coronation of the new king and all the pomp and ceremony and festivities that would accompany the occasion.

Thomas was indeed displeased with his nephew's refusal to return on schedule and his laxness in writing home, but more disturbing was John's seeming inattention or incompetent handling of the business affairs. John had not managed to collect more than a fraction of the money owed to his uncle. He then destroyed the long standing business relationship between

Thomas Hancock and the firm of Trecothick, Apthorp, and Thomlinson by bungling a cash transfer and insulting Trecothick when his firm attempted to offer Hancock an alternative solution. The problem arose due to Hancock's inexperience and arrogance and although the rupture in the long standing relations between the house of Hancock and the firm of Trecothick, Apthorp, and Thomlinson could have been avoided by more mature and reasonable negotiations, John Hamcock was not up to the job. Bereft of the facts, Thomas decided to sever relations with that firm and transfer his funds to the firm of Jonathan Barnard, who was eager to acquire a business relationship with Hancock.

Hancock returned to Boston in July 1761. His uncle greeted him with the news that he was not prepared to make him a partner and Hancock returned to his subordinate position. Hancock had an ace up his sleeve, however, in the form of a wily business plan he had hatched with Barnard and his partner Harrison before boarding the ship for home.

John Hancock: Merchant

Hancock took on more responsibility as Thomas's health declined and literally did most of the leg work for the company as Thomas was so ill that it was often difficult for him to leave the house. Thomas finally made his nephew a full partner on January 1, 1763. As a partner, Hancock was free to pursue the post-war business plan he made with Barnard and Harrison in London, which was to export whale oil to England with the intention of gaining control of the American whale oil export market. It was a grandiose plan, but whale oil was a highly desired commodity in Britain, used in manufacturing, processing, and residential and street lighting.

Hancock made a valiant, but in the end, futile attempt to seize control of the oil trade from the hands of William Rotch, a Nantucket oil merchant who knew the trade and who knew how to get the best of a newcomer like John Hancock. Just as the plan was getting in motion, Thomas Hancock died suddenly on August 1, 1764. This left John Hancock solely in charge of the business and under pressure to make well-informed decisions in spite of his lack of experience in general and in the whale oil trade specifically, and to continue to make his mark on Boston society as a man of commercial influence.

Outwardly, Hancock was the picture of a successful merchant, but the reality was not as promising. More often than not he did not get good prices for his oil. Many of his problems were the result of his lack of preparation and his overconfident, if not cavalier, approach to business. His fortunes were complicated by the depressed post-war economy in New England that followed the French and Indian War. In addition to this, many of his uncle's business contacts refused to honor their debts after he died. By the mid-1760s, Hancock was cash strapped and short-tempered.

An advertisement from December 25, 1764, describes Hancock's retail operations: "Store No. 4, at the east end of Faneuil Market, a general assortment of English & India goods, also choice Newcastle coals, and Irish butter, cheap for cash. Said Hancock desires those persons who are still indebted to the estate of the late Hon. Thomas Hancock, Esq., deceased to be speedy in paying their respective balances to avoid trouble."

If Hancock and Boston were in financial straits, so was Britain. The French and Indian War was horrendously expensive and Parliament decided if the war was fought to the benefit of the American colonies, the colonies should help pay the bill. In April 1764 Parliament passed the Sugar Act, which was intended to raise revenue and to create an administrative structure to enforce collections. The Sugar Act had relatively little impact on trade, but the depressed economic mood was sufficient to create resentment against any tax that came from Parliament.

Introduction to Politics

In 1764 Hancock was a founding member of the local Society to Encourage Trade and through the connections he made there he was elected to one of Boston's seven selectman seats in 1765. As news of the impending Stamp Act reached the colonies, Hancock seemed uninterested. He had other problems. He was still preoccupied with trying to get the best of William Rotch. His balance sheet was a mess. He was stunned to learn from Barnard and Harrison, who refused to let him operate on credit, how little money he had, and he continued to bleed cash at an alarming rate to buy up oil before Rotch could get to it.

By the time the Stamp Act became effective, Hancock owed Barnard and Harrison £19,000. American trade was stagnant and it seemed everyone rigorously protested the Stamp Act, and Hancock started paying attention to the general discontent. He thought he was overtaxed to begin with, why should he or anyone else have to pay more? He was not so much affected by the Stamp Act itself as he was disturbed by the idea he would have more taxes to pay. Thus Hancock joined the growing number of voices who protested the Stamp Act because it was symbolic of the widespread economic distress already prevalent in the colony.

"I seldom meddle with Politicks, & indeed have not time now to Say anything on that head." —**John Hancock**

More significantly, Hancock was befriended by Samuel Adams. Adams supported his bid for selectman and introduced him to members of the patriot clubs and allowed him to attend a few secret meetings. Adams needed Hancock, who was wealthy, socially prominent, and well connected. Hancock's public position was vital to Adams, who needed a voice that was respected in the merchant community and could form a consensus between the merchants and the radicalized factions of the town.

Mob violence erupted on more than one occasion in Boston over the Stamp Act. In August 1765, the Massachusetts stamp distributor Andrew Oliver was hanged and burned in effigy and his property destroyed. He was so thoroughly terrorized that he resigned before he performed a single official duty as the colony's stamp officer. The home of Lieutenant Governor Thomas Hutchinson was also destroyed by mobs.

Hancock could not resist Adams's overtures. He craved approval, power, and attention. Adams opened doors for Hancock to walk on a larger political stage than he ever imagined. Suddenly Hancock found himself in a position to exert influence. Other merchants looked to him for guidance on what to do about the Stamp Act and the larger issues that surrounded it. The radicals had to have the merchants on their side to form a coalition powerful enough to challenge the tax. Merchants had to be convinced to follow a policy of non-compliance with the tax. Radicals preferred public outbursts of mob action to get their point across. Hancock's political skills were honed in this situation where he cultivated a voice of action that also decried violence.

Hancock knew nothing less than a repeal of the Stamp Act was necessary to secure his new political power. He was a generally popular figure because he had the ability to appeal to various levels of society. He was learning to walk the fine lines between the classes and between the radical and moderate political factions, and he was good at rhetoric. His communications to his agents in London became more pointed once he decided he would no longer import British goods until the Stamp Act was repealed.

"I should now have sent my Demand for a Spring Supply of Goods to come on the Brigantine Harrison, but upon mature deliberation I am resolved at least to for the present not to send another invoice to London or Carry on any Business in that way under the additional burthen of the Stamp Act." **—John Hancock, in a letter to Barnard and Harrison, October 14, 1765**

Hancock's message played well to the merchants and the radical classes alike. However, his boldness was guided as much by his own financial distress as politics. His whale oil scheme continued to perform poorly and if Barnard and Harrison would not let him operate on credit, it was just as well to exploit the financial and political advantages of the boycott.

When news of the repeal of the Stamp Act reached Boston, Hancock remained in the public eye. He won re-election as a selectman and also won a seat in the Provincial Assembly. One of his first initiatives in the assembly was to draft a bill, along with Samuel Adams and James Otis, to make the future importation of slaves into Massachusetts illegal.

Conflicts with Royal Officials

When Parliament enacted the Townshend Acts in 1767, Hancock was again determined not to be taxed. He encouraged merchants to boycott, but this time merchants did not agree with him. Undeterred, Hancock made it his business to insult the customs commissioners charged with enforcing the law, hoping to incite further public reaction against the latest parliamentary interference in American trade. These tensions came to a head on June 10, 1768 when the commissioners seized his sloop *Liberty*. As the British man of war *Romney* towed the *Liberty* from the dock, a mob assembled on the Hancock wharf. The commissioners wanted to search the sloop but did not board with a writ of assistance, and Hancock knew without that document he was not obliged to allow them below deck. As the drama on the *Liberty* played out, the mob became more agitated and rowdy. As a show of support for Hancock, the mob ultimately seized a pleasure craft belonging to one of the commissioners, hauled it though the streets and burned it near Hancock's mansion while mob leaders urged the crowd to "take up arms and be free." Hancock was instrumental in dispersing the crowd before they became more riled and the Liberty Affair, as it came to be known, only bolstered his growing popularity.

The war between Hancock and the customs commissioners was not over. On November 3, 1768 he was arrested for smuggling. Hancock was defended by John Adams and in spite of irregular proceedings by the prosecution; Hancock was acquitted and became more of a public hero than ever.

1767–1773

In the period immediately following the Liberty Affair, Hancock's relations with Boston's radical factions cooled and he drifted toward the political center. He was more comfortable identifying with his fellow merchants and although he resented parliamentary interference in American commerce, he was not yet prepared to walk the path toward American independence—he was more interested in maintaining the political and social status quo of the colony.

Hancock's maturity as a politician during this period is reflected in his decreased dependence on politicians who could do favors for him. He looked to his constituents for guidance and he believed they wanted peace as much as he did. The stress of the court proceedings over his arrest for smuggling and the public horror over the Boston Massacre in 1770 convinced Hancock that the middle road was the best course. During this period he served as moderator at Boston town meetings, was appointed to the Massachusetts Committee of Correspondence, became treasurer of Harvard, and continued to serve in the Provincial Congress. Through these positions he remained in the public eye, and could do so without exciting controversy, though he would take a different direction by 1773.

1773–1776

In 1773 the relative quiet of Boston was broken as Parliament announced its latest revenue scheme, the Tea Tax, assigned to save the faltering East India Company and to give them a monopoly in the American colonies. Merchants in New York, Philadelphia, and Charleston canceled their tea orders, but not so in Boston, where the agents receiving the tea were friends or family of Governor Thomas Hutchinson, a loyalist and symbol of parliamentary oppression.

Hancock was not directly involved in the Tea Party, but he had associations with the group that was involved. His reputation as a troublemaker was already well known in Parliament, and as far as the British government was concerned, he may as well have dumped the tea himself. Hancock, along with Samuel Adams, John Adams, and Josiah Quincy, was vocal in his opposition to further parliamentary interference with colonial legislatures. The political tide was turning and Hancock with it.

Hancock gave a rousing speech on the fourth anniversary of the Boston Massacre to a crowd that overflowed from Faneuil Hall and had to be relocated to the larger South Meeting House. In this popular speech he urged, "Let us be unified and strengthen the hands of each other by promoting a general union among us."

This speech secured Hancock's popularity and assured his re-election to the various public offices he held, and marks the moment he returned to the radical camp. The increased publicity from the speech also brought notoriety; he had Britain's attention. Hancock's call for unity was a rallying cry when Parliament passed the Intolerable Acts, which among other things closed the port of Boston until the East India Company was reimbursed for damages and removed governing council elected by Massachusetts colonists and replaced it with a council appointed by the king.

Unity, Hancock told the crowd, was the only recourse "to free ourselves from these unmannerly pillagers who impudently tell us, that they are licensed by an act of the British Parliament, to thrust their dirty hands into the pockets of every American." **—John Hancock, speaking on the occasion of the fourth anniversary of the Boston Massacre, March 5, 1774.**

Tensions in Boston ran high. General Thomas Gage replaced Governor Thomas Hutchinson as the military royal governor of Massachusetts and ordered his soldiers to fortify the town's defenses. Gage also canceled a General Assembly meeting of the Provincial Congress slated to convene in Salem. British troops were told that rebellion could break out at any time and a handbill was given to them identifying the individuals who were responsible for inciting public sentiment against the British government. Hancock's name was on the list of the principle troublemakers. Soldiers were advised "the instant rebellion happens, that you will put the above persons immediately to the sword, destroy their houses, and plunder their effects."

Angered, the congressional delegates met anyway and took steps to form a legitimate revolutionary government. They established the Massachusetts Committee of Safety, charged with the task of forming an army of 15,000 and securing supplies, arms, and artillery. Hancock, convinced war was imminent, settled his debts with George Hayley, his London agent, and went into the revolution cash poor but ready for action.

Hancock was re-elected to the Provincial Congress, and was also selected as a delegate to the Second Continental Congress, scheduled to meet in Philadelphia in May 1775. He was a busy man, serving on every important governing body and committee. These activities set him firmly in the sights of the occupying British forces, for whom he became a popular target and was harassed to the point that he and Samuel Adams fled to Lexington. General Gage ordered the seizure of the Boston Safety Committee's munitions stores and British soldiers were sent to find Hancock and Adams.

Hancock was so preoccupied that he had to postpone his marriage to Dorothy Quincy, a young lady of immense social stature selected for him by his Aunt Lydia. He wrote to her explaining his attentions were required elsewhere and promised to "return as soon as possible" hoping she would not be "saucy" when he finally did return.

Chaos reigned in Boston and its environs. As the British army retreated from Concord, growing numbers of Massachusetts militia men went on the offensive. Hancock and Adams began to pick their way southward to Philadelphia, to take their seats in Congress. On the outskirts of the city, they met up with other congressional delegates from Connecticut and New York, and were escorted to Philadelphia by 300 horsemen, who took them to the City Tavern.

Hancock was elected president of the Second Continental Congress to replace Peyton Randolph, who was suddenly required to return to Virginia. Once settled in the town, Hancock took the opportunity to set the agenda, arguing now that Massachusetts had already raised forces to fight the British and asking whether the other colonies would support them. While Hancock proved adept at walking the fine line between the radicals who desired independence and moderates who favored reconciliation groups, he became a target for John and Samuel Adams, who sought to curtail his rapidly growing power and influence. Their intentions became clear when Hancock proposed to be commander in chief of the Continental army and the Adamses supported George Washington, partly in an effort to mollify the southern delegates who thought too much power was vested in the Massachusetts delegation and partly to clip Hancock's wings. Hancock's subsequent offer to serve in the army under Washington was refused, and these rebuttals pulled him back into the moderate camp.

Spurned from military service, Hancock devoted himself to the details of his position as president of the Congress and he set the foundation for making the office an independent executive branch. He was so thoroughly immersed in his duties, he neglected his relationships both with Dorothy and his Aunt Lydia. He managed to travel to Connecticut in August 1775, whereupon his aunt insisted he marry right away. Dorothy's attentions were drifting dangerously toward Aaron Burr, who was visiting an uncle in the vicinity, and Lydia Hancock would brook no interference with the marriage she had arranged.

Hancock and his new wife returned to Philadelphia in time for the reconvening of Congress. They lived grandly in a fully staffed large house. Dorothy had to quickly learn the ropes of entertaining in the role of the president's wife. She earned John Adam's admiration for being "genteel" and "totally silent as a Lady ought to be." When she and her husband were not entertaining or receiving dignitaries, they spent the evenings, scissors in hand, trimming the rough edges from the bills of credit printed by Congress. Hancock signed them and sent them to the army so it could provision itself.

By 1776, the rift deepened between Hancock and John and Samuel Adams. Irked by Hancock's support of John Dickinson's Olive Branch Petition, they worked to undermine his authority in Massachusetts or any future he planned in Massachusetts politics by securing a coalition that excluded Hancock and attacked his allies and associates. As Hancock became more alienated from his sources in Boston he found it harder to stay abreast of the popular mood, the gauge by which he set his political direction. He was nearly caught behind the times on the issue of independence. His father-in-law, Edmund Quincy, advised him after the British left Boston "nothing will answer the end so well as a Declaration to all the world for absolute Independency." Hancock learned by May of 1776 he had been deliberately excluded from the Massachusetts lower house and the Governor's Council. Seeing the mood of the times and the radicals moving into popular sentiment, Hancock became an ardent convert to the cause of independence.

Hancock's huge signature on the Declaration of Independence was a way for him to bring attention back to himself. As president of the Continental Congress he was first to sign the document. Contrary to popular myth, Hancock did not care what the king thought about his name being written in large script. He cared about his image being rehabilitated as the man who invented the idea of independence.

Return to Massachusetts

In the months after congressional approval of the Declaration of Independence, Hancock's world settled into the dreariness of managing the war, a necessary task without the fame and glory of the days leading up to it. He began to think he had run his course as president and set his sights on returning home to renew his political aspirations in Boston. At this time, he was living well beyond his means. His commercial interests had dried up and the rents on many of his Boston properties were outstanding. He was also worried the British would pillage his holdings and was under pressure from Harvard to tend to his long neglected duties as treasurer. He gave his reasons for leaving as ill health and needing to spend more time with his family.

Hancock's plans to return to Boston were delayed by the anticipated arrival of British troops in Philadelphia. Congress fled to Baltimore and Philadelphia was spared by Washington's successful Christmas Eve attack on the British at Trenton. Although it was safe to return to Philadelphia, Hancock's plans to return to Boston were further delayed by the birth of his daughter Lydia. Lydia only lived a few months, and in the summer Dorothy returned to Boston without her husband. He promised to follow her shortly. Those plans were delayed when the war again came close to Philadelphia and Congress once more had to evacuate, this time to York, Pennsylvania. General Howe left New Jersey and set his forces in the Chesapeake Bay. Washington was ineffective in stopping them at Brandywine Creek, and the British were poised to take Philadelphia.

Hancock received a warning from Alexander Hamilton before the British invaded Philadelphia. "If Congress have not left Philadelphia they ought to do it immediately without fail, for the enemy have means of throwing a party this night into the city."

Washington provided Hancock an armed escort to Boston and by all accounts he entered the city to a brilliant reception. Hancock returned to Boston because he had his sights set on becoming governor. A landslide victory swept Hancock into office as the first popularly elected governor of Massachusetts.

Hancock was re-elected governor for several successive terms. He won despite his lack of a discernable platform or program; the force of his personality was apparently enough. He left the governing to the legislature, which was dominated by eastern commercial and maritime interests. Hancock spent his entire gubernatorial career largely as a figurehead with enough sense to let the powers of the legislature have their way.

Post-War Career

Hancock held the governor's office from 1780 to 1784. Shortly after the 1784 election, he abruptly announced his resignation. Although the true purpose behind his leaving is unclear, Hancock's timing was impeccable. It was his successor who had to contend with the crisis of Shays' Rebellion.

By 1785 Hancock was forty-eight and in chronic ill health, mostly due to bouts of gout. He nevertheless persisted in occupying the political limelight as much as possible, serving additional terms as president of the Congress and as governor. He was also elected to the Massachusetts ratification convention. He nursed hopes of serving as the first president of the United States, but soon realized the national political current would not support him.

Legacy

Hancock died in October 1793 at fifty-six years of age, leaving a substantial legacy of public service. Although his detractors criticized him for using his political position to advance his agenda and personal ambitions for fortune and power, Hancock proved himself to be a master politician. His talent was to sense the popular current and bring it to reality. To do this he learned how to skillfully maneuver around and among the various factions and to build a consensus. It was his nature to be persistent and undaunted, necessary characteristics to have in times of crisis. His place in history will always rest on his large signature on the Declaration of Independence.

CHAPTER 14

Benjamin Harrison

A member of one of the first families of Virginia, Benjamin Harrison V continued the family tradition of political service to the colony of Virginia and later, to the newly formed American nation. Perhaps not as well known as some of the other signers, Harrison nonetheless played an important role in the nation's early struggles. His legacy continued on, as a son and a great-grandson would eventually serve in the nation's highest office as presidents of the United States.

Early Life and Education

Benjamin Harrison's family was among the first to settle in the new colony of Virginia, arriving in 1632. Almost from the time they arrived, they began to distinguish themselves in public office. Harrison's great-great-grandfather Benjamin Harrison I served as clerk of the Council in Jamestown in 1633. In 1644, Benjamin Harrison II was a member of the House of Burgesses, the governing body of colonial Virginia. His election began the tradition of members of the Harrison family holding prominent political office that continued for more than 200 years. In time, the Harrison family rose to prominence in Virginia because of their own wealth and marriages that linked them to some of the most important families in colonial Virginia.

Harrison's father, Benjamin Harrison IV, married Anne Carter, the eldest daughter of Robert "King" Carter, one of the most influential and wealthiest men in the colony. Their first child and son, Benjamin Harrison V was born at the family home, Berkeley, in Charles City County, Virginia on April 5, 1726. Nine children would follow: five sons, four of whom survived infancy, and four daughters.

Berkeley, the Harrison family home, was built by Benjamin Harrison V's father on land given to him by his father-in-law. Using bricks made and fired on the land, Harrison built a Georgian-style, three-story brick mansion on a hill overlooking the James River in 1726. Berkeley shares an honor with Peacefield, the Adams family home in Quincy, Massachusetts. Both residences are the ancestral homes for two United States presidents.

Benjamin Harrison V went on to attend the College of William and Mary. In 1745, he was called home upon the sudden death of his father and two sisters in a lightning strike during a thunderstorm. Harrison now found himself in the position of having to manage his father's estate and any thought of continuing his studies was gone. Harrison eventually married his second cousin Elizabeth Bassett; together the couple had seven children.

The Political Arena

Even as Harrison continued to oversee the running of the family plantation, he found time to enter local politics. In 1749, he was elected to the House of Burgesses, a seat that he held until 1775. Harrison was also frequently chosen to serve as speaker of the House during his tenure. By 1763, Harrison, whose influence in the house was considerable, was becoming more critical of British colonial policy in general and of the unfair tax practices in particular, and for the next decade worked tirelessly for the American cause for freedom.

When compared to the more radical and outspoken politicians of the period such as Patrick Henry, Harrison was clearly of a more temperate and moderate disposition. Still, he did not shy away from controversy or conflict. Beginning in 1764, Harrison served as a member of the House committee that protested the proposed Stamp Act. By 1773, Harrison was working alongside other Virginia leaders such as Patrick Henry and Richard Henry Lee as one of the members of the Virginia committee of correspondence, which worked with other colonial committees to draw up plans of resistance to the British.

Harrison quickly caught the attention of some other notable delegates such as John Adams of Massachusetts, who later wrote: "These gentlemen of Virginia, appear to be the most spirited and consistent of any. Harrison said he would have come on foot rather than not come."

In 1774, when the Crown dissolved the House of Burgesses, Harrison was among those who called for a meeting of representatives from all the colonies to discuss the deteriorating political situation. Harrison was then elected as a delegate to the first Continental Congress, where he joined other delegates such as Richard Henry Lee and George Washington in Philadelphia. At the meeting, Harrison served as chairman of foreign affairs and as a member of the Board of War. He showed himself to be a man of firm convictions, good sense, and an even temperament that held up well particularly when the group was facing great tensions among the delegates.

Harrison was also chosen to preside over the debates that led to the eventual writing of the Declaration of Independence, and was among the signers. From 1775 to 1776, following the outbreak of the revolution, Harrison served as a county representative in meetings held to reorganize the colonial state governments. He was also a member of the Committee of Secret Correspondence for the Congress that was dedicated to seeking European aid for the American cause.

Wartime

By 1778, Harrison returned home to Berkeley from Philadelphia. Unfortunately, Berkeley had fallen onto hard times in part because of Harrison's absence. His oldest son was away fighting the British in the South, and his surviving sons were too young to be able to help with the day-to-day running of the plantation. For the next three years Harrison did what he could to take care of the plantation and his family, while making sure his own affairs were in order. In 1781, Harrison was drawn away from his family and home when the governor of Virginia asked him to go to the Continental Congress to seek financial aid for Virginia.

The appearance of the British fleet in Chesapeake Bay interrupted Harrison's plans. Not long after, a detachment of Hessian soldiers accompanied by local Loyalists arrived at the stately home of the Byrd family, called Westover, located only a few miles from Berkeley. The troops continued on to Richmond, then the new capital of Virginia, in search of food, weapons, and other supplies. It seemed that Berkeley had been spared. Still, Harrison took no chances and had his family moved to the home of relatives. However, on their return from Richmond, the troops, under the leadership of former American military officer Benedict Arnold, did stop at Berkeley, where they were to rendezvous with a British warship.

While waiting for the ship, Arnold and his men wreaked havoc at Berkeley. They destroyed much of the house and its contents, burning paintings, clothing, and furniture. The walls were stripped, and what was not burned was confiscated. Livestock was turned loose or slaughtered. Horses were stolen. The troops also confiscated the Harrison family's forty slaves. The family graveyard was desecrated, with tombstones overturned and broken. In addition, the troops encamped on the grounds, which were ruined from campsites and troop movement. The damage was so extensive that it was four years before Harrison and his family could return.

Governor Harrison

In the fall of 1781, Harrison moved his family once more—this time to Richmond, for he had been elected as governor of Virginia. For the next four years, the family resided in Richmond at the governor's mansion. Harrison proved to be a popular governor, but because of term limitations he left office in 1785. He and his family returned to Berkeley and Harrison resumed private life.

Harrison did run for a seat in the state legislature, but was defeated by John Tyler, Sr., the father of the future president John Tyler. Harrison was elected from a neighboring district and served as speaker of the house during the time that the state legislature adopted the Virginia Statute for Religious Freedom.

In 1788, Harrison became a delegate to the state convention debating whether or not to ratify the constitution. Once again due to his popularity and reputation as a politician, Harrison was appointed chairman, but because of increasingly bad health, he refrained from taking part in any of the debates. Harrison was a strong supporter for ratification, provided that certain amendments that later became the Bill of Rights were attached to the document. In the end, he voted against ratification, on the grounds that a bill of rights was needed for the document to be truly effective.

In 1819, when artist John Trumbull was painting his famous work, *Declaration of Independence*, he had no portrait of Benjamin Harrison V to work with. Instead, Benjamin Harrison VI, Harrison's son, who was said to have resembled his father, served as Trumbull's model for Benjamin Harrison V.

In 1790, Harrison was proposed by fellow politicians as a candidate for the governor's office. However, when he learned that the current governor, Beverley Randolph (who was also a close family friend), would seek office again, Harrison declined to run. By the spring of 1791, Harrison's health, which had been marked by periods of gout and other illness, took a turn for the worse. During that time, he was elected again to the state legislature but took ill once more and died at Berkeley on April 24, 1791.

Legacy

Unlike many of his Virginia contemporaries, Benjamin Harrison V was not known for his great oratory like Patrick Henry, nor was he possessed of a great writing talent like Thomas Jefferson. His talents, rather, made him useful, as opposed to the brilliance of other members of the Virginia delegation. He was a moderate in a sea of clashing personalities and philosophies. Yet Harrison's usefulness allowed a Continental Convention to stay focused on its agenda and made it possible for other members to be heard. Like the generations of Harrisons before him, Benjamin Harrison placed duty above comfort, freedom above tyranny, and the future of a fledgling nation above his own life. While not the most recognizable of the Founding Fathers, his contributions made it possible for a new nation to begin.

CHAPTER 15

Richard Henry Lee and Francis Lightfoot Lee

Richard Henry Lee and Francis Lightfoot Lee were the sons of Virginia planter Thomas Lee. Francis Lightfoot is remembered as the "Forgotten Revolutionary" and Richard Henry as a skilled politician who operated amid a sea of "gentleman amateurs." Richard Henry was the author of the Westmoreland Resolves, Westmoreland County's formal protest against the Stamp Act, and Francis Lightfoot was a signer. Richard Henry is credited with proposing the motion for declaring independence from Great Britain, and in cooperation with John Dickinson is credited with the idea of forming intercolonial committees of correspondence. Both brothers signed the Declaration of Independence and served in the Virginia House of Burgesses and in the Continental Congress, and Richard Henry represented Virginia in the Senate.

Early Life

Richard Henry and Francis Lightfoot were the fifth and sixth sons, respectively, of Thomas and Hannah Ludwell Lee. By the eighteenth century, the Lee family was established as wealthy and influential gentry in Westmoreland County, on the Northern Neck of Virginia. Thomas Lee was a tobacco planter and land speculator who owned in excess of 16,000 acres in Virginia and Maryland. He used slaves, indentured servants, and contract labor to extract the wealth from his lands. Thomas served as a justice of the peace and as acting governor of Virginia from 1749 until his death in 1750. His children inherited the sense of duty expected of persons of elevated social position. In addition to Richard Henry's contributions and those of his brother Francis Lightfoot, their older brother Thomas served in the Virginia Assembly and brothers William and Arthur were diplomats in the cause of European support for the American Revolution. Their sisters were no less distinguished; Hannah Lee Corbin was an early advocate for women's rights and Alice Lee Shippen, who was married to Dr. William Shippen of Philadelphia (the chief physician and director general for the Continental army hospitals), was the link between her brother Richard and John and Samuel Adams.

The Northern Neck of Virginia is a peninsula on the western bank of the Chesapeake Bay, bounded by the Potomac River to the north and by the Rappahannock River to the south. The Northern Neck was the cradle for many of Virginia's foremost citizens of the revolutionary and early national period, most notably the Lees, George Washington, James Madison, and James Monroe.

Richard Henry was loud, brash, and confrontational. Francis Lightfoot was a quiet man who liked his books and his library and to spend quiet days at Menokin, his country estate, in the company of his wife. History has judged Richard Henry to be a consummate politician, and Francis Lightfoot the "forgotten revolutionary." While the two brothers could not have been more opposite in temperament, the course of America's history could not have been the same without them.

Education

Both Richard Henry and Francis Lightfoot were educated by private tutors at Stratford Hall, the family estate. Richard Henry was subsequently sent to Wakefield Academy in Yorkshire, England; a privilege accorded to an elder son. After his studies at Wakefield, Richard Henry toured northern Europe and returned to Virginia at the age of nineteen. Francis Lightfoot was not sent on to university although he clearly had the intellect to successfully complete studies at that level. Stratford had a well-provisioned library and all of Thomas Lee's children are purported to have devoted considerable time to study. By all accounts, Francis Lightfoot was the most studious. He was educated and loved books and intellectual pursuits. Arthur Lee once said of his brother, "He was calmness and philosophy itself." Francis Lightfoot kept an impressive library at Menokin and in his essay about Francis Lightfoot Lee written in 1877, Mark Twain tells us, "He loved books; he had a good library, and no place had so great a charm for him as that."

Careers

With their formal education complete, Richard Henry and Francis Lightfoot moved into the adult realm of responsibility and duty expected of the gentry. Richard Henry made his home in Westmoreland County and became a justice of the peace there in 1757. He was elected to the Virginia House of Burgesses in 1758 and served as a delegate until 1775. The first bill Richard Henry introduced in the House of Burgesses was to curtail the slave trade into Virginia. It was a bold and radical proposal that immediately marked him as a firebrand, especially when he pronounced such things as Africans were "equally entitled to liberty and freedom by the great law of nature." It was no surprise to anyone when he became a friend and ally of Patrick Henry, another radical voice in the assembly.

Francis Lightfoot inherited lands in Loudon County and began his career in public service as the first justice of a thirteen-man county court. He was the commander of the Loudon militia and was elected to the House of Burgesses in 1758. He served on various committees including those on grievances, encouraging manufactures and arts, and regarding wars and Native

Americans. For a man so deeply engaged in committee work, he was reportedly bored by it and was often absent from the assembly.

Francis Lightfoot wrote to his younger brother William, "the people of Loudon are so vex'd at the little attendance I have given them that they are determined to dismiss me from service, a resolution most pleasing to me."

The Stamp Act

It became more difficult for Francis Lightfoot to retreat from the duty of public service once Parliament passed the Stamp Act. He joined his brother Richard Henry and 114 other Virginians as a signer of the Westmoreland Resolves. Richard Henry was a coauthor of the Resolves, an official protest of the Stamp Act and yet another articulation of the sentiment that American colonists as British subjects could not be taxed without their consent and that Parliament could not levy such taxes if Americans were not allowed direct representation in that body. The document stated that anyone attempting cooperation with the tax would be stigmatized and punished. Francis Lightfoot published an advertisement in the *Virginia Gazette* in April 1766 asking his acquaintances not to take letters to him to the post office as he was determined to "never willingly pay a Farthing of any TAX laid upon this COUNTRY in an UNCONSTITUTIONAL MANNER."

"And every abandoned wretch, who shall be so lost to virtue and public good, as wickedly to contribute to the introduction or fixture of the Stamp Act in this Colony, by using stampt paper, or by any other means, we will, with the utmost expedition, convince all such profligates that immediate danger and disgrace shall attend their prostitute purposes." **The Westmoreland Resolves, 1766**

The following year, Richard Henry rigorously protested the Townshend Acts. In 1768 he wrote to John Dickinson of Philadelphia that the colonies should establish special committees to communicate with each other. Nothing came of this suggestion for more than five years, but Richard Henry Lee and John Dickinson planted the seed of the Committees of Correspondence that would bring the colonies together in a common cause.

The Calm Before the Storm

In 1769, Francis Lightfoot married Rebecca Tayloe, the daughter of Richmond County planter John Tayloe II. Shortly after their marriage, the couple moved into their country estate, Menokin, a gift from John Tayloe. As Menokin was located in Richmond County, Francis gave up his Loudon County seat in the House of Burgesses and represented Richmond County until he was sent to the Second Continental Congress in 1775.

FACT

Menokin is a Rappahannock word that translates as "he gives it to me." The house was designated a National Historic Landmark in 1971 and is in fragile condition. It is currently managed by the Menokin Foundation.

Richard Henry did not lead a similarly docile political life. On May 16, 1769 he and Patrick Henry composed the Virginia Resolves, a document affirming the prerogative of the House of Burgesses to levy taxes, redress grievances, and communicate with the other colonies. The following day, the royal governor dissolved the House of Burgesses. Undeterred, the radicals moved their meetings to Raleigh's Tavern, where they drafted the Virginia Association, a non-importation agreement in which Virginians would boycott British goods until their grievances were satisfactorily addressed by Britain. Widespread colonial resistance and boycotts to parliamentary revenue acts resulted in the repeal of the Stamp Act and the Townshend Acts. The absence of these irritants returned politics to a relative quiet.

The Revolutionary War

As elsewhere the quiet was shattered by the events in Boston in 1773. The closing of the Boston harbor pushed Richard Henry Lee, Patrick Henry, and Thomas Jefferson to establish a committee of correspondence. The royal governor again dissolved the House of Burgesses and again they reconvened at Raleigh's Tavern. This time they resolved to appeal to the other colonies to form a colonial congress. Before they could act on their resolution, they received an invitation from Massachusetts to send representatives to the Continental Congress scheduled to meet in Philadelphia. Virginia sent seven delegates, among them Richard Henry Lee and Patrick Henry.

Richard Henry Lee

This was the setting for Richard Henry Lee's most distinguished accomplishment of the Revolutionary period: three resolutions introduced on June 7, 1776 that later took the shape of the Declaration of Independence. These resolutions were seconded by John Adams and the course for the formal declaration of independence from Britain was set.

Richard Henry Lee proposed that the colonies should be free and independent states, form foreign alliances, and should organize a plan of confederation.

Congress appointed a committee to prepare a Declaration of Independence. Richard Henry Lee would have been a member of this committee, except his wife was ill and his presence was required at home. The work was left in the hands of Thomas Jefferson, Benjamin Franklin, Roger Sherman, Robert Livingston, and John Adams, although the final document is recognized as the work of Thomas Jefferson.

In addition to setting the stage for the Declaration of Independence, Richard Henry Lee was instrumental in the selection of George Washington as the commander in chief of the Continental army, a position coveted by John Hancock. Richard Henry Lee worked with John and Samuel Adams to secure support for Washington. The arrangement suited the Adamses' desire to curb Hancock's seemingly insatiable desire for power and Lee's desire to secure more influence for the southern colonies.

Francis Lightfoot Lee

While his brother occupied himself with robust and fiery pronouncements against Parliament and George III, Francis Lightfoot Lee was, by comparison, inconspicuous. He preferred to work behind the scenes; he was not given to oratory and he did not enjoy debate. His quiet, steady tone was often the moderating force that subdued the impetuous rhetoric of Richard Henry and other vocal patriots. Francis Lightfoot Lee was active on various committees in Congress including the Board of War, the Committee on Secret Correspondence, and other committees. He was a signer of the Articles of Confederation.

The Revolutionary government created a three-year limit of service in Congress, and after his three-year term, Francis Lightfoot returned to state and local politics where he served until his retirement in 1782 at the age of forty-eight. Although he felt disdain for the limelight, as a man of means and privilege he took his politics seriously and remained interested in the affairs of his country until his death.

Post-War Careers

Richard Henry served in the legislature from 1780 to 1784 and joined with the conservative planter faction. He was elected to Congress in 1784 and represented Virginia until 1789. He was elected a delegate to the Constitutional Convention but refused to attend because he feared the document would create a strong central government at the expense of power vested in the states. Two antifederalist pamphlets titled *Letters of the Federal Farmer to the Republican* have often been credited to Richard Henry, but their authorship is not certain. He served in the United States Senate from 1789 until illness forced his retirement in 1792. He was relieved to see the ratification of the Bill of Rights before he left the Senate.

Francis Lightfoot had withdrawn from public life well before the Constitutional Convention of 1789, but he kept abreast of developments nevertheless. Historians point to a letter George Washington sent to James Madison as indication of Francis Lightfoot's support of the Constitution, in which Washington claimed Lee was "decidedly in favor of the new form under a conviction that it is the best that can be obtained."

Legacy

The Lees were early champions of the patriot cause. They protested taxes levied by Parliament both in deed and in official actions such as the Westmoreland Resolves. They served their colony, state, and nation in various public offices. Their hand is on every significant document from the revolutionary period, with their signatures on the Declaration of Independence and the Articles of Confederation, and less directly on the Constitution.

Francis Lightfoot quietly did his duty, although his preferences were to live a quiet gentleman's life among his books. His niece Ann Hume Shippen Livingston referred to him as the "sweetest of all the Lee race" in a sonnet she wrote in his honor in 1781.

Mark Twain wrote most eloquently about Francis Lightfoot, "The man's life-work was so inconspicuous, that his name would now be forgotten, but for one thing—he signed the Declaration of Independence. Yet his life was a most useful and worthy one. It was a good and profitable voyage, though it left no phosphorescent splendors in its wake." **Mark Twain, *The Pennsylvania Magazine of History and Biography*, 1877**

Richard Henry was more political and extroverted by nature. His early career was dominated by his desire to maintain his status and power as a planter and man of influence in local affairs. Prior to the Seven Years' War, his interests and British imperial policy more often than not coincided. In the period following the war, his interests corresponded more closely to the patriot cause. In a bid to preserve the social and economic structure that was best for him, and he presumed best for all, he embraced the patriot cause and became a leading figure of the revolution. Unlike his brother Francis Lightfoot, who enjoyed country life at Menokin, Richard Henry spent very little time at his plantation, Chantilly. He busied himself instead with affairs of politics and government, and left a legacy of achievements that shaped the new union in the American colonies.

Richard Henry died at Chantilly in 1794 at the age of sixty-two. Francis Lightfoot died at Menokin in 1797, at the age of sixty-three, a few months after the passing of his wife.

CHAPTER 16

Robert Morris

Entrepreneur, war profiteer, politician, and land speculator—Robert Morris wore many hats, as did many of his fellow Founding Fathers. He did not initially support independence from England, thinking it ill-advised and dangerous. Nevertheless, he signed the Declaration of Independence, next to John Hancock's signature, although in a far less flamboyant script. In spite of Morris's reluctance to sever ties with England, the American Revolution would not have occurred without him. Morris was responsible for financing the war and was pivotal in the logistical delivery of arms and supplies to the troops.

Early Life

Robert Morris was born in England on January 20, 1734. His family immigrated to Oxford, Maryland in 1744 where his father was a tobacco factor. Robert was briefly educated by a private tutor but was not a model student. His father decided Robert's future lay not in the classroom but in the business world. He sent Robert to Philadelphia where he was apprenticed to Charles Willing, who owned a prominent firm in the shipping and banking business. Morris applied himself diligently to his responsibilities at the Willing counting house and became a trusted and valued employee. When Charles Willing died in 1754, his son Thomas assumed many of his father's civic positions and relied on Morris to handle more of the day-to-day functions of the business. In 1756, at the end of Morris's seven-year apprenticeship, Thomas took Morris on as a partner and in 1757 made the transition official by changing the firm's name to Willing, Morris, & Company. Morris's rapid rise to power within the firm was impressive. He did not come from Philadelphia society; his promotion was based entirely on his abilities and his pluck. Together he and Thomas Willing developed a lucrative import and export trade and experimented with creative financial instruments that maintained a healthy bottom line and influenced Morris in his later contributions to the fiscal development of the early national period.

In addition to European commodities, Charles Willing's ships also brought significant numbers of indentured servants into Philadelphia. In 1754, many of them arrived with "ship fever," also known as "jail fever" or typhus, and the disease spread rapidly through town. As Mayor, Charles Willing was required to visit the sick houses, where he contracted the fever and subsequently died.

Early Career

Morris was described as a large man with a large personality. He excelled in his role as a Philadelphia businessman and by all accounts led an active professional and social life; in fact the two were often entwined. His day usually began at his desk. By mid-morning he would adjourn to the wharf to oversee the loading of departing vessels and the unloading of arrivals. After that there were business meetings with other merchants and associates at any one of the local taverns. By evening it was off to dress for dinner, followed perhaps by a play, or a soiree. Morris liked entertaining and being entertained. He had a reputation as a sober and honest businessman, but he also enjoyed the reputation of the genial host. He gave lavish parties, sumptuous banquets, and kept one of the best-stocked wine cellars in the city.

Evidence of Morris's wilder days included the birth in 1763 of his illegitimate daughter, Mary. Although Morris did not marry her mother, he was honorably attentive to his daughter. He willingly supported her and saw to her education. She married in 1781 and the two remained in contact throughout her life. In addition to this child, Morris had seven other children with his wife Mary White, whom he married in 1769.

Revolutionary War

Robert Morris's public career began with his opposition to the Stamp Act. He was appointed to a committee of merchants to formally protest the tax. He signed the non-importation agreement with other merchants but was relieved when the Stamp Act was repealed and the difficulties with Parliament subsided and he could return to business as usual. In the period from 1765 to 1776, Morris identified with the conservative arm of the Pennsylvania Whigs. He believed in the prerogative of merchants to conduct business without regulatory interference from Parliament. He also believed it was a violation of the colonists' rights as British citizens if they were taxed without their consent. However, he was not an advocate of the radical idea of independence.

As tensions between America and England renewed in the 1770s, Morris resumed political life. In 1775, largely motivated by hostilities in New England, he became involved with every principle political committee and office associated with the revolution. He remained in favor of reconciliation with Britain, but was actively occupied with the governance and protection of colonial interests. He was elected to the Pennsylvania Council of Safety, the Committee of Correspondence, and the Provincial Assembly. He was also a delegate to the Continental Congress, a seat he held from 1775 until 1778.

While in Congress he served on a number of vital committees, among them the Committee of Trade and the Marine and Maritime Committee. As chairman of the Committee on Trade he was in charge of finding commodities for export to pay for war supplies. He was not above resorting to unorthodox measures to fulfill this responsibility.

By 1775, the firm of Willing, Morris & Company had a contract with Congress to import weapons and ammunition. In the fall of 1775, Congress received intelligence through one of Morris's trading partners in Britain that two unarmed British ships were en route to America with gunpowder and weapons. Congress determined to purchase and outfit their own ships to intercept these supplies and deliver them to George Washington who was by then in command of the Continental army outside of Boston. Conveniently on the Marine and Maritime Committee, Morris sold two vessels belonging to Willing, Morris & Company to Congress to be outfitted as man-of-war ships. Later in the war, Morris used personal funds when necessary to finance the war and used his extensive trading network for intelligence connections regarding British military operations in America.

The Declaration of Independence and Beyond

While he appeared devoted to promoting the American cause, Morris was not prepared to vote for independence from Britain in July 1776 as "it was an improper time," in his opinion, for such a drastic and dangerous action. He voted against the motion on July 1, 1776. However, the following day he and John Dickinson abstained from voting to allow Pennsylvania to cast unanimous votes for independence. Morris signed the document in August committed to the path of war he had hoped to avoid. It is an irony of history that from this point forward the revolution could not have progressed without him.

The ongoing problem that plagued the Continental army was the lack of appropriations to outfit the troops with clothes, food, arms, artillery, and ammunition. Morris lent the government £10,000 of his own money to sustain it through the winter of 1776 and into early 1777. Without this infusion of capital, Washington would not have managed to field an army for the Battle of Trenton (December 1776) and the Battle of Princeton (January 1777).

"I am not one of those politicians that run testy when my own plans are not adopted. I think it is the duty of a good citizen to follow when he can not lead." —**Robert Morris, explaining his decision to sign the Declaration of Independence**

Morris used his business contacts as the base of a network to keep supplies coming into the colonies (notably, he smuggled regular shipments of gunpowder and war materiel from foreign allies). He was allegedly the chair of a secret committee that concluded arms agreements with European agents. In many cases the agreements were made with persons or businesses who were partners with committee members, including several contracts with Willing, Morris & Company.

In November 1776, George Washington's troops retreated from Fort Lee in New Jersey, across the Delaware River and into Pennsylvania with the British rumored to be hot on their heels. The Continental Congress disbanded and evacuated for Baltimore. Morris stayed behind as a member of the Pennsylvania Council of Safety to see to the defense of the city. In late December Washington decided to attack the Hessian garrison at Trenton, a strategy that Morris financed. Washington's success at Trenton secured Philadelphia and was a significant turning point in the early stage of the war.

Morris was criticized for making a staggering profit during the war, but much of what he made was used to support the war effort. In more than one circumstance, had it not been for Morris, the Continental army would have had no means of procuring supplies. Morris personally underwrote the activities of privateers, he was able to squeeze resources out of the colonies, and managed to convince other men of means to lend financial support to the cause. Even as late into the war as the Battle of Yorktown, Morris skillfully managed to procure cattle from Connecticut and flour from Virginia and Pennsylvania, for the Continental forces.

In spite of these heroic efforts to finance and supply the army, Morris was the subject of a congressional inquiry into his weapons contracts. The attack against him was led by Thomas Paine. The investigation into Morris's activities was conducted in 1779 and he and Willing, Morris & Company were acquitted of any wrongdoing. His reputation suffered as a result but the damage was not long-lived; Morris was too talented with financial management to be dismissed.

Superintendent of Finance

Morris was appointed superintendent of finance in 1781, a position defined in the Articles of Confederation with oversight over the treasury and national financial matters. The financial outlook for America was grim in 1781. The army was funded by select individuals, one of them Morris, and foreign allies. The government did not have the authority to collect taxes; it could requisition revenue and supplies from the colonies, but its power of enforcement was weak. The currency was worthless and no one used it. Morris was charged with the monumental task of finding remedies to these problems. On May 17, 1781 he presented Congress with his proposal for the creation of the Bank of North America. The Bank of North America opened in 1782 and was the first bank chartered by the government of the United States. Morris's business partner Thomas Willing was its first president. The majority of the bank's funding came from a loan from France. With the establishment of a national bank, Morris could borrow money and was subsequently able to continue to finance the war against Britain. He also wrote a pamphlet, titled *On Public Credit*, that outlined a national economic system upon which Secretary of the Treasury Alexander Hamilton would later expand.

After the war, Morris was elected to the Pennsylvania legislature. He was also sent as a delegate to the Constitutional Convention in 1787. He was a signer of the Constitution and a supporter of a strong national government. Morris was concerned a weak central government and strong state governments would result in clashes of provincial interests at the expense of greater issues, such as national defense, commerce, and foreign relations.

This sentiment is hardly surprising coming from a businessman with global connections. With the establishment of the new government, Morris served in the United States Senate from 1789 to 1795. He was appointed to more than forty committees and devoted much of his energy to promoting Federalist economic proposals, which were largely infrastructure and internal improvement programs.

As superintendent of finance, Morris developed a program of three interdependent approaches for the management of the national treasury: to rein in expenditures, to secure revenue, and to restore public confidence.

Post-War Career

Morris left public life in 1795 to return to the world of commerce and investment. He had business interests in canal construction and steam engine development, as well as several manufacturing concerns. He also became involved in a massive land speculation project. Morris amassed holdings of 6 million acres in a tract that stretched from New York to Georgia because he believed masses of immigrants would flee Europe after the war and he intended to sell land to most of them. In addition to this grandiose arrangement, Morris was also in the middle of building a mansion in Philadelphia.

Unfortunately for Morris, war and revolution in Europe prevented the mass immigration he predicted and his creditors relentlessly insisted on repayment. For the first time in his life, Morris could not afford to proceed with his plans. His financial troubles were so deep he is alleged to have considered suicide but decided against it when he considered the increased difficulty this would present to his family. He could not afford his real estate scheme and he could not afford to complete his mansion. He resorted to hiding in his country estate, The Hills, but this did not protect him from his creditors, and the man who was once one of the premier entrepreneurs of Philadelphia and the financier of the American Revolution ended up in debtor's prison for three years. This was a devastating blow for Morris, but he was not abandoned by his friends. George Washington kept in contact with him during his incarceration and visited him in 1798. Mrs. Morris was invited to Mount Vernon in 1798 in the assurance of the "affectionate regard General and Mrs. Washington for Robert Morris." In 1799 Gouverneur Morris also visited Robert Morris in prison and dined with him and Mrs. Morris. Nor were Morris's talents entirely forgotten. In spite of the damage to his reputation, Thomas Jefferson considered offering Morris a position in his cabinet if he could leave prison in time to accept it.

Morris's mansion was never completed and eventually dismantled. The materials from the house, particularly the marble, were repurposed in buildings from Rhode Island to South Carolina.

Congress passed the nation's first Bankruptcy Act in 1800 and within a year Morris was able to leave prison. He still owed approximately $3 million to his creditors. Once free, Morris lived a quiet life in retirement. His health was poor and he had no resources to start over. He died on May 9, 1806.

Legacy

Robert Morris was a talented and influential contributor to the American bid for independence. His financial acumen and personal resources were a consistent stabilizing force during the economically precarious period of the American Revolution. Without his connections and resources, the Continental army would have dissolved before the end of 1776. He was a signer of the Declaration of Independence, the Articles of Confederation, and the Constitution. He was largely responsible for the creation of the Bank of North America and laid the groundwork for the nation's economic system, charting the course that would eventually establish the United States as a global economic leader. A daily reminder of Morris's contribution to the American financial structure is the introduction of the dollar sign as the official symbol of the currency of the United States.

CHAPTER 17

Benjamin Rush

Benjamin Rush was a man of a contradictory nature: while extolling the virtues of medical practices considered backward, he also preached the importance of proper treatment of the mentally ill. A fervent patriot, he was capable of mean-spirited gossip and conspired to remove George Washington as commander of the Continental army. Benjamin Rush was a physician, writer, and social activist, and a Founding Father.

Early Life and Education

Benjamin Rush was born on December 24, 1745, the fourth of seven children born to John Rush and Susanna Hall. The Rushes were early residents of the small town of Byberry in Philadelphia County, located approximately fourteen miles from Philadelphia. The Rush family had come to the area from Oxfordshire, England in 1683; drawn in part by the efforts of William Penn, the founder of Pennsylvania, whose mother was related to Susanna Rush and who was seeking people to come and settle in the new colony. In 1751, tragedy struck the Rush family when John Rush, a gunsmith and farmer by profession, died.

Susanna Rush did what she could in overseeing her children and their education while managing a small grocery shop in Philadelphia. As a devout Presbyterian, she was particularly attentive to their religious instruction, and she and Benjamin regularly attended the Second Presbyterian Church in Philadelphia. There, Benjamin would hear the sermons of the church minister Gilbert Tennent, one of the leaders of the Great Awakening then sweeping the northeast.

The Great Awakening was a widespread religious revival that swept through the American colonies, particularly those of New England, during the first half of the eighteenth century. Unlike the solemn and rigid Puritan spirituality of the previous century, the Great Awakening saw the formation of new religious groups, a more intimate and fervent kind of preaching, increased church membership, and a growing social activism.

Rush also spent a great deal of time with his uncle, the Reverend Samuel Finley. Finley was the head of the Nottingham Academy in Maryland, which Rush began attending when he was eight years old. For the next five years, Rush studied Greek, Latin, history, and literature. In 1759, Rush enrolled at the College of New Jersey (now Princeton); his intelligence and earlier instruction under Finley allowed him to move through his studies quickly. So quickly in fact, that by 1760, at the age of fifteen, Benjamin Rush graduated.

Practicing Medicine

Upon returning to Philadelphia, Rush first thought of pursuing the law but instead decided to study medicine under one of the more prominent doctors, Dr. Redman. He also attended classes taught by Dr. Shippen, who at that time was lecturing on the study of anatomy. In 1766, Rush left Philadelphia for Edinburgh, Scotland, where he spent two years at the University of Edinburgh. In 1768, he graduated with his Doctor of Medicine degree.

From late winter in 1768 to the spring of 1769, Rush traveled to London to continue his studies by taking additional training at St. Thomas Hospital. He also learned a number of languages including French, Italian, and Spanish, and made the acquaintance of Benjamin Franklin, who helped him pay for his to return to America. While in London, Rush met the artists Benjamin West and Sir Joshua Reynolds, who in turn introduced him to writers Samuel Johnson and Oliver Goldsmith. Rush then traveled to France where he met French philosopher Diderot, who gave him a letter of introduction to Scottish philosopher and historian David Hume. Rush returned to the colonies in 1769, where at the age of twenty-four, he opened up his own medical practice in Philadelphia. He also undertook the position of professor of chemistry at the College of Philadelphia (now the University of Pennsylvania).

Benjamin Rush published the first American textbook on chemistry as well as several volumes on medical student education. In addition, his appointment to the medical faculty at the College of Philadelphia, along with that of a number of other notable physicians, made possible the creation of the first medical school in America.

Benjamin Rush soon earned a reputation in the city as a brilliant physician who provided his services to the poor and as an excellent teacher whose classes proved popular among the medical students at the college.

The Patriot Doctor

Not content to confine himself to medical writings, Rush began writing on the events of the day, which included penning several patriotic essays.

He also wrote about local politics and the abolition of slavery (he was instrumental in helping establish the Pennsylvania Society for Promoting the Abolition of Slavery). Rush was active in the patriot organization the Sons of Liberty and was sought out by pamphleteer Thomas Paine, who was writing his famed work *Common Sense*, in which he called for American independence. It was Rush who provided Paine with a title for his pamphlet.

Rush also became more involved in the political activities in Philadelphia. He attended the provincial conference to send delegates to the Continental Congress and was elected chairman of the committee that supported the resolution for Congress to declare independence from the Crown. In 1774, he was appointed to represent Pennsylvania at the Continental Congress held in Philadelphia. He made a point of riding out from the city to meet the delegates from Massachusetts, which led to a lifelong friendship with John Adams.

In the midst of all this political activity while still practicing medicine, Rush found time in January 1776 to marry Julia Stockton, the daughter of another local patriot and signer of the Declaration of Independence, Richard Stockton. The couple would have thirteen children, nine of whom survived.

Less than seven months after his marriage, Benjamin Rush joined his father-in-law and another physician, Dr. Witherspoon, in Philadelphia for the signing of the Declaration of Independence. The two men would share the distinction of being the only son-in-law and father-in-law to sign the document. Soon after, on July 20, 1776, Rush was elected to the Congress, where he dedicated himself to the fight for independence. Thanks to Rush and his notes taken during the convention, historians have been able to piece together information about some of the lesser-known delegates based on the observations Rush made. However, Rush did not endear himself to everyone. Several members of the Congress, including friends such as Benjamin Franklin and John Adams, found Rush to be a gossip and judgmental about others.

Fighting the War

In 1777 Rush was appointed surgeon general of the Middle Department of the Continental army. Rush, upon seeing the horrid conditions of the army hospitals, immediately began criticizing the incompetent and corrupt management of the medical facilities. Growing increasingly frustrated that his department and position gave him no means of battling the problem, Rush wrote letters of complaint to Congress and to General George Washington. Rush's term of enlistment ended not more than a year later, when continued conflicts with the Army Medical service and his old teacher Dr. William Shippen Jr. led him to resign his post in 1778.

What was the Middle Department?
The Middle Department was created on February 27, 1776, as one of seven territorial and administrative units of the Continental army during the Revolutionary War. The Middle Department consisted of the colonies of New York, New Jersey, Pennsylvania, Delaware, and Maryland.

During the war, Rush actively but secretly campaigned for the removal of George Washington as commander in chief, especially after the Continental army lost a series of important battles. Rush even went so far as to write an anonymous letter to Governor Patrick Henry of Virginia. Unfortunately for Rush, his activities were soon discovered by Washington, who then confronted him. At that point, any further military service that Rush may have provided was effectively ended. Rush later expressed regret for his actions against Washington, stating in a letter to John Adams that Washington's role was vital to the winning of independence for the new nation.

Continued Service

In 1783, after the Washington debacle, Rush was appointed to the staff of Pennsylvania Hospital, where he remained a member for the rest of his life. Rush did not abandon politics either. In 1789 he wrote several articles for the Philadelphia newspapers that advocated the adopting of the new proposed United States Constitution, and he was also a convention delegate and voted for the document. In 1797, Rush was appointed treasurer of the United States Mint, where he served until 1813. It was during this period that Rush may have performed one of his greatest services in American history by helping to reconcile the friendship between John Adams and Thomas Jefferson. Rush encouraged the two men to begin writing to one another and thus helped to rekindle one of the most famous friendships of all time.

In 1803, as the Lewis and Clark expedition was getting ready to go, Thomas Jefferson sent Meriwether Lewis to Philadelphia to visit Rush. The doctor informed Lewis about frontier illnesses and presented Lewis with a medical kit to be taken on the journey.

Even as Rush continued his involvement with politics, he remained committed to his teaching career and medical practice. In 1791, he was appointed professor of medical theory and clinical practice at the University of Pennsylvania. During the course of his medical career, it has been estimated that Benjamin Rush taught more than 3,000 medical students. He also established the Philadelphia Dispensary for the relief of the poor, the first of its kind in the United States. He worked tirelessly for the poor, and the mentally ill, often without pay. During the yellow fever epidemic of 1793, Rush worked nonstop to help tend to the ill.

Rush's medical career was filled with contradictions. On one hand he was one of a handful of doctors who stressed the importance of inoculation against smallpox as well as a vocal proponent of preventive medicine. In 1812, Rush published *Medical Inquiries and Observations upon the Diseases of the Mind,* which was one of the first seminal American works in the field of psychiatry, and which earned Rush the title of "father of psychiatry." But even with these far-thinking ideas, Rush also still hung on to outdated medical practices, such as bloodletting, in which the patient was literally "bled" to rid the body of toxins and disease. In some cases, Rush would remove as much as four-fifths of a patient's blood during the course of treatments.

Rush was a committed social activist who continued to lobby for the abolition of slavery, as well as a strong proponent of the importance of scientific education for all people, including women, and for the creation of public medical clinics to serve the poor. Rush was also instrumental in the creation of Dickinson College in Carlisle Pennsylvania. He was a founding member of the Philadelphia Society for Alleviating the Miseries of Public Prisons (known today as the Pennsylvania Prison Society). Benjamin Rush died in Philadelphia in 1813 as the most famous physician in America. He was buried at Christ's Church, not far from the grave of Benjamin Franklin.

Some of Rush's contemporaries found Rush's use of bloodletting extreme and complained. One fellow doctor even accused Rush of killing more of his patients than curing them. Rush, enraged at the accusation, sued the person for libel and won a judgment of $500.

Legacy

Benjamin Rush's legacy of service to country, to fellow man, and to the causes of social justice highlight an accomplished life as an important figure in American history. Rush, though at times showing himself to be less than perfect, was also dedicated to improving the life of his fellow man, whether as free citizens of a new nation, or in making sure that the public received the best medical attention possible. An ardent social reformer, Rush worked tirelessly whether serving in the Continental Congress or teaching or tending to his patients. Although history has not always been kind to him, there is little doubt that without Benjamin Rush, the history of freedom and medicine would have been very different in America.

PART IV

★ THE FRAMERS ★

America successfully waged a war for independence and established its first government under the Articles of Confederation. The Confederation government formed a "firm league of friendship" among the thirteen states. By 1787, however, it was clear that the Confederation was in danger of collapse or fragmenting into several regional confederations. Congress had very limited powers, largely confined to the authority to conduct foreign affairs, make treaties, and declare war. The Confederation Congress could requisition capital but it had no authority to collect it, and by 1786, the returns from all thirteen states amounted to less than one-third of the interest of the national debt. When delegates from the thirteen states gathered in Philadelphia in May 1787 to revise the Articles of Confederation, the questions many delegates were forced to consider were whether the Articles were worth fixing and whether the fledgling nation would survive.

Quiz: Test Your Constitution Comprehension

1. **Who had perfect attendance at the Constitutional Convention?**
   A. John Hancock
   B. Gouverneur Morris
   C. Samuel Adams
   D. Rufus King

2. **How many times is the word *slavery* mentioned in the Constitution?**
   A. 4
   B. 0
   C. 7
   D. 1

3. **Who is credited with the final version of the Preamble?**
   A. Thomas Jefferson
   B. James Madison
   C. Gouverneur Morris
   D. Robert Morris

4. **The Constitutional Convention convened in:**
   A. Philadelphia
   B. Baltimore
   C. Boston
   D. Annapolis

5. **The Three-Fifths rule applied to:**
   A. Taxation
   B. Ratification
   C. Taxation and representation
   D. Election procedures

6. **The Federalist faction supported:**
   A. The concept of a strong central government
   B. The creation of the Federal Reserve
   C. Directing all export revenues to military appropriations
   D. Concentrating power within state government

7. **The oldest delegate at the Constitutional Convention was:**
   A. George Washington
   B. Benjamin Franklin
   C. John Dickinson
   D. Robert Morris

8. **The youngest delegate at the Constitutional Convention was:**
   A. Robert Morris
   B. Rufus King
   C. Gouverneur Morris
   D. Alexander Hamilton

9. **Shays' Rebellion was:**

    A. A rural insurrection against excise taxes on whiskey
    B. A colonial revolt against the threat of an autocratic national government
    C. A revolution originating in Shays, Massachusetts, demanding liberty for all men, regardless of class
    D. A rebellion in Massachusetts protesting foreclosures

10. **Which of the following men was a delegate to the Constitutional Convention but refused to attend or sign the final document?**

    A. Richard Henry Lee
    B. William Few
    C. Daniel of St. Thomas Jenifer
    D. Thomas Fitzsimons

Answers

1.D 2.B 3.C 4.A 5.C 6.A 7.B 8.B 9.D 10.A

CHAPTER 18

Rufus King

Rufus King was a country boy from Maine who became a lawyer, a representative in the Massachusetts General Court, and a delegate to the Continental Congress and the Constitutional Convention. He was skeptical that any revisions to the Articles of Confederation were really necessary, and was more interested in protecting the political and economic interests of the Northeast than building a national union. In spite of his initial resistance, King became one of the leading proponents of the creation of a strong central government.

Early Life

Rufus King was born in the Massachusetts frontier town of Scarborough (now in Maine) on March 24, 1755. His father, Richard King, was a successful farmer and merchant who was a lifelong Loyalist. Richard served as a captain in the expeditionary forces raised by Governor Shirley against the French at Cape Breton during the French and Indian War. He participated in the attack on the French fortress at Louisbourg and returned to Massachusetts following this successful campaign and ultimately settled in Scarborough. Richard managed to amass more than 3,000 acres of land and was one of the foremost lumber exporters in Maine. He was married twice; Rufus was his eldest child from his first wife, Isabella Bragdon of York, Maine.

Rufus King was ten years of age when the Stamp Act was passed. Richard King had no interest in protesting the tax, a position that put him at odds with his neighbors. Some accounts suggest the townspeople of Scarborough were envious of Richard King's wealth, other accounts allege Richard King's loyalty to England and to parliamentary policy was sufficient to incite local hostility against him. A mob gathered at his home and when he refused to recant his position, his house was attacked and most of his furnishings destroyed. Allegedly his barn was burned a year later by local patriots who disapproved of his politics. In spite of the violence directed against him, Richard King remained unmoved in his sympathies for the Crown. All of his sons, however, would join the patriot camp.

Rufus King was educated in the village school and was sent to Dummer Academy in Byfield, Massachusetts when he was twelve. After his preparatory studies at Dummer, King was admitted to Harvard in 1773 at the age of eighteen. He was a diligent student and persevered in his studies even as the environment in Boston and Cambridge grew increasingly hostile in the years 1773–1775.

FACT

After the Battle of Lexington in April 1775, the Harvard campus was overtaken with American soldiers who used all available school buildings for barracks. The school term was suspended and the students were sent home. The library and archives were sent to Concord, where the college temporarily reconvened. Students did not return to campus until June 1775.

King had other troubles in 1775. His father died in January and although he left a respectable estate, it did not supply enough cash to support the household, business concerns, and to send King to Harvard. King was able to complete his studies at Harvard thanks to his brother-in-law, Dr. Southgate, who paid King's tuition when his family could no longer afford it.

Revolutionary War

King graduated from Harvard in 1777 and began to study law with Theophilus Parsons in Newburyport. Parsons was also a graduate of Dummer Academy and Harvard. A highly regarded lawyer, Parsons would later become a chief justice of Massachusetts. King suspended his studies in Parsons's firm to volunteer in the Continental army and was an aide de camp for Brigadier General Glover at the Battle of Rhode Island, an island off the coast of the state of Rhode Island. The offensive failed when the French fleet sent to support the Continental army was forced to withdraw after a violent storm damaged the ships, leaving the British with control of the water and the island. In these circumstances, Major General John Sullivan decided to abandon the mission and retreat to the mainland. The volunteer portions of the army were discharged at this point, and King was dismissed from service on September 5, 1778. This was the only military experience King had during the course of the war, and as he wrote to his brother-in-law, Dr. Southgate, in October 1778, "I saw and experienced enough to satisfy my curiosity." King returned to Newburyport to resume his studies with Parsons and was admitted to the bar in 1780. King also joined a Boston men's club whose members later comprised the core of the Massachusetts Federalist Party.

The Battle of Rhode Island, also known as the Battle of Quaker Hill, was fought to recapture Rhode Island, now called Aquidneck Island and part of the state of Rhode Island, from the British. Present at this battle were the First Rhode Island Regiment, comprised entirely of free blacks.

Career

King began his public life in 1783 when he was elected to the General Court of Massachusetts. His national career began in 1784 upon his election as a representative to the Continental Congress, where he frequently spoke out against slavery and was the leading voice in preventing the extension of slavery into the Northwest Territories. He was re-elected to Congress in 1785 and 1786. Working in the Congress eroded some of the provincialism that came with the limiting experience of practicing law in Newburyport and brought him into contact with new people and new ideas. He met and befriended Henry Knox, John Jay, and Robert Livingston, and expanded his interests into finance, diplomacy, and commerce.

Constitutional Convention

King was thirty-two years of age when he was selected as a delegate to the Constitutional Convention of 1787. He was admired for his oratory and for attending every session. King served on several committees, most notably the Committee on Postponed Matters and on the Committee of Style along with Gouverneur Morris, William Samuel Johnson, Alexander Hamilton, and James Madison. Together they presented the convention with a polished final version edited from twenty-three articles to seven and with a new preamble.

Prior to 1787, King was not entirely convinced the Articles of Confederation required significant changes. He was not convinced a national government was in the best interest of the New England states, particularly if such a government required them to be inexorably tied to the interests of the Southern planter aristocracy. King was concerned the disparity between the Northern and Southern economies and cultures would not lend itself to finding common ground and that planters had no understanding of northeastern mercantile interests. Nor was King an adherent of the popular sentiments regarding the natural rights of man. He had no faith in the common man who seemed, he thought, to naturally resort to mob action as a solution to all problems. The Declaration of Independence, therefore, did not inspire him to think the next step should be to fashion a system of government that would promote liberty and the rights of man.

However, King, like many of his colleagues at the Constitutional Convention, was shaken by the events of Shays' Rebellion and began to question the existing government's ability to protect life and property. King went to the convention unsure to what extent the Articles of Confederation would have to be revised, but as he became increasingly engaged in the process and the debate, he became a principal leader in the nationalist caucus. Always meticulous in his work, he kept notes on the proceedings that became an invaluable resource for scholars of the period.

QUOTE

"The great body of the people are without virtue, and not governed by any restraints of conscience." —**Rufus King**

Once at the convention, King spoke up early and often. He was won over to the process of writing a new document as he was able to witness what he believed to be a mature, meticulous, and reasoned dialogue, the results of which produced a text that he considered neither abstract nor utopian. His voice was heard most particularly on the questions of ratification, slavery and representation, and presidential power.

Ratification

In August 1787, the convention debated the question of how many states were needed to ratify the document. James Wilson (Pennsylvania) argued for seven, Roger Sherman (Connecticut) ten, Pierce Butler (South Carolina) nine, and Daniel Carroll (Maryland) asserted all states must agree for the document to be valid. King seconded Carroll's motion. Gouverneur Morris questioned if it would be more expeditious to eliminate ratification by state conventions and allow each state to determine the best means for their process of ratification. King disagreed, arguing that would be "equivalent to giving up the business altogether." After much debate, when a vote was taken on the issue of Morris striking out the requirement states ratify by conventions, the motion was defeated and it was decided ratification by nine states was necessary to start a new government.

Representation and Slavery

The question regarding how to determine congressional representation for slave states was complicated, passionate, and turbulent. As the debate rocked back and forth between whether or not representation should be based on population or on financial criteria or a combination of both, King moved that voting in the lower house should be based on "some equitable ratio of representation,"—a motion that passed seven to three. The next problem was to decide the equitable ratio. James Wilson argued that the representation of states should be determined in proportion of the free population and three-fifths of "all other persons."

The words slave, slaves, and slavery are not used in the Constitution. Instead, reference is made to "such persons" or "all other persons," which were the agreed upon euphemisms for slaves or slavery. The concept of counting slaves as three-fifths of a person originated in 1783 during a congressional debate regarding the levying of direct taxes (taxes on land or individuals). The Northern states insisted Southern states must include all slaves in their population count. The Southern states objected, but James Madison offered the compromise of counting slaves as three-fifths of a person. By the time of the convention all but New Hampshire and Rhode Island approved it. The Articles of Confederation required unanimous approval to implement a proposal, so this rule was not adopted, but the precedent for the three-fifths formula was set.

One of King's main contributions to the Constitution was in the compromise over importing slaves and the prohibition of exports. He contended it was improper that states were required to defend each other even if some states persisted in introducing dangers into their borders (i.e., slaves that may organize violent rebellion), but would not be taxed to cover the costs of defending against such dangers, particularly if the exports were produced by slaves that entered the country without restriction. If slaves could be imported freely, southern states as a consequence gained economic benefit and political advantage through representation based on the three-fifths rule. King insisted, "I can never agree to let them be imported without limitation and then be represented in the national legislature." For King the question of slavery was a question of political and economic advantage, not a humanitarian one.

"If slaves are to be imported shall not the exports produced by their labor, supply a revenue the better to enable the Genl. Govt. to defend their masters . . . at all events either slaves should not be represented, or exports should be taxable." —**Rufus King, 1787**

In the end, Article 1, Section 2C of the Constitution reads the apportionment of representatives and of direct taxes among the states will be determined by their population and in the case of slave states, "adding to the whole number of free persons, including those bound to service for a term of years, and excluding Indians not taxed, three-fifths of all other persons." Southern states were able to count population to their advantage when it came to determining representation but they were also taxed according to the same formula. King was not successful on the issue of taxing exports.

Post-Convention Career

King returned to Massachusetts and worked diligently to encourage the state to ratify the new Constitution. He was successful in this endeavor by advocating the adoption of a bill of rights. He was not successful in his bid to position himself for election as one of Massachusetts's first representatives in the United States Senate. His friend and political ally Alexander Hamilton suggested he move to New York, where more favorable prospects might be arranged.

King, who had just married, relocated to New York where he won election to the New York Assembly in 1789. After New York ratified the Constitution there was debate as to who should be sent to represent New York in the Senate. Hamilton endorsed King, a recommendation that ran contrary to the political will of the powerful Livingston family, and the end result of this struggle between the titanic forces of New York politics was that Rufus King was sent to the Senate in 1789. In 1791 he was elected director of the Bank of the United States. He was re-elected to the Senate in 1795 but resigned the seat when he was appointed United States minister to Great Britain, 1796–1803.

King served admirably as minister to Great Britain during a tense period of Anglo-American relations. American commercial activities were jeopardized by naval conflicts between the British and the French during the wars of the French Revolution. Of particular concern was the British impressment of American sailors. King was unable to effect a change in this practice, but he nevertheless managed to maintain otherwise smooth relations between the two nations.

King returned to the United States in 1803 and resumed his career in politics. He was the Federalist candidate for vice president in 1804 and 1808, but was not successful and retreated to his Long Island estate, King Manor, to the life of a country gentleman. In 1813 he was elected to the Senate, where he remained until 1825. He entered the Senate as a critic of the War of 1812, but changed his mind and his position in 1814 when the British attacked Washington. Later in his senatorial career he spoke out in ardent opposition to the admission of Missouri as a slave state.

King was the Federalist candidate for president in 1816, but was defeated by James Monroe. In 1825 President John Quincy Adams appointed him once again as minister to Great Britain. He became ill shortly after his arrival in London, and was home within the year. He died on April 29, 1827.

Legacy

Statesman and diplomat Rufus King emerged from the parochial quiet of his Newburyport law office to a political career that began in the state legislature but quickly carried him to the Continental Congress and to the Constitutional Convention. At the convention, he shed his regional attitude to shape the document that laid the blueprint for a strong national government. He was rarely silent on any issue, and over the course of time and debate his imprint is on much of the final version. He was one of New York's first senators and served that body and in his tenure as minister to Great Britain with distinction.

CHAPTER 19

Gouverneur Morris

Gouverneur Morris is perhaps best known for his work on the Constitution, but he had an active political career that spanned all phases of the development of the new republic. He sat in the Provincial Assembly of New York, the Continental Congress, and the United States Senate. He helped to write the state constitution of New York, he signed the Articles of Confederation, and as a member of the Committee of Style, he wrote the final draft of the Constitution of the United States and is famously associated with the Preamble.

Early Life

Gouverneur Morris came from a long line of wealthy and patrician New Yorkers. On his mother's side he was of Huguenot ancestry; her ancestors were among the first to settle the New Amsterdam colony in the 1660s. His father's ancestors were supporters of Cromwell's rebellion against the Crown during the English Civil War. After the Restoration, they left for Barbados, the Caribbean refuge for Civil War veterans and other people disaffected by the war. By the 1670s they moved to New York.

In New York the Morris family acquired 500 acres, the first installment of a holding that would eventually expand to more than 1,900 acres. This estate, Morrisania, was designated a manor in 1697, an anachronism that bestowed a sort of feudal status on the exclusive echelons of the wealthiest landowners in New York. Manor lords drifted naturally into the world of public office, and Gouverneur's grandfather Lewis Morris Sr., the first lord of the manor, served in the Colonial Assembly and as chief justice of the New York Supreme Court, and later was governor of New Jersey. Lewis Morris Sr. had two sons: Lewis Jr., who became the next lord of the manor, and the younger son Robert Hunter Morris, who became deputy governor of Pennsylvania. Lewis Morris Jr. dutifully entered politics, serving as a New York assemblyman and as a judge of the Court of Admiralty. He had four children by his first wife, Katrynje Staats, five children by his second wife, Sarah Gouverneur. Gouverneur Morris, the only son from the second marriage, was born January 31, 1752.

The Morris family purchased their land from a farmer named Jonas Bronck. Bronck's property, approximately ten miles north of New York City and running along the Harlem River to Long Island Sound, would later be part of the borough known as the Bronx.

Gouverneur was ten years of age when his father died. Lewis Morris believed Gouverneur, of all his children, was the brightest and held the greatest promise to walk in the footsteps of his esteemed ancestors. Gouverneur's grooming as a Morris and as a polished, well-educated son of the gentry was of particular importance to Lewis, who specifically indicated as much in his will. It was imperative Gouverneur be properly educated, according to the will, and he could matriculate to any school except Yale.

In his will, Lewis Morris stated "It is my desire that my son Gouverneur Morris may have the best education that is to be had in England or in America but my express will and directions are that he never be sent for that purpose to the colony of Connecticut least he should imbibe in his youth that low craft and cunning so incident in the people of that country which is so interwoven in their constitutions that all their art cannot disguise it from the world tho many of them under the sanctified garb of religion have endeavoured to impose themselves on the world for honest men."

Education

Gouverneur Morris's precociousness put him on the fast track. He began his education at a school in New Rochelle run by a Swiss Huguenot minister who taught his pupils French and "useful sciences." In 1761, at nine years of age Morris was sent to the Academy of Philadelphia, a college preparatory school founded by Ben Franklin. In 1764 he entered King's College (now Columbia University), an Anglican school in New York, at the ripe age of twelve.

Morris was sixteen years of age when he delivered the commencement address to his graduating class at King's College. As the youngest son of Lewis Morris, he was not the heir and lord of Morrisania. Although he inherited a slave, his father's shaving box, a seal ring, a pair of gold buttons, and stood to inherit £2000 when his mother died, he had to make his own way in the world. Like his grandfather, father, and half-brother, he became a lawyer. He was apprenticed to William Smith Jr. and clerked for him for three years, after which he was sworn in as a lawyer. He was only nineteen at the time and celebrated with his friends at one of their favorite haunts, Fraunces Tavern.

Morris was an exceptional student and he excelled at his studies, particularly languages and mathematics, even though he had to contend with serious setbacks in his early life, such as the death of his father when he was at the Academy of Philadelphia, and severe and debilitating burns he received on his right arm and side when he upset a pot of boiling water. He missed a year of college while he recovered from this accident, but nevertheless managed to graduate with his class.

Career

Morris was a talented and successful attorney. He was invited to join the Moot, a lawyer's club, and he traveled in the highest social circles with the likes of other New York luminaries as Robert Livingston and John Jay. Morris was not initially interested in politics, but like many other young men of his day he was drawn into them by the uproar over the Stamp Act. When news reached New York about the Sons of Liberty dumping tea into Boston Harbor and the British closing the port, a meeting was held to elect a committee of protest and response. Morris attended one of these meetings, conveniently held at Fraunces Tavern, to see what the fuss was about, and what he saw unsettled him.

"The mob began to think and reason. Poor reptiles! It is with them a vernal morning, they are struggling to cast off their winter slough, they bask in the sunshine, and ere noon they will bite, depend upon it. The gentry begin to fear this." **—Gouverneur Morris, 1774**

There was a cross-section of society in attendance. On the one side were people of property and influence such as the Livingstons and the DeLanceys and on the other ordinary tradesmen, two groups who were rarely of one mind but now were of one voice chanting a common cause. Morris was watching a mob in action, the prospects of which he believed boded ill for the future.

The more Morris thought about the situation, he realized he was a man who believed that all men had rights. As a young lawyer with a promising career ahead of him, he appreciated the concept of liberty realized through law, not through violence, in pursuit of a democracy. While he remained uncomfortable with the radical concept of the creation of an egalitarian society as a consequence of independence from Britain, he was inclined toward compromise. He hoped for a reconciliation with Britain, one in which the colonies would tax themselves and see to their own defense but Britain would regulate their trade. This was a short-lived hope that faded with the implementation of the Intolerable Acts.

Revolutionary War

Morris's political career began on May 8, 1775 when he was elected to represent South Westchester County in the New York Provincial Congress. One of his main accomplishments was participating in the drafting of the constitution of the new state of New York. After the Battle of Long Island in August 1776, the British occupied New York City and his family's estate. As his property was in the hands of the British, Morris was not allowed to run for reelection to the legislature.

By 1776, Morris realized reconciliation with Britain was less likely. He watched in despair as war became a reality and families and friends were torn apart by conflicting loyalties. This was a problem in his family. His oldest brother, Lewis, sided with the patriots, his brother Richard was sympathetic to the patriot cause but never formally declared it, his other brother Staats Long was married to an Englishwoman and was also the colonel of a British regiment, his sisters had Loyalist husbands, and his mother remained a staunch Loyalist all of her life. Some of his closest friends remained loyal to the Crown.

Morris's Political Career

Morris was elected as a delegate to the Continental Congress in 1777. The hostilities in New York delayed his arrival in Philadelphia for several months, but he finally arrived in January 1778. The Congress lacked many of the celebrities from the early days; Patrick Henry and Thomas Jefferson had returned to Virginia, Benjamin Franklin and John Adams were abroad as diplomats, and George Washington was commander in chief of the Continental army. Meetings were irregular as it was difficult to get a quorum, but the twenty-six year old Morris pursued his duties enthusiastically. His first assignment in Congress was to investigate the condition of the Continental army. He visited Washington at Valley Forge and was appalled at what he saw. The winter conditions were bad enough on their own, but Morris was horrified at the sight of starving troops in threadbare clothes. It was inconceivable to Morris that the army was on the verge of starvation when it had been traveling through some of the most productive farmland in America. Part of the problem was farmers preferred to sell to the British, who paid them in pounds sterling rather than to the Continental government, which paid in worthless Continental currency. Morris had his hands full trying to resolve problems that were grounded in the inefficiencies of finance and logistics. The solution required a thorough overhaul of revenue collection and revamping the structure of the army.

"An American Army in the Bosom of America is about to disband for want to something to eat." —**Gouverneur Morris, 1778**

Morris was in his element in Congress, where he turned his talents to the critical matters of finance. While in Congress he also signed the second constitution of his political career, the Articles of Confederation. The ink of his signature was barely dry when he started to think of changes and modifications that he thought would be ultimately necessary. For example, he envisioned an American government with an executive branch, "either a Committee of three or a single officer such as [a] Chief of the States." Such a concept was abhorrence to the spirit of the Articles of Confederation that sought to avoid centralized political power. In 1781 the freshly named superintendant of finance Robert Morris invited him to take the position of assistant superintendant, a position that would make maximum use of Gouverneur Morris's talents and energies. They were no relation to each other but they worked seamlessly together as partners.

A Hiatus from Politics

Morris was widely recognized as a bright and talented young man with a quick mind and a quicker tongue. He was often impatient and as a result of his bluntness and sarcasm, coupled with his emerging Federalist views, cost him re-election to Congress in 1779. He retired to Philadelphia where he resumed his law career and an active social life. He enjoyed a reputation as a ladies' man. In 1780 he suffered a horrible accident in which he was allegedly thrown from a carriage and his left leg was caught in the spokes of the wheel. His leg was so seriously fractured it had to be amputated. The incident did not dent his enthusiasm for life; on the contrary it lent him a cachet that made him all the more intriguing and popular.

The tragic loss of Morris's leg was a source of interest among his closest friends, who believed he injured himself "in consequence of jumping from a window in an affair of gallantry." More to the point, John Jay wrote to him, "I have learned that a certain married woman after much use of your legs had occasioned your losing one." Morris denied these allegations although later in his life he was less inclined to do so.

Constitutional Convention

The richest moments of Morris's political life occurred during the period he was a delegate to the Constitutional Convention. By this time he was considered a high Federalist. Some of his views included the need for a strongly nationalist government, with a president that would either serve for life or would be eligible for re-election and a senate that was appointed by the president and would hold office for life, without pay. He is famous for giving more speeches (173) than any other delegate, many of them attacks on slavery and the slave trade, he was absent for a full month of meetings, and he was the principal drafter of the final version of the document.

Morris took positions that invariably and inevitably put him at odds with the Southern delegates. With his colleague Rufus King of New York, he advocated a tax on exports, an end to the slave trade, and a discontinuation of the three-fifths compromise for representation. Like King he questioned why slaves should be counted at all and feared the Southern states would embroil the rest of the country in wars over territorial disputes or create a drain on military resources that might be sent to quell slave rebellions.

"Upon what principle is it that the slaves shall be computed in the representation? Are they men? Then make them citizens and let them vote. Are they property? Why then is no other property included? The houses in this city of Philadelphia are worth more than all the wretched slaves which cover the rice swamps of South Carolina." —**Gouverneur Morris, 1787**

The question of the nature of the president was very complicated and engendered far more debate than slavery. Morris was one of the leading proponents not only for the creation of an executive, but a powerful one. He did not entirely have his way on this matter but was more successful than on the issue of slavery.

His most spectacular contribution was perhaps on the Committee of Style, where as a writer he and William Samuel Johnson, Rufus King, James Madison, and Alexander Hamilton crafted the document we now recognize as the Constitution of the United States. The committee streamlined a draft of twenty-three articles into seven. Morris's contributions on the Committee of Style are often eclipsed by his elegant reworking of the Preamble.

"In adopting a republican form of government, I not only took it as a man does his wife, for better, for worse, but what few men do with their wives, I took it knowing all its bad qualities." —**Gouverneur Morris**

The Constitutional Convention released the document on September 17, 1787 with instructions it was to be submitted to a convention of delegates chosen by each state to review the new Constitution for ratification. When the conventions of nine states had ratified it, the document and the new government would be legitimate and elections for a president could then proceed. The road to ratification was not smooth, and Morris did not actively promote the process. Morris rejected Alexander Hamilton's request for a contribution to the Federalist essays for ratification published in New York's newspapers (which later became known as *The Federalist Papers*). Morris was confident all would go well, with or without his further input. With the Constitution complete and the convention at an end, Morris withdrew from public life.

Later Career

Morris returned to private life to pursue various business interests in Europe. He was appointed minister plenipotentiary to France from 1792 to 1794 and was the only minister who remained at his post during the Reign of Terror. He kept a diary of his experiences in which he recorded a mixture of horror and disgust with the fanaticism of the Jacobin government. The French, aware of Morris's sentiments, asked the American government to recall him, a circumstance that pleased him greatly. He had seen enough of what he believed to be a revolution run amok. He returned to the states a more conservative man than when he had left.

He returned to New York, restored Morrisania, and was elected senator from New York in 1800. He lost his re-election bid in 1802 and retired once again to private life, this time at Morrisania. He devoted his later years to work the massive Erie Canal project and was chairman of the Erie Canal Commission.

In December 1809, at the age of fifty-seven, he married Ann Cary Randolph, with whom he had a happy and affectionate life. Their son Gouverneur Morris II was born on February 9, 1813 when Morris was sixty-one years of age.

Legacy

Morris would have preferred to live a private life, perhaps one that tended more toward pleasantries, women, and the company of good friends, but he was not a frivolous man. Like the other Founding Fathers in his cohort, he was an extraordinary man who was called upon to respond to the challenges of extraordinary times. He contributed to three constitutions in his long career, the state constitution of New York, the Articles of Confederation, and the Constitution of the United States. He lent his talents to the reform of America's tangled finances, served his country abroad as minister to France during one of the darkest periods of that country's history and served his native state of New York in the new national government and guided the major infrastructural project of his day, the Erie Canal.

CHAPTER 20

John Dickinson

Many historians consider John Dickinson one of the more interesting Founding Fathers. Dickinson was certainly among the most learned; as a lawyer, writer, statesman, and soldier, Dickinson earned the respect of many of his peers. However, because of his stand against the American Revolution, despite the fact that Dickinson played an important role in the events from the Stamp Act of 1765 to the Constitutional Convention in 1787, he remains one of the most overlooked historic personalities of this period.

Early Life

John Dickinson was born in Talbot County, Maryland on November 2, 1732, the son of a prosperous landowner. He was one of three children born to Samuel Dickinson and his second wife Mary Cadwalander. Dickinson's family came from England sometime in the seventeenth century. His great-grandfather Walter Dickinson was a Quaker, who originally settled in Virginia and later Maryland. Walter Dickinson slowly began buying land in Maryland and Delaware. Over time the family's land holdings were said to include approximately 12,000 acres spread between the colonies of Maryland and Delaware. The Dickinson family showed an aptitude for agricultural enterprises—their lands yielded rich crops of wheat, corn, and tobacco, adding to the family's wealth.

Dickinson grew up on his family's tobacco plantation, Croisadore (Cross of Gold), near the village of Trappe in Talbot County, Maryland. In addition to being a successful landowner, Dickinson's father later served as the first judge to the Court of Pleas in Kent County, Delaware. To be closer to court and to his wife's family in Philadelphia, Samuel Dickinson decided to build another plantation in Delaware, Poplar Hall, an imposing and elegant brick mansion, located in Jones Neck, southeast of Dover, Delaware. By 1740, Samuel Dickinson had moved and settled his family at Poplar Hall. Dickinson, like other wealthy children of the time, was educated at home, by his parents and later by tutors. By all accounts, Dickinson was an eager and intelligent pupil.

Learning the Law

In 1750, at the age of eighteen, Dickinson moved to Philadelphia to study law. Three years later, in 1753, Dickinson went to London where he continued his legal studies at the Middle Temple. At that time it was common for the wealthy to send their sons to London to continue their education. In this case, Dickinson was sent to one of the prestigious Inns of Court, in order to complete his legal education.

While in London, Dickinson made the most of his time, visiting many of the city's cultural and historical landmarks, which he described in the many letters sent back to his parents at Poplar Hall. The sights of London did not easily impress Dickinson. After a trip to the House of Lords, Dickinson wrote that the nobility looked no different than other ordinary men. A visit to the royal residence of St. James for a birthday celebration was also unexciting. Dickinson later wrote how embarrassed King George II appeared as he mumbled to his guests or stared at his feet. In spite of his lack of enthusiasm for British government and royalty, Dickinson did enjoy his time in London, taking in the theater and applying himself to his studies.

What was the Middle Temple?
Dickinson studied law at the Middle Temple, one of the Inns of Court that trained lawyers in Great Britain. There are four Inns of Court: Lincoln's Inn, Inner Temple, Middle Temple, and Gray's Inn. Anyone wishing to train for the bar had to join one of the Inns. The Inns not only provided legal education, but also residential and dining facilities as well.

Early Career

In 1757, Dickinson returned to Philadelphia and began practicing law. By 1762, he had also entered politics, and was elected to the Pennsylvania Assembly. He quickly made a name for himself, siding with the delegates who wished to keep the colony's status as a commonwealth, rather than a colony that would place it immediately under the Crown's control. Even though Dickinson was wary of self-government by the colonies, he also saw the potential for the abuse of colonial freedoms by the British government. This marked the beginning of a lifelong belief that the preservation of established freedoms was far more important than creating new ones. For Dickinson, protection lay in the law, not with men.

In 1770, Dickinson married Mary ("Polly") Norris, daughter of Isaac Norris, speaker of the Pennsylvania General Assembly and a wealthy Quaker. Dickinson and his wife eventually moved to the Norris estate of Fairhill, near Germantown. The couple had five children, but only two daughters survived to adulthood. The marriage to Polly Norris was also beneficial to Dickinson financially, though by this time he was a prosperous man in his own right.

Road to Revolution

Dickinson's support of maintaining commonwealth status for Pennsylvania, while heightening his reputation, also cost him his seat in the General Assembly. However, in October 1765, Dickinson was chosen to represent Pennsylvania at the Stamp Act Congress meeting in New York, where he drafted a resolution for the Congress against the Stamp Act.

In December 1768, Dickinson began publishing in the *Pennsylvania Chronicle* newspaper a series of twelve letters known as the "Letters from a Farmer in Pennsylvania to the Inhabitants of the British Colonies," which were published under the pseudonym "A Farmer." The letters were powerful arguments illustrating why the Stamp Acts were a contradiction of traditional English civil liberties. Although in his writings Dickinson hinted at the possibility of a more extreme response on the part of the colonies to British taxation policies, he still hoped for a peaceful outcome to the difficulties between the Crown and her troublesome American colonies.

FACT

The "Letters" were so popular not only in the colonies but also abroad that Dickinson emerged as the first American political hero. He would receive an honorary Doctor of Law degree from the College of New Jersey (now known as Princeton) and public thanks from a meeting in Boston. Not all the accolades were words or pieces of paper: Paul Revere engraved his likeness.

Much to Dickinson's dismay, tensions between the Crown and the colonies were increasing to such a degree that any hope of peaceful reconciliation between the two seemed all but lost. Dickinson was particularly incensed at the actions of the Boston rebels and the Sons of Liberty whose actions appeared to be a deliberate attempt to push the colonies into war with England. When the First Continental Congress convened in Philadelphia in September in response to the crisis, John and Samuel Adams immediately began courting Dickinson. In July 1774 during the meetings of the Continental Congress, Dickinson drafted three resolutions that he hoped might prevent hostilities. Still, Dickinson was a realist and at the same time he helped to fortify the defenses for the city of Philadelphia and offered his services as a commander of the city's new militia regiment.

Declaration of Independence

In May 1775, during the meetings of the Second Continental Congress, Dickinson argued not only for a new petition to be sent to the Crown in an attempt to avoid war, but that the Congress should send a delegation to London, authorized to initiate negotiations. Certain delegates, including Thomas Mifflin of Pennsylvania, Richard Henry Lee of Virginia, and John Rutledge of South Carolina, attacked Dickinson's plans vociferously. At one point tempers rose so high that half of Congress walked out. In the end, Dickinson's idea was rejected, but Congress did agree to a petition for the sake of unity, an action that more radical members of the Congress, such as John Adams, thought an exercise in futility. Dickinson wrote a "Petition to the King," in which he appealed to the Crown directly for a peaceful resolution to the growing problems in the colonies. The Crown rejected Dickinson's appeal; war was all but inevitable at this point.

The following year, when Richard Henry Lee proposed a declaration on independence, Dickinson opposed the suggestion, believing that such an action would be reckless and unwise. Dickinson also argued that going to war with England would leave the colonies vulnerable to possible hostile actions from other European powers such as France and Spain. He also noted that many differences among the colonies had yet to be resolved and could lead to civil war.

Instead, Dickinson proposed that the colonies create a confederation before breaking free from the British. In the weeks leading up to the vote on independence, Dickinson chaired the committee that Congress appointed to draft Articles of Confederation for a new republican government. He also stood as the last major opponent of separating from the Crown. Other delegates such as Robert Morris of Pennsylvania and John Jay of New York also did not want the colonies to break away, but realized that the tide of opinion was such that they accepted the consensus and despite private qualms, publicly supported the cause of colonial freedom. In the end, Dickinson abstained from voting on adopting the document; in doing so, it allowed all the colonies to adopt the Declaration unanimously.

As a result of his stand against the Declaration of Independence, the new government of Pennsylvania quickly let Dickinson go from the congressional delegation. Dickinson then turned his energies to serving his country, taking command of the Pennsylvania militia group he had helped organize. However, his stance on independence had cost him dearly, marking him for criticism from the more radical political elements that now dominated colonial politics. In the end, Dickinson was left with few allies who could help him salvage his reputation. He also resigned his commission over what he believed were a number of incidents directed at him because of his refusal to support the signing of the Declaration of Independence.

In July 1776, on the day of the vote, John Dickinson and Robert Morris stood in the back of the room and abstained themselves from voting and signing the Declaration of Independence. Dickinson later stated: "My conduct this day, I expect will give the finishing blow to my once too great and, my integrity considered, now too diminished popularity."

According to some historical accounts during the summer of 1777, Dickinson again enlisted for military duty, this time serving as a private with the Delaware volunteers. The group was mobilized in response to an advancing British force under General Sir William Howe whose plan it was to attack Philadelphia, at that time the American capital. The Delaware militia along with other American soldiers, were to hold off the British until Washington could arrived with reinforcements. Dickinson's company fought at the Battle of Brandywine and then returned home after the battle. Dickinson remained a part-time soldier until the war's end. The war also impacted Dickinson financially; his home, Fairhill, was burned to the ground by the British and his other properties in Delaware were also damaged either by Tories or outlaws. His residence in Philadelphia had also been confiscated and turned into a hospital.

Still Dickinson remained one of the wealthier landowners in Delaware, as well as the largest slaveholder. In 1777, however, Dickinson freed his slaves, an act that was both courageous yet also practical as Dickinson's farm was moving away from the more labor-intensive crop of tobacco, to those of wheat and barley, which did not rely so heavily on an intensive labor force.

The Constitutional Convention

During the post-war years, Dickinson's transgressions appeared to be forgiven. In 1779, he returned to the Continental Congress and in 1781 was elected governor of Delaware. The following year, Dickinson stepped down from the governorship to take office as the president of the Supreme Executive Council of Pennsylvania. In 1786, Dickinson traveled to Annapolis, Maryland where, along with James Madison, he revised the Articles of Confederation. Dickinson was also elected president at that gathering.

In 1782, Benjamin Rush approached Dickinson about the possibility of founding a new college in Cumberland County. Rush wanted to call the college "John and Mary's College," in honor of Dickinson and his wife. Dickinson, appalled at the parallel with William and Mary, which was named in honor of the British monarchs, refused. Instead, the college was named "Dickinson."

From May to September 1787, Dickinson served as a delegate from Delaware to the Constitutional Convention in Philadelphia where he made numerous contributions, particularly in the debates over the powers of the new office of the presidency. At the gathering in Philadelphia, Dickinson pushed for equal representation among the states, keeping in mind that the smaller states might have a diminished voice in government representation. His arguments led to the compromise in congressional representation.

In 1788, Dickinson wrote a series of twelve letters under the pen name "Fabius" calling for the support of the ratification of the new constitution. Using examples from history, Dickinson explained how the system of check and balances would work among the different branches of the new government and how it would help safeguard the civil liberties of the people. Delaware became the first state to ratify the Constitution.

Later Life

Following the success of the Constitutional Convention, Dickinson retired from political life. For the remainder of the decade, he lived with his wife and two daughters in Wilmington, Delaware. He spent his days reading, mostly historical and religious works, as well as writing letters to friends and family commenting on political and current affairs.

Dickinson returned to the state senate in 1793 but served for just one year before resigning due to poor health. His final years saw him working within the abolition movement and donating money to the poor. Dickinson died February 14, 1808, at his home in Wilmington. Upon learning of his death, President Thomas Jefferson expressed his sorrow. Both houses of Congress wore black armbands in mourning. Dickinson was buried in the cemetery of the Friends Meeting House, Wilmington.

John Dickinson continued to write to the end of his life. In a second series of "Fabius" letters, written in 1797, Dickinson wrote about the importance of maintaining friendly relations with France, even as that nation was undergoing its own revolution. In 1801, he published two volumes of his collected political writings.

Legacy

Although Dickinson is probably one of the most overlooked of the Founding Fathers, his contributions were key to the founding of the new nation. Criticized for his conservative views and as being overly cautious, Dickinson still stood by his views. His devotion to the rule of law and to the principles of liberty also established him as a man of strong principles, who was not easily swayed. His convictions over the Declaration of Independence cost him dearly; however, that did not stop him from fighting for a nation that he believed was destined for greatness. His staunch support of the new Constitution also demonstrated his willingness to do whatever it took to help the new nation on its way. While not as familiar, John Dickinson, nonetheless demonstrated his devotion to his country and his writings continue to resonate among many Americans today.

CHAPTER 21

Charles Cotesworth Pinckney

Charles Cotesworth Pinckney was a son of South Carolina's planter aristocracy. He spent most of his youth in England, but upon his return to Charleston he took up the cause of the patriots. He served in the Continental army and fought in campaigns along with George Washington. He dutifully served his colony and state in the legislature. He was also sent as a delegate to the Constitutional Convention in 1787. Although he was a southerner, he attended the convention as a Federalist and was instrumental in guiding the Constitution through the ratification process in South Carolina.

Early Life

Charles Cotesworth Pinckney was born on February 25, 1746 in Charleston, South Carolina, the eldest son of Charles and Eliza Lucas Pinckney. Charles Cotesworth's branch of the Pinckney family settled in America in 1692 with the arrival of his grandfather Thomas and his wife Mary. Thomas and Mary had three sons, Thomas, Charles, and William. Charles, who would become Charles Cotesworth Pinckney's father, was sent abroad for his education, married an Englishwoman, and returned to South Carolina where he was a prominent member of the bar, speaker of the assembly, and King's Councilor.

Charles Pinckney's first wife died and he subsequently married Eliza Lucas, the daughter of a British officer who previously held plantations in Antigua. They had three children, Charles, Thomas, and a daughter Harriott. Charles Cotesworth Pinckney was born in his father's house in Charleston, a fine two-story home that overlooked the bay. From infancy his mother indulged him with popular educational toys of the period, including what Eliza Pinckney proudly described as a "sett of toys to teach him his letters by the time he can speak, you perceive we begin by times for he is not yet four months old." Charles Cotesworth is alleged to have commented later in life that he was greatly surprised he was not made stupid by the ardent efforts his parents expended to make him brilliant.

FACT

Charles Cotesworth Pinckney's mother, Eliza Lucas, is responsible for the introduction of indigo as a cash crop in South Carolina. An extraordinary woman, Eliza Lucas was managing plantations for her father by the age of sixteen. She was educated at a finishing school and her favorite subject was botany.

In 1753 Charles Pinckney was appointed as a colonial agent, essentially a political and commercial lobbyist for the colony, and temporarily moved his family to London. Charles Cotesworth and his brother Thomas studied under a private tutor and were later placed in a school for young boys. Charles, Eliza, and Harriott returned to South Carolina in 1758 and left Charles Cotesworth and Thomas in school in England. Leaving their sons behind was difficult for Charles and Eliza, but the Pinckney brothers were well on their way in the education and training that was expected of boys in their social class. Charles and Eliza planned to return to England in two years and left their sons in the care of their English guardian, Mrs. Evance.

Shortly after their return to South Carolina, Charles Pinckney became ill and died from a fever on July 13, 1758. In his will Pinckney divided his lands in England and America between his children and left instructions for Charles Cotesworth to be "virtuously, religiously and liberally brought up," and to study and practice the laws of England. Charles Cotesworth was expected to take on the mantle of social responsibility and to be an asset and honor to his country and his family.

"That he will employ all his future abilities in the service of God and his country, in the virtuous cause of liberty, as well as religious as civil, and in support of private right and justice between man and man." **—Instructions for Charles Cotesworth Pinckney in the will of Charles Pinckney**

Education

When the Pinckney brothers were old enough they were sent to the Westminster School, one of the premier schools to prepare them for the next step, matriculation to Oxford. At Oxford, Charles Cotesworth was in the company of several other young men from prominent South Carolina families. The roll call of his fellow Carolinians, including names such as Thomas Lynch, William Henry Drayton, Thomas Heyward, Hugh Rutledge, and Paul Trapier, to name a few, comprises a list of men who would one day take up the cause against Britain. Charles Cotesworth graduated from Christ Church College, Oxford, in 1764 with degrees in science and law. Later that year he was admitted to the Inns of Court in the Middle Temple for his formal legal training. He was admitted to the English bar in 1769. Afterward, he traveled Europe studying chemistry and botany and attended the Royal Military College in Caen. In 1769 he returned to South Carolina after a sixteen-year absence.

Career

Charles Cotesworth returned to South Carolina as a gentleman with massive property holdings, but he was not content to merely pass his time as a planter. He qualified to practice law, and settled into a life of public service following the example that had been set by generations of Pinckneys before him.

Charles Cotesworth hit the ground running. He was the steward of his plantations, he practiced law, he was a vestryman and warden in the Episcopal Church, and joined the first regiment of the South Carolina militia. In 1770, at the age of twenty-three, he was admitted to the South Carolina bar and he was elected to the colonial legislature as the representative from St. John's Colleton. In 1773 he was appointed deputy attorney general for the circuit that included Camden, Georgetown, and the Cheraws. In the midst of this flurry of activity, he found time to marry in 1773. His first wife, Sarah Middleton, descended from a family as distinguished as the Pinckneys. Her father was the second president of the Continental Congress and her brother signed the Declaration of Independence.

Revolutionary War

Charles Cotesworth scarcely had time to settle into his legal and public career before America and Britain were at war. Although he spent most of his life in England and he came from a high born class, he joined the patriot cause. There is no evidence he struggled with the decision with which side to take in the impending conflict. As a young boy, he watched his father in his role as a colonial agent negotiate economic circumstances that were best for South Carolina. On a personal level, his interests as a member of the mercantile planter class were not served by parliamentary interference in his political and economic affairs. In 1775 he severed another association with Britain by leaving the royal government to become a member of the first South Carolina Provincial Congress, the body charged with managing South Carolina's transition from royal colony to independent state.

Military Career

Charles Cotesworth volunteered in the first Continental army unit organized in South Carolina. As a junior officer, he went to the defense of

Charleston at the Battle of Sullivan's Island in 1776. Charles Cotesworth was an aide on Washington's staff during the Battle of Brandywine and the Battle of Germantown. During this period he met Alexander Hamilton and James McHenry who became his friends and later his political allies.

The Pinckneys were planters and statesmen, people of privilege who believed their elevated social and political standing demanded public duty. Their ancient heritage can be traced far into European history. They arrived in England with William the Conqueror and a Pinckney (Picquigny) was one of the barons who compelled King John to sign the Magna Carta. The Pinckneys of South Carolina were similarly prepared to "defend the inherited rights of Englishmen."

In 1778 he commanded a regiment in an unsuccessful attempt to capture east Florida from the British. This was followed by a disastrous encounter with the British in Savannah, which was followed by the even more disastrous siege of Charleston in 1780, which ended badly when he was taken prisoner. He was held for two years until he was finally released in a prisoner exchange. Although the war was over by the time of his release, he remained on active duty until November 1783. He was promoted to brevet brigadier general in recognition of his service.

"The freedom and independence of my country are the gods of my idolatry." —**Charles Cotesworth Pinckney**

The main lesson Charles Cotesworth learned from his wartime experiences was that South Carolina would never be safe as long as it remained isolated. The general welfare and security of South Carolina rested on a union with the other colonies in which they would work cooperatively together for their common defense and prosperity. The germ of this idea followed him from the battlefield and developed over the years between the end of the war and the start of the Constitutional Convention.

After the war, Charles Cotesworth resumed the peacetime pattern of his life. He managed his plantations, he practiced law, and he was Charleston's representative in the lower house of the state legislature. These were by no means easy times. His personal property and finances were greatly damaged by the war. Sarah Middleton Pinckney died in 1784. Charles Cotesworth was wounded in 1785 in a duel with Daniel Huger. 1786 was a better year; he married Mary Stead, the daughter of a wealthy Georgia planter.

Constitutional Convention

Charles Cotesworth remained a leading figure in South Carolina's legal and political realm in the immediate post-war period. His brother was elected governor of the state in 1787 and within months of taking office commissioned Charles Cotesworth as a delegate to the convention to revise the Articles of Confederation. Charles Cotesworth was a well-educated, thoughtful, and accomplished man, but he had no political experience outside of state and local affairs. Contrary to what one might assume about his sectional feelings as a southerner, he went to the convention already in favor of a strong national government, believing the future of the nation depended upon it. Initially he was not sure how forcefully the convention should proceed with revisions. As the debate progressed and arguments between differing factions seasoned into serious and judicious discussions intent on solutions and compromise, he grew increasingly confident in the new document that began to emerge from the deliberations.

Charles Cotesworth's colleagues at the convention respected him as a veteran who served with distinction, a man highly esteemed in his home state, and who was thoroughly grounded in legal matters. However, his fellow delegate from South Carolina, Pierce Butler, was lukewarm regarding Charles Cotesworth's public speaking skills: "When warm in debate he sometimes speaks well—but he is generally considered an indifferent orator."

Slavery and Export Taxes

Charles Cotesworth confined his debates to issues that were important to South Carolina, particularly matters concerning representation, the taxation of exports, and the importation of slaves. The slave trade debate, which took place mostly during the heat of the Philadelphia summer, was contentious. Nineteen delegates from ten states were persistently vocal on the subject. Charles Cotesworth's younger cousin Charles argued if slavery was wrong, they only had to look to the empires of Greece and Rome for the antecedents of the institution, and that modern states such as Britain, France, and Holland held slaves as well. The southern states should be allowed to manage their own affairs regarding slavery and in due time they would address the subject of ending the importation of slaves. Charles Pinckney warned that he wanted to support the new Constitution but would not be able to if the convention insisted on placing the obstacle of slavery in front of him.

Charles Cotesworth supported his cousin's position. He argued that South Carolina and Georgia "can not do without slaves." They did not have a surplus slave population, as he claimed Virginia enjoyed. To stop the importation of slaves would compromise the economies of the states in the lower south.

"The more slaves, the more produce to employ the carrying trade. The more consumption also, and the more of this, the more of revenue for the common treasury." —**Charles Cotesworth Pinckney**

The question of the importation of slaves was referred to committee and it was recommended that Congress could not end the slave trade before 1800. Charles Cotesworth moved to extend the prohibition to 1808. After much debate, the convention adopted Charles Cotesworth's motion seven to four.

Most of the delegates realized they were not going to solve the problem of slavery; at best they could organize compromises around it. The underlying consensus was the slave states would eventually stop importing them, and perhaps find a more cost-efficient and less morally reprehensible source of labor. But that was a much larger problem than they felt they could address at the time. A related issue the convention had to address was how to account for slaves with regard to representation and whether the commodities they produced for export were taxable.

Charles Cotesworth Pinckney and Pierce Butler argued against the three-fifths clause and moved slaves should be counted equally with whites in the census used for determining a slave state's representation in the lower house of Congress. Their motion was defeated, and the three-fifths formula prevailed.

Charles Cotesworth was more successful with regard to the matter of the taxation of exports. He strenuously opposed export taxes. Simply put, South Carolina produced exports with the labor of imported slaves. He would not agree to any document that interfered with the state's ability to freely export commodities or import the labor that made them.

Ten days later, the Committee of Detail presented what would become provisions of Section 9 of the final draft. The federal government could not prohibit the importation of slaves until 1808 and commodities exported from any state could not be taxed.

In addition to the major questions posed by slavery and export taxes, Charles Cotesworth was quiet on other issues, except for the matter of election of the legislature. He opposed the election of either branch of the legislature by the people and did not believe popular elections were a safeguard against a bad government. The legislature, in his opinion, was better at determining what was good for the people than the people themselves.

"If the committee [the Committee of Detail] should fail to insert some security to the Southern states against an emancipation of slaves and taxes on exports, I shall be bound by my duty to my state to vote against their report." —**Charles Cotesworth Pinckney**

Ratification

The South Carolina convention to ratify the Constitution was set for May 12, 1788 in Charleston. Charles Cotesworth was in attendance as a representative of the parishes of St. Philip and St. Michael. After a brief debate, South Carolina voted to ratify 149 to seventy-three. At the close of this chapter in his life, Charles Cotesworth returned to private life.

Post-Convention Career

After the creation of the new government, Charles Cotesworth was offered, and refused, command of the United States Army, a position on the Supreme Court, the position of secretary of war, and that of secretary of state. He did accept the appointment of minister to France in 1796, but the French government would not accept him and he was forced to detour to the Netherlands. In 1796, President John Adams named him, along with John Marshall and Elbridge Gerry, to a committee to restore the impaired relations between the French and the Americans, and to particularly negotiate an agreement that the French would suspend the seizure of American ships and sailors. The mission culminated in the XYZ Affair, a meeting in which three French agents identified at the time only as X, Y, and Z insisted on a substantial bribe before they would entertain any dialogue on the matter. Charles Cotesworth is reported to have answered "No! No! Not a sixpence!" The discussion was over and he returned to South Carolina in 1798.

Charles Cotesworth made two unsuccessful runs as the Federalist nominee for vice president in 1800 and 1804. He also ran unsuccessfully for president in 1808. He returned to Charleston to practice law and enjoyed an active life for the remainder of his days. He was a charter member of the board of trustees for South Carolina College (now the University of South Carolina), the first president of the Charleston Bible Society, the chief executive of the Charleston Library Society, and the president general of the Society of the Cincinnati from 1805 to 1825.

Legacy

Charles Cotesworth Pinckney was a statesman, planter, lawyer, and politician who ardently did his duty for his colony, his state, and his nation. He was a prominent figure in the American Revolution and helped shape the government of the new republic. Although a southerner, he was a strong Federalist who sought to protect the interests of his state by promoting the creation of a greater national unity that ultimately stood for the protection of all states.

PART V

★ THE REVOLUTIONARIES ★

Without Thomas Paine's pen and Patrick Henry's oratory, it is hard to imagine what the American Revolution would have been like. These two men, both possessed of stubborn and creative natures, gave the Revolution a voice that even today remains powerful and true. Their words, born out of deeply felt emotions and beliefs about liberty and the relationship between men and their government, continue to reverberate today in political discussions. Unfortunately, the tragedy of their lives is that for their championing of the American cause, both men's usefulness ended when liberty was won. As important as their roles were in bringing the old world to an end, there was no place for them in the building of the new.

Quiz: Why We Want Our Freedom

1. **Thomas Paine disagreed with George Washington over what issue?**

   A. Slavery
   B. State's rights
   C. Secession
   D. Stamp Act

2. **What is the name of the book that outlined the American cause for independence?**

   A. *Give Me Liberty*
   B. *The Stamp Act Resolves*
   C. *Common Sense*
   D. *The Rights of Man*

3. **What did George Washington read to his troops while they crossed the Delaware?**

   A. Benjamin Franklin's *Poor Richard's Almanac*
   B. Thomas Jefferson's *Notes on the State of Virginia*
   C. Patrick Henry's *Stamp Act Resolutions*
   D. Thomas Paine's *The Crisis*

4. **Who served as the first governor of post-colonial Virginia?**

   A. George Washington
   B. James Madison
   C. Patrick Henry
   D. Thomas Jefferson

5. **Who advocated universal education for all men?**

   A. Thomas Jefferson
   B. Patrick Henry
   C. James Madison
   D. Thomas Paine

6. **Who declined to attend the Constitutional Convention because he "smelled a rat"?**

   A. Patrick Henry
   B. Thomas Jefferson
   C. Benjamin Franklin
   D. Thomas Paine

7. **Who said, "These are the times that try men's souls"?**
   A. George Washington
   B. Thomas Paine
   C. John Adams
   D. Patrick Henry

8. **At the end of his life, Patrick Henry belonged to what political party?**
   A. Federalist
   B. Whig
   C. Democratic-Republican
   D. Tory

9. **Who was dismissed from his job for advocating a salary increase?**
   A. Thomas Paine
   B. Patrick Henry
   C. Benjamin Franklin
   D. John Adams

10. **Thomas Paine's *The Crisis* is credited with what victory during the American Revolution?**
    A. Battle of Yorktown
    B. Battle of Charleston
    C. Battle of Trenton
    D. Battle of Saratoga

Answers

1.A 2.C 3.D 4.C 5.D 6.A 7.B 8.A 9.A 10.C

CHAPTER 22

Thomas Paine

He was notoriously unreliable, an alcoholic, and terrible with money. But his talent with a pen and his gift for words kept Thomas Paine's ideas about liberty foremost in many American colonists' minds. His writings also helped win support for the American fight for freedom from England. It is hard to say what might have happened had Thomas Paine not been a part of the Revolutionary generation. Because of his writings, Paine would embody for generations the meaning of freedom, civil liberties, and political equality.

Early Life and Education

Born on January 29, 1736 in the town of Thetford, Norfolk in England, Thomas Paine was the son of Joseph Paine and Frances Cocke Paine. His father, a devout Quaker, worked as a maker of corsets and also as a tenant farmer. Thetford at that time was an important center of commerce and transportation serving, as a market town and stage post in that area of rural Norfolk. Despite his father's status as a Quaker, Paine was confirmed in his mother's church, the Church of England.

From 1744 until 1749, Paine attended Thetford Grammar School, where he received a rudimentary education. His father forbade his son to learn Latin and Greek, though Paine did show an aptitude for mathematics and literature. He was also fascinated by the stories told by some of the teachers of life at sea.

Paine was originally born as Thomas Pain. Though Paine claimed to have changed his name once he came to North America, there is evidence that he had already added the "e" to the end of his name by 1769.

At the age of thirteen, Paine went to work for his father, but determined to escape from Thetford and a life working in his father's business, he left, and served as a privateer on the ship *The King of Prussia* for at least one voyage. Paine returned to England in 1759 and went into business for himself as a corset maker in the town of Sandwich in Kent. According to some accounts, Paine also became a lay Methodist minister, which at that time was an evangelical movement within the Church of England. That same year, Paine took a wife, marrying Mary Lambert. Misfortune soon followed; in 1760, his business collapsed and his wife died giving birth to their first child.

An Unsettled Life

By 1762, Paine had returned to Thetford to work as an excise officer, meaning he collected duties and taxes on goods coming into the country. The following year, Paine moved to Grantham, Lincolnshire, and in August 1764, he was transferred to the city of Alford. Paine's tenure as an excise officer was rocky at best. On August 27, 1765, he was fired for claiming to have inspected goods that he had not. Paine again returned to work as a corset maker and also was employed as a servant. He also applied to become an ordained minister of the Church of England and according to some accounts actually preached. He was reinstated to his former position as an excise officer almost a year later.

What was an excise officer and what were his duties?
An excise officer worked for the Board of Excise, which was established by Parliament. The first excise duties were collected in 1643. Excise officers collected inland duties or taxes on any number of things at the time of their manufacture. This included such items as alcoholic drinks and tobacco, salt, paper, and windows.

In 1767, Paine took another excise position at Grampound, Cornwall. A year later, on February 19, 1768, Paine was sent to Lewes, East Sussex, where he lived above a tobacco shop owned Samuel and Esther Ollive. Paine partnered with Ollive in the setting up of a tobacco mill to further supplement his income. After Ollive died in 1769, Paine started a shop with Ollive's widow and in 1771 married her daughter, Elizabeth.

Paine's first foray into political matters came when living in Lewes. His landlord, Samuel Ollive introduced Paine to the Society of Twelve, a local group of intellectuals that met to discuss local politics. Paine also served in the vestry church group that collected taxes and tithes to be given to the poor. Although a poor speaker in public, Paine still participated in the local debating society. It was also during this period in Lewes that Paine first began seriously writing some poetry and essays.

During this period, Paine's political stance, which tended to side with the Whig Party, began veering in a more radical direction. He penned his first political pamphlet, *The Case of the Officers of Excise*, which argued for better salaries for excise officers. He even traveled to London toward the end of 1772 with a petition signed by 3,000 excise officers, though little was accomplished for his efforts.

Voyage to America

By 1773, Paine once again found himself in a precarious financial position, as the tobacco mill was not doing well. A year later, the Excise Board, after complaints about Paine's neglect of his duties, fired him again. Desperate, Paine sold the tobacco mill. His marriage to Elizabeth was foundering and the couple separated. It seemed as good a time as any to leave. A fortuitous meeting with Benjamin Franklin led Paine to leave for America, with a letter of recommendation from Franklin in his pocket.

Paine landed at Philadelphia on November 30, 1774. Not long after, he made the acquaintance of Franklin's son-in-law, Richard Bache. Paine also met a local bookseller Robert Aitken. Together the two men created the periodical the *Pennsylvania Magazine,* of which Paine served as a co-editor.

One of Paine's first articles for *Pennsylvania Magazine* was "African Slavery in America" published in the spring of 1775, in which Paine severely criticized the institution of slavery in America as being unjust and inhumane. As a result of the article, Paine met Benjamin Rush, who would be a signer of the Declaration of Independence and who would encourage Paine to write *Common Sense.*

By the time Paine arrived in America, tensions were high between the colonies and Great Britain. Already reeling from the numerous tax acts passed by Parliament, American colonists were also showing their teeth with the meeting of the Stamp Act Congress. Barely a month before Paine's coming to America, the First Continental Congress had met in Philadelphia, issuing the document "The Declaration and Resolves," calling for Parliament to treat her North American colonies as true representatives of the British Empire which meant, among other things, equal representation.

Common Sense

Paine was fascinated by the events unfolding before him and quickly found himself a staunch supporter of the colonial cause. In his eyes, the colonies had every right to revolt against a government that imposed unfair taxes and refused its citizens a basic right of Englishmen, that is, the right of representation in the halls of Parliament. But Paine's attitude was more radical than those of many of the members of the Continental Congress: he saw no reason for the American colonies to rely on England anymore.

With the encouragement of prominent Philadelphia physician Dr. Benjamin Rush, Paine decided to write down his ideas about American independence. On January 10, 1776, Paine's pamphlet *Common Sense* was published. Copies were sold for the price of two shillings.

"We have it in our power to begin the world over again." **—Thomas Paine, *Common Sense*, 1776**

Common Sense was an unprecedented success in colonial America. Never before had a pamphlet been written that aimed for an audience beyond the elite and the educated. Paine's work was also unprecedented in that Paine's arguments for independence had never been so clearly articulated for the masses. Over half a million copies were sold; both patriots and Loyalists bought the pamphlet.

Common Sense proved to be so popular that pirated editions began appearing within three weeks of the pamphlet's publication. It is believed that almost 120,000 copies of *Common Sense* were sold within the first three months of its appearance.

It is easy to understand why Paine's rhetoric caught the public's attention. *Common Sense* argues, among other things, that it was time for the American colonies to break away from England as Americans now had little in common with the British Crown and people. The arguments for independence, in Paine's opinion, were sound. Even more important in Paine's eyes, it was America's destiny to break away from a corrupt and greedy government and set forth on a new experiment and the creation of a new and pure republic. Government was a necessary evil to Paine, but it could be managed with a sound and representative structure. Above all, government should be kept simple and answerable to the people. In all, Paine's rhetoric reduced the arguments for independence in language that anyone—from merchant banker to simple farmer—could understand and appreciate.

Into the Fray

As if writing propaganda was not enough, Paine volunteered with a company of Philadelphia volunteers to join what was called the "flying camp," a mobile strategic reserve unit created by George Washington that was stationed near Amboy, close to the New York border. But because there was no military action underway, Paine ended up serving as a headquarters secretary. He later ended up as an aide de camp to General Nathaniel Greene and spent his time writing propaganda reports that celebrated American victories and downplayed their defeats.

In 1776, Paine returned to Philadelphia where he began a new series of essays known as *The American Crisis* that were published during the period 1776 to 1783. During the period he was writing, he also served as secretary of the Committee of Foreign Affairs in Congress, but was later forced to step down for disclosing confidential information. He also found work as a clerk in the Pennsylvania Assembly and tried to secure funds for the creation of a Bank of North America to help raise funds for the war effort.

The American Crisis tackled a number of important political topics and is considered among some of Paine's greatest writings. Much of Paine's writing continues to ring true today, including the following quote: "The times that tried men's souls are over-and the greatest and completest revolution the world ever knew, gloriously and happily accomplished." —**Thomas Paine, *The American Crisis*, No. 13, 1783**

By 1784, Paine found himself a landowner as he was rewarded for his work with the patriot cause with an estate that had been confiscated from a Loyalist. He was also flush with grants received from both the federal and

Pennsylvania governments. He began spending his time between his home in Bordertown, New Jersey and New York City where he continued to write, dabble in scientific experiments, and sketch plans for an iron bridge that he hoped would be built across the Schuylkill River.

Later Years

Unable to find funding for his bridge project, Paine left America in 1787 for England, where he hoped to raise monies to build his bridge. Events in France caught Paine's attention and he entertained ideas of going to France not long after the French Revolution began. To show his support for the revolutionary cause, Paine wrote *The Rights of Man*, in which he defended the French Revolution and credited the Americans with striking the initial spark against the overthrow of tyranny, poverty, and illiteracy. The book was banned in England and learning that he was to be arrested, Paine escaped to Paris where he was elected a member of the National Convention. However, in 1793, Paine was imprisoned in Paris for failing to support the execution of the King Louis XVI.

Paine's time in prison was spent writing his book the *Age of Reason*, a critical attack against organized religion. He only escaped death due to an error by a jailer who marked a cross, the sign that the occupant was due for execution, on the wrong side of the door.

FACT

Paine's bridge project was actually built by a Rotterdam firm that constructed a more scaled-down version of Paine's original design across the Thames River. The bridge was completed in 1790, but like many of Paine's endeavors failed, as structurally the bridge proved faulty and was dismantled.

After Paine's release from prison, he continued to stay in France. However, in 1802 he returned to America at the behest of President Thomas Jefferson who was an admirer of his. Unfortunately, by the time Paine returned to the United States he found himself overlooked and forgotten for his service and writings to the American cause. Paine had also given plenty of people reason to dislike him: the Federalists attacked his ideas of government and for Paine's support of the French Revolution. Nevertheless, Paine continued to write, often railing against the Federalist party and the current political atmosphere. But he also was overtaken by poverty, ill health and alcoholism. On June 8, 1809, Thomas Paine died in New York City, an outcast. One newspaper commented that "He had lived long, did some good and much harm," a statement that fortunately time has proven wrong. Thomas Paine had six mourners at his funeral.

Legacy

Thomas Paine never became a great head of state nor was he rewarded for his great service to his adopted country. But his words live on and continue to resonate among people everywhere. Without his abilities to articulate the principles of revolution and the ideals of a democratic republic, it is hard to say how well the Founding Fathers' dreams of a new country and a new kind of government would have taken hold. For it was Thomas Paine who took the words of the elite and translated them into a language that even the common man could call his own. He was perhaps the greatest propagandist during one of the most turbulent periods in history.

CHAPTER 23

Patrick Henry

His fiery oratory gave voice and emotion to the revolutionary movement, and along with fellow radicals Samuel Adams and Thomas Paine, Patrick Henry stands as one of the most influential and controversial figures of the Revolutionary War period. His denunciation of the English monarchy, government corruption, and denial of the rights of men earned Henry a reputation as a fierce political speaker and a man of strong principles. Even after the Revolution, Henry continued as an outspoken critic of big government and supporter of individual freedom.

Early Life and Education

Patrick Henry was born in Hanover County, Virginia on May 29, 1736. His father John Henry had come to the Virginia colony from Aberdeen, Scotland and quickly established himself as a the owner of a small estate located on the South Anna River that went by the name of Mount Brilliant. Known as a man of moderate means, good character and deep loyalties, John Henry was active as a vestryman of the local church, a justice of the peace, and a colonel of the local militia. Patrick Henry's mother, Sarah Winston Henry, was the daughter of Presbyterian immigrants from England, and like her husband, was known throughout the county as a woman possessed of great social charm and character.

As a young boy, Patrick Henry gained a reputation as being a bright boy, though lazy and unmotivated. He learned to read Latin and would throughout the rest of his life enjoy reading Roman classic literature. By the age of ten, his father realized that his son would be ill-suited to the life a farmer, as Patrick showed a clear distaste to the process of raising tobacco. John Henry instead tried to direct his son toward applying himself to his studies, but young Henry showed little interest.

One of the early influences on Patrick Henry's life were the religious sermons of Samuel Davies, who came to Hanover County as a pastor for the New Light religious congregations. Even though Henry had been christened in his uncle Patrick's church, St. Paul's, his mother enjoyed hearing Davies preach and would often take her young son with her.

Failed Beginnings

At the age of fifteen, Patrick began working as a clerk at a crossroads general store. A year later, with the help of his father and in partnership with his older brother William, Henry opened up his own store. Henry showed himself to be no better at business than at farming, and within a year the brothers had lost their monies.

In 1754, when Henry was eighteen, he married Sarah Shelton, the daughter of a local tavern owner. As a wedding gift, Henry's father-in-law gave the couple six slaves and 300-acre Pine Slash Farm, which proved to have infertile sandy soil. Henry and his wife could not make a go of the farm. By the age of twenty-one, Henry had lost his house and belongings in a fire. He and Sarah turned to storekeeping to earn a living thanks to the generosity of his father who bankrolled Henry in this latest endeavor. Unfortunately, Henry did no better the second time around and the business was soon bankrupt.

FACT

For young men wishing to take the bar exam in colonial Virginia, a trip to Williamsburg, then the capital of the colony, was in order. Patrick Henry took his examination in front of some of the greatest legal minds in colonial America at the time, including Robert Carter Nicholas, Edmund Pendleton, John and Peyton Randolph, and George Wythe. Wythe also taught a young James Monroe.

Deeply in debt, Henry was making a name for himself in the county as a person of less than trustworthy character. He needed to find another means of earning a living since by 1760 he had not only his wife to support but several children. He decided to try his hand at the law and spent six weeks studying. In the spring of 1760, Henry went before four local members of the bar to take the test. He passed and obtained a license to practice law. He and his family moved in with Sarah's father at Hanover Courthouse, where Henry opened his door for business.

Patrick Henry, Lawyer

Henry proved quite successful at his new profession; over a period of three years, he took on some 1,185 lawsuits and won most of them. His reputation spread beyond Hanover County to the city of Fredericksburg. By 1763, Henry, although living in Hanover, became a landholder in neighboring Louisa County. One of Henry's most famous cases was the 1763 Parson's Cause in Hanover County, which involved a local pastor bringing suit against a local law that determined the pay of the clergy. What started as a legal argument over wages paid to the local clergy soon evolved into an argument about whether the price of tobacco paid to clergy should be determined by the colonial government or by the Crown.

Clergy pay during this period was paid in tobacco. If the crop was good, the pay tended to be higher, if the crop was bad, many clergy were left to fend for themselves. In addition, a cap was placed on the amount that could be paid to the clergy when the crop was good. So many pastors disliked the law that they petitioned the Crown to intervene. The Crown did intervene and struck down the law.

The argument eventually went to trial. The court, overseen by Henry's father, John Henry, decided in favor of the clergy. In speaking to the jury, who were to determine the settlement to the clergy, Henry, speaking on behalf of Louisa County, reminded the jury members of the right of the colony to fix tobacco prices, despite the ruling from London. Henry's plea for justice and the right to self-government was so potent that the jury in the end awarded not a large sum as was expected but the total sum of one penny to the plantiff. In return, Henry won legions of supporters and the enmity of the local churches.

Politician

In 1765, Henry was chosen to represent Louisa County at the House of Burgesses, where he soon emerged as one of the assembly's most outspoken and radical members. When Henry arrived in Williamsburg the legislature was already in session debating over the passage of the Stamp Act, among other things. Just nine days after his arrival, Henry introduced the Virginia Stamp Act Resolutions, in language considered so extreme that some members considered Henry's resolutions treason against the Crown.

Henry waited until most of the conservative members of the assembly were away before putting the resolutions to a vote. With mostly supporters in the chambers, the Virginia Stamp Act Resolutions passed. Word spread throughout the colonies of Henry's success, adding to the growing tensions between the American colonists and the Crown. Henry's resolutions were by far the most dramatic expression of anti-British political sentiment at that time. Some historians have even called the Resolutions one of the main catalysts leading to the American Revolution.

What were the Virginia Stamp Act Resolutions?
The Virginia Stamp Act Resolutions were a series of proposals challenging the Crown and the Stamp Act. Among the most important resolutions was that Virginia was subject to taxation only by a government in which Virginians had elected representatives. Since Parliament had no colonial representatives, the only legal body allowed to tax Virginians was the Virginia General Assembly.

Trouble at Home

In 1771 Henry, his wife Sarah, and their six children moved into their home in Scotchtown in Hanover County. It was during their time at Scotchtown that Sarah began exhibiting strange behaviors and her mental condition began deteriorating. To protect herself and others from harm, Sarah was restrained in what was known as a "Quaker shirt," an early form of a strait jacket.

Henry's friends and physician urged Henry to commit his wife to the public hospital in Williamsburg. But after inspecting the facilities, which Henry found brutal and dehumanizing, he instead had a two-room apartment prepared for her in the basement of their home.

Unlike the mental hospitals of the period—where the mentally ill were chained to walls in rooms with no windows, proper ventilation, or heat—Sarah's accommodations in Scotchtown were quite luxurious by the day's standards. Each of her rooms had a window that provided light, air, and a view of the grounds. There was also a fireplace to provide heat and a bed for her to sleep in. Henry himself took care of Sarah when he was home. At times when he was away, a slave would make sure that Sarah was cared for.

In the spring of 1775, Sarah died. Because it was thought that she had been possessed, she was denied a Christian funeral or burial. In his grief and anger, Henry ordered Sarah to be buried near the home at Scotchtown and planted a lilac tree next to her grave. The lilac bush still stands today on the grounds of Scotchtown.

Preparing for Revolution

Henry quickly established himself as a leader in Virginia. In 1773, in response to the requests from the colony of Massachusetts asking for the creation of colonial committees of correspondence, Henry, working with Thomas Jefferson and Richard Henry Lee, led the Virginia House of Burgesses to adopt resolutions creating that colony's committee of correspondence. By 1774, the formation of these committees eventually led to the creation of the First Continental Congress. Henry was elected as a representative, where he became known for his more radical leanings, burning oratory, and support for an independent America.

Possibly the most famous speech made by Henry came in a meeting of the House of Burgesses on March 23, 1775, in Saint John's Church in Richmond, Virginia. The House was debating whether to mobilize for military action against the British. Many believed that Britain would bend to the colonists' demands; Henry was not as sure. After three days, the complacency of the convention was shattered when Henry proposed that Virginia be prepared to defend itself against the British. Among those in attendance was Thomas Jefferson, who found Henry to be a difficult personality, though Jefferson did have grudging admiration for him. Many years later, Patrick Henry's first biographer, William Wirt, attempted to reconstruct Henry's speech. According to Wirt, Henry's speech ended with the famous words: "Is life so dear, or peace so sweet, as to be purchased at the price of chains and slavery? Forbid it, Almighty God! I know not what course others may take; but as for me, Give me Liberty, or give me Death!" According to Wirt, the crowd responded to Henry by shouting, "To Arms! To Arms!"

Henry was also chosen to attend the Second Continental Congress, but before leaving he received news of the outbreak of hostilities in Lexington. Henry then learned that the royal governor of Virginia had seized the ammunition from the Williamsburg arsenal and had loaded it onto a ship on the James River. Gathering the Hanover militia, Henry marched toward the capital to retrieve the ammunition. A messenger was sent ahead to warn the governor to return the ammunition. The governor complied with Henry's demand, leaving Henry free to attend the Continental Congress in Philadelphia, where he helped vote into legislation the creation of the Continental army with George Washington as general and commander in chief of the troops. Henry's actions in Williamsburg followed the activities at Concord by only a few hours. His march on Williamsburg is considered to be the beginning of the American Revolution in Virginia.

For over a century and a half, Wirt's account of Henry's speech stood. But by the 1970s, historians began questioning the authenticity of Wirt's work. Historians today believe that the speech Henry gave was in fact filled with graphic name calling and that Henry was not above using the fear of Native American and slave revolts to support military action against the British, possibly making Henry's speech much less heroic.

The War Years

In August 1775, Henry was selected as a colonel of the First Virginia Regiment, then based in Williamsburg. The appointment meant that he was commander of all the military forces in the Virginia colony. George Washington opposed the appointment, but did not offer protest when Henry was chosen. However, disputes over military actions and what he perceived as affronts by the military committee of the Continental Congress led Henry to resign his commission on February 28, 1776.

On June 29, 1776, Henry was elected as the first post-colonial governor of Virginia. With the support of George Mason and Thomas Jefferson, during his first term Henry sent George Rogers Clark on a secret military mission that eventually helped expel the British from the Northwest Territory. However, Henry was unable to prevent a military invasion by the British of Hampton Roads and Portsmouth.

Henry also married for the second time on October 25, 1777. Henry married Dorothea Dandridge, with whom he would have eleven children. In the summer of 1779, Henry retired from the governorship to the 10,000-acre Leatherwood Plantation in Henry County, Virginia where he grew tobacco.

Henry was called back into political service in 1784 when he was again elected governor, but stepped down in 1786 when his term expired. When the Constitutional Convention of 1787 convened in Philadelphia, Henry declined to attend stating that he "smelt a rat in Philadelphia." Always a strong supporter of state's rights, Henry took a strong stand against the United States Constitution and would lead the Virginia opposition to its ratification. Henry saw all kinds of potential problems with the new document, arguing that it gave the federal government too much power and that the office of the presidency could turn into a monarchy. Henry favored strong state government and a weaker federal government. Henry also criticized the fact that the convention was conducted in secret. As a staunch Antifederalist, Henry was instrumental in forcing the adoption of the Bill of Rights to amend the new Constitution.

FACT

In early November 1775 Henry and James Madison were elected founding trustees of Hampden-Sydney College in Hampden Sydney, Virginia. Seven of his sons attended the new college. Today, the college is known as the oldest private charter in the South, as well as being the last college established before the American Revolution. The school is only one of three four-year, men's-only liberal arts colleges in the United States.

Later Years

Henry's last years were spent trying to regain a measure of prosperity, something that had eluded him for most of his life. His health increasingly precarious and with children and grandchildren to support, Henry turned once again to the practice of law, where he established himself as a leading attorney and master orator in the courtroom. However, in spite of his successes, Henry remained plagued by financial insecurity and ill health. He retired to his last home, the Red Hill plantation located on the Staunton River and gave up his law practice. To the end however, Henry remained steadfast in his political beliefs. When President George Washington offered Henry the post of secretary of state in 1795, Henry declined because of Washington's

Federalist policies. Washington also would offer Henry the office of chief justice, which Henry turned down. However, with events in France and its subsequent revolution, Henry feared for his own country and gradually began supporting some Federalist policies of the Washington and Adams administrations.

In 1798 President John Adams nominated Henry special emissary to France, but Henry declined, not because of politics but because of his increasingly worsening health. He stood for office one more time and was elected to the Virginia House of Delegates as a Federalist in 1799. Three months before he was to take his seat, Patrick Henry died of stomach cancer on June 6, at Red Hill.

Legacy

Patrick Henry, like Thomas Paine, struggled to find his place after the Revolution was over. It is hard to imagine what might have happened if not for Henry's strong stand and powerful oratory. Like Paine, Henry translated the words of politicians into a language that was understood by many. His relentless and courageous approach to see that the basic rights of men were upheld helped remind many colonists of their rights as Englishmen, and later as Americans. His later championing of the rights of states, and his criticism of the new Constitution helped push political leaders to adopt the Bill of Rights. His fight for the rights of men still resonates today as new generations of Americans continue to discover Patrick Henry, which assures all of us that his words of liberty and justice will continue to live on.

PART VI

★ THE LAWYERS ★

Although not "Signers," or "Framers," these men are also considered to be among the Founding Fathers of the United States. Their efforts to help guide the newly formed country from a loose confederation of colonies to a group of united states proved crucial in the beginning years of the nation. Their contributions came through the fields of law and diplomacy and helped establish the foundation for a strong American legal system and judiciary branch, and defined America's role as a world power for years to come.

Quiz: Legal Trivia: Do You Know Fact from Fiction?

1. Who was the first chief justice of the Supreme Court?

A. James Madison
B. Aaron Burr
C. John Marshall
D. John Jay

2. Which "James" was considered to be the last of the "Virginia Dynasty"?

A. James Monroe
B. James Madison
C. James McHenry
D. James Wilson

3. Who authored a five-volume biography of George Washington?

A. John Adams
B. Thomas Jefferson
C. Benjamin Franklin
D. John Marshall

4. Who of the following was born in a log cabin on the Virginia frontier?

A. George Washington
B. James Madison
C. John Marshall
D. Thomas Jefferson

5. Which of the following two were cousins?

A. Thomas Jefferson and John Marshall
B. George Washington and John Jay
C. James Madison and James Monroe
D. John Adams and John Quincy Adams

6. Which article guaranteed the establishment of the judicial branch in the Constitution?

A. Article I
B. Article II
C. Article III
D. Article IV

7. Under which Founding Father president was the White House painted white?

A. George Washington
B. Thomas Jefferson
C. John Adams
D. James Monroe

8. John Jay belonged to what political party?

A. Federalist
B. Whig
C. Democratic-Republican
D. Tory

9. Which Founding Father served as secretary of state, secretary of war, minister to France, and president of the United States?

A. Thomas Jefferson
B. James Monroe
C. Benjamin Harrison
D. John Adams

10. Which president was known as the "Era of Good Feeling" president?

A. George Washington
B. Thomas Jefferson
C. James Madison
D. James Monroe

Answers

1. D 2. A 3. D 4. C 5. A 6. C 7. D 8. A 9. B 10. D

CHAPTER 24

John Marshall

Although not a signer of the Declaration of Independence or a framer of the Constitution, John Marshall is one of the most important figures of American history. A lawyer and statesman, Marshall shaped the field that became known as constitutional law. Through his brilliant legal mind and strong personality, he also made the newly formed judicial branch and its Supreme Court a viable and enduring component of the federal government.

Early Life

Born on September 24, 1755, in a log cabin near the small frontier community of Germantown, in Fauquier County, Virginia, John Marshall was the oldest child and first son of Thomas Marshall and Mary Randolph Keith. In time, the family would grow to fifteen children, including eight girls and seven boys. John's parents also took on the responsibility of raising a number of family relatives. The cabin and its rural setting in colonial Virginia made for a lively childhood for all the Marshall children. As a child, Marshall was known for his quick humor and wit. He was a handsome boy, blessed with penetrating black eyes, a feature that as an adult would serve him well in arguing legal issues in court.

Marshall's father was active in the community, serving as sheriff and a justice of the peace. He was also employed by Lord Fairfax, who owned much of the land in what was known as the Northern Neck of Virginia. Fairfax employed Thomas Marshall as his agent in Fauquier County. Among Marshall's duties were surveying land, helping people find land to settle on, and collecting rents. In time, Thomas Marshall would himself owning some 200,000 acres of land in Virginia and Kentucky.

Marshall's mother was a member of the aristocratic Randolph family of Virginia, one of the first families to settle in the Virginia colony. The family was known for its intermarriages with a number of other prominent Virginia families including the Blands, Byrds, Carters, Fitzhughs, Harrisons, Jeffersons, and Lees. Marshall's cousins included Thomas Jefferson.

Sometime around 1763, Thomas Marshall moved his family from Germantown to the settlement of Leeds Manor, located on the eastern slopes of the Blue Ridge Mountains. There, near the banks of Goose Creek, Marshall's father built his family another wood cabin, similar in size and design to the one left behind in Germantown, called The Hollow. The family resided there for ten years. In 1773, the Marshall family moved once again—this time to a 1,700-acre estate near North Cobbler Mountain, not far from their home at Goose Creek. By the time John turned seventeen, his father had completed the family's seven-room house known as Oak Hill. John would eventually own the property, and even though he had homes in Richmond, Virginia, and Washington, D.C., it was Oak Hill that he would return to whenever possible.

Education

Thomas Marshall took a strong hand in his eldest son's education. Thomas Marshall was particularly fond of history and poetry, and he passed that love on to his son. He also utilized his business relationship with Lord Fairfax by sending his son to Greenway Court, Fairfax's home. While visiting there, Marshall eagerly devoured volumes of classical literature from Fairfax's extensive private library. At that time, Greenway Court was an exceptional private academy in Virginia. Marshall took advantage of the resources at Greenway Court and borrowed freely from the extensive collection of classical and contemporary literature.

ESSENTIAL

Besides making use of Lord Fairfax's library, John Marshall also had access to his father's collection of books. At a time when books were rare and valuable objects, Thomas Marshall's library included works by Livy, Horace, Pope, Dryden, Milton, and Shakespeare. Not only John, but all of his brothers and sisters proved to be exceptional students, thanks to their parents' efforts.

At the age of fourteen, Marshall was sent to a private academy run by the Reverend Archibald Campbell in Westmoreland County, where future politician and president James Monroe was among his classmates. After one year, Marshall returned home where he continued his studies in Latin, English history, and literature. His father then arranged for a minister, the Reverend James Thomson, to come and teach his children while serving as a pastor to the local church. Thomson tutored the Marshall children in return for his room and board. After a little over year, Thomson left the area. The young minister had succeeded at his teaching tasks, for John Marshall now could read and transcribe the writings of the classical writers Horace and Livy.

Young Marshall and Politics

Early on, it had been decided by Marshall's parents that their eldest son would be a lawyer. In fact, they were so certain of it that Thomas Marshall purchased a copy of the book *William Blackstone's Commentaries on the Laws of England*, which had recently been published in the colonies, for John to study. In addition, Thomas Marshall also guided his son in more practical matters such as local and Virginia politics, and by 1767, was serving as a member of the Virginia House of Burgesses.

On his visits home, Thomas Marshall would tell his family of the latest political goings on. He found an apt pupil in his eldest son when it came to talk of politics. Thomas Marshall was particularly vocal when it came to the topic of rights of the English colonists; he was extremely critical of British efforts to keep the increasingly unruly colonies under control through new tax laws. Thomas Marshall would later be a member of the Virginia convention that declared the colony's independence from Great Britain.

Revolutionary War Service and Early Legal Career

Like his father, John Marshall was dedicated to the cause of American liberty. As soon as hostilities broke out in 1775 between the colonists and the British, he joined a local Virginia regiment, the Culpepper Minutemen, fighting alongside his father, who was head of the regiment. A year later in 1776, Marshall joined the Continental army, where he served under his father's old classmate, George Washington. Marshall was involved in fighting in New Jersey, New York, and Pennsylvania and was also present during the brutal winter quartering at Valley Forge in 1777–1778.

Marshall eventually achieved the rank of captain and was mustered out of the army by 1781. He then turned his energies to studying the law. He attended law lectures given by George Wythe, an acclaimed Virginia law professor and classical scholar, at the College of William and Mary in Williamsburg, Virginia. Despite Marshall's sketchy law education, he was licensed to practice and admitted to the local bar the following summer. His natural eloquence, charismatic personality, and keen legal mind soon established him as one of the area's rising young attorneys.

Marshall returned to Fauquier County where he decided to enter politics. He was elected to the Virginia House of Delegates in 1782 and 1784. While attending sessions in Richmond, Virginia, Marshall also found time to establish a law practice in the city. During this period, he met and married Mary Ambler; the couple later took up residence in Richmond. Marshall served on the important Committee on the Courts of Justice, and at the age of twenty-seven was elected by the legislature to the governor's Council of State.

Still a young man, Marshall already began forming the basis for what would be a brilliant legal career. Given his father's tutelage and his association with George Washington and other colonial leaders during the Revolutionary War, Marshall was left with a passionate love of the newly formed American republic as well as a burgeoning distrust of the strident call of states' rights. These two beliefs would form the bedrock of Marshall's legal philosophy and the eventual shaping of the field of constitutional law in the United States.

A Rising Star

Even though Marshall was not in a position to be selected to attend the Constitutional Convention in Philadelphia in 1787, he was selected as a delegate to the Virginia convention responsible for ratifying or rejecting the newly framed United States Constitution that met in June of 1788. From its early beginnings, Marshall believed strongly in the new document. As a soldier in Washington's Continental army, Marshall had seen firsthand the problems with a loose confederation of states, each with its own agenda, as opposed to a strong national and united nation that worked to serve all. It was vital that the Constitution be ratified, Marshall believed, if the new United States of America was to survive as a country.

Federal Power Versus States' Rights

Working together with fellow Federalists James Madison and Edmund Randolph, Marshall argued for ratification of the proposed Constitution. Among his strongest opponents was Antifederalist Patrick Henry, who believed the proposed document dangerous and who supported instead strong state governments. In a number of speeches, Marshall stated that the Constitution was not only democratic but a well-crafted plan for a sound government that would be answerable to the people. Further, state governments were not in danger of losing their powers as Henry and other Antifederalists argued.

Marshall strongly believed in the power of a popular, elected government that consisted of both representative and balanced government. Still, he had his doubts as to whether or not men were capable of governing themselves in a judicious fashion. The basis of Marshall's commitment to ratification of the Constitution was grounded in the idea that the Constitution sought to establish a national government, rather than an alliance of states, like the earlier Articles of Confederation had mandated. Marshall's legislative experience had already shown him how irresponsible and selfish state powers could be over any number of matters.

Among Marshall's arguments at the convention was that the new American government would hold sovereign powers of two kinds: legal, as exemplified by a judicial branch, and political, which would be embodied by the legislative and executive branches. He was especially supportive of Article III, which established the judicial branch of the United States government. Ultimately, the convention approved the Constitution by a vote of eighty-nine to seventy-nine. Marshall would later align himself with the newly formed Federalist Party, which advocated a strong national government and business and commercial interests. He would find plenty of occasions to bump heads with his cousin Thomas Jefferson, who established the Democratic-Republican Party, which supported states' rights and was committed to the ideal notion of an agrarian society.

It is not surprising that John Marshall supported Article III of the Constitution. Under this provision, the Constitution established a judicial branch of the federal government that is made up of the Supreme Court of the United States and lower courts as created by Congress.

Marshall the Attorney

Meanwhile, Marshall's private law practice continued to flourish in Richmond as he rapidly made a name for himself as a shrewd and diligent attorney. In 1796, Marshall appeared before the fledgling United States Supreme Court in the case *Ware v. Hylton*, which argued the validity of a Virginia law that allowed for the confiscation of debts owed to British subjects. Marshall argued that the law was a legitimate right of the state. The Court ruled against him, but despite the defeat, Marshall's arguments garnered him increasing respect among state and national leaders who were impressed with his reasoning and commitment to the law.

On the National Stage

In 1795, President George Washington offered John Marshall the position of attorney general of the United States, but Marshall declined Washington's offer. Washington tried again in 1796, offering Marshall the post of minister to France. Again, Marshall respectfully declined the president's proposal. Finally, Marshall agreed to become a member of a commission appointed by President John Adams to represent the United States in France, along with Charles Cotesworth Pinckney and Elbridge Gerry. However, when the Americans arrived, their French hosts refused to conduct diplomatic business with them unless the Americans paid the French enormous bribes. In addition, the French delegation demanded a formal apology for comments made by President Adams about the French.

One of the most popular patriotic slogans in American history came about as a result of the XYZ Affair. In response to the French demands for bribes, the American delegation answered: "Not a sixpence." However, given the inflated rhetoric of the day, the quote became infinitely more resounding, "Millions for defense, sir, but not one cent for tribute."

In response, Marshall prepared a memorandum in which the Americans flatly refused to honor the French demands. The resulting incident became known as the XYZ Affair, one of the first scandals involving the new American government. When news broke of the scandal, anti-French opinion in the United States increased rapidly. Hostilities between the two countries further intensified after the French government expelled Marshall and Pinckney from France. In spite of his dismissal by the French government, Marshall's handling of the scandal made him a very popular figure with the American public.

A Supreme Court Appointment

In 1798, President Adams offered Marshall a Supreme Court appointment; Marshall refused the offer. However, the following year, he found himself running for a seat in the United States House of Representatives. Although his congressional district strongly supported his cousin Thomas Jefferson's Democratic-Republican Party, Marshall still won the election, in part because of his popularity and reputation as well as the strong support of the state's important political leaders such as Patrick Henry. As a result of his election to Congress, Marshall soon emerged as a leader for the Federalist Party. Adams again approached Marshall to serve as his secretary of war. Marshall declined, but in 1800, he finally accepted an appointment to serve as Adams's secretary of state.

Not more than eight months later, Marshall found himself as chief justice of the Supreme Court as a result of the passage of the Midnight Judges Act. In the wake of the presidential election of 1800, with Thomas Jefferson elected as the new president, the Federalists had been roundly defeated and were going to lose control of the executive and legislative branches of the government. In an attempt to stop the Democratic-Republicans from taking over the judicial branch, President Adams and the lame duck Congress passed the Midnight Judges Act. The act, among other things, reduced the number of justices from six to five; this effectively blocked any chance for Jefferson to appoint a new justice until two vacancies occurred. After offering the chief justice appointment to John Jay, who declined, Adams nominated Marshall, who accepted on the spot. Marshall was confirmed by the Senate on January 27, 1801, and received his commission on January 31, 1801.

Chief Justice Marshall

On March 5, 1801, John Marshall took his seat on the Supreme Court, and for the next three decades handed down a number of important decisions that have continued to be bedrock American law. At the time Marshall assumed his duties, the Court was in desperate need of unification and strengthening. This was due in part to the court having two chief justices in just eleven years. With Marshall's ascension to the bench, the Court would have a chief justice for thirty-four years, one of the longest tenures of any chief justice in Supreme Court history. Another problem was the lack of cohesive decisions by the court. Up until Marshall, the common practice was for each justice to deliver separate opinions on cases heard in front of the court. Marshall was able to persuade his colleagues to abandon this practice, and instead begin offering "an opinion of the Court," in which one decision was given. Accordingly, Marshall wrote a majority of these opinions during the next decade.

High-Profile Cases

In 1803, Marshall also gave the Court a needed victory that boosted its image and demonstrated the Court's strength as the arbiter and interpreter of American law with the landmark case *Marbury v. Madison*. The decision declared for the first time that an act of Congress was unconstitutional. The case resulted from a petition put forward to the court by a William Marbury, who had been appointed as a justice of the peace in the District of Columbia, who had not yet received his commission. Marbury petitioned the court to force the secretary of state, James Madison, to deliver his commission. The Court refused stating that the law upon which Marbury was basing his claims, the Judiciary Act of 1789, was unconstitutional.

There followed a number of other landmark decisions including *United States v. Peters* (1809) in which Marshall further solidified the power of the judicial branch, this time against the claims of a state, by establishing that the Supreme Court was the final interpreter of federal law.

Marshall also helped further the idea of corporate capitalism in the new nation with his opinion in *Fletcher v. Peck* in 1810, in which he stated that the contract clause of the Constitution prevented state legislatures from repealing land grants to private-interest groups. This was the first in a series of contract decisions made by the court that encouraged the growth of corporate capitalism. And although Marshall's decisions rarely ventured into the realm of civil rights, in his decision on the 1807 Aaron Burr treason case, Marshall stood on the side of political freedom when he argued for narrow definition of treason as well as requiring strict proof of such action in order for an individual to be convicted.

Marbury v. Madison not only marked the first time the Supreme Court declared an action as "unconstitutional," but also established the concept of judicial review. This meant that the judicial branch may oversee and nullify, or invalidate, the actions of another branch of government. This landmark decision helped to cement the "checks and balances" idea of American government, one of the most important legacies of the Founding Fathers.

During the period 1812 to 1824, Marshall continued to be an influential voice on the Court and personally wrote in some of the most important constitutional cases in American legal history. Among them was *McCulloch v. Maryland* (1819), in which Marshall ruled that states could not tax federal institutions. He also ruled that Congress had the authority to create the Second Bank of the United States, even though the authority to do this was not expressly stated in the Constitution. The formation of the bank was crucial to the securing of a national currency and the creation of a credit structure for interstate capitalism. Also, by ruling that Congress had the authority to go beyond enumerated powers through a broad interpretation of the "necessary and proper" clause, Marshall created the opportunity for federal branches of government to have "implied" national powers.

Later Life

Whenever possible, Marshall returned to Richmond where he and his wife had built a home. Sundays found him in attendance at St. John's Church in Church Hill. For approximately three months every year, Marshall returned to Washington, D.C., for the Supreme Court's annual term. He also found time to serve on the circuit court in Raleigh, North Carolina.

Marshall also was active in a number of other endeavors including serving in 1823 as the first president of the Richmond branch of the American Colonization Society, which was dedicated to resettling freed American slaves in Liberia, on the west coast of Africa. In 1828, he presided over a convention to promote internal improvements in Virginia, and in 1829, Marshall was a delegate to the Virginia state constitutional convention. Marshall also authored a five-volume biography of George Washington. With the death of his wife Mary on Christmas Day in 1831, Marshall began a slow decline. His health, which had not been good for several years, rapidly declined in 1835, and in June he journeyed to Philadelphia, Pennsylvania where he underwent surgery for the removal of kidney stones, a rigorous medical procedure for the time. Although he recovered, Marshall had lost his vigor for life. He died on July 6, 1835 and was buried next to his wife in Richmond, Virginia.

Legacy

It might be said that without John Marshall as chief justice, the American legal system would not exist as we know it today. In his role as chief justice and by the sheer force of his personality, Marshall raised the office of chief justice and the Supreme Court to a prominence and power it previously lacked. His landmark opinions established the foundation for constitutional law in the United States for decades to come. His decisions are still studied and debated in law schools today and provide some of the earliest introductions to American legal history in classrooms across the country. Despite the demise of the Federalist Party, Marshall continued to espouse the philosophy of Federalism with its strong emphasis on a central government during his tenure as chief justice. He served as chief justice through all or part of six presidential administrations, including those of John Adams, Thomas Jefferson, James Madison, James Monroe, John Quincy Adams, and Andrew Jackson. During his tenure as chief justice, Marshall participated in more than 1,000 decisions, writing 519 of the opinions himself, and established the Supreme Court as the final authority on matters of constitutional law.

It is interesting to note that in his later years, Marshall was increasingly troubled by what he perceived to be a decline in the quality of American leaders. He saw the passing of the great statesmen from the period of the American Revolution and the Constitutional Convention to be replaced by what he believed to be superficial party politicians. Dismayed by the election of Andrew Jackson in 1828, Marshall even advocated restricting the power of the presidency with limits of only term and even replacing popular elections by selection of the president by lot in the Senate.

Four law schools today bear John Marshall's name: The Marshall-Wythe School of Law (now William and Mary Law School at the College of William and Mary in Williamsburg, Virginia); The Cleveland-Marshall College of Law in Cleveland, Ohio; John Marshall Law School in Atlanta, Georgia; and The John Marshall Law School in Chicago, Illinois.

John Marshall died believing that the Constitution and the republic for which he had labored were gone; fortunately history and time appear to have proved him wrong. This much is certain: Without John Marshall, the United States may have faced much rockier beginnings, faltered through critical legal issues, and struggled increasingly with the tensions between popular democracy and government. That the nation did not is due in no small measure to John Marshall's efforts and his belief in the greatness of his country. His reputation as the "great chief justice" seems secure.

CHAPTER 25

James Monroe

He was not considered to be the intellectual equal of fellow Virginians Thomas Jefferson or James Madison. He lacked the oratory skills of Patrick Henry. He was cautious in his thoughts and actions. Yet for all his seeming lack of traits that distinguished other members of the "Virginia Dynasty," James Monroe still carved out an illustrious career as soldier, statesman, politician, and president. Monroe was also the last Founding Father, the last of the Virginia dynasty, and the last of the Revolutionary War generation to become president of the United States.

Early Life and Education

Unlike many of the Founding Fathers, little is known of the early life of James Monroe. He was born on April 28, 1758, in a wooded area of Westmoreland County, Virginia. His father, Spence Monroe, was known as a moderately prosperous planter with land holdings of about 500 acres, and was known to be handy as a carpenter. His mother, Elizabeth Jones Monroe, married Spence Monroe in 1752; the couple would eventually have five children, four of whom lived to adulthood. James was their first child.

In 1774, Monroe's father died. Monroe, his sister, and two younger brothers were then sent to live with a maternal uncle, Joseph Jones, who emerged as a prominent figure in the young Monroe's life. Jones was a member of the colonial Virginia House of Burgesses and later a member of the Continental Congress. It was Jones who introduced James to the world of politics and who later encouraged his nephew to try politics on his own.

Monroe's education is equally as sketchy. At the age of eleven, Monroe was sent to the Reverend Archibald Campbell's school, the Campbelltown Academy, where he excelled in his studies, especially Latin and mathematics. John Marshall, later chief justice of the United States, was among his classmates. In 1774, at the age of sixteen, Monroe attended the College of William and Mary in Williamsburg, Virginia to purse a classical education and to study law under the illustrious George Wythe, one of the most celebrated lawyers in the colonies. Monroe enjoyed being in Williamsburg, which was at the time the capital of colonial Virginia. For Monroe, it proved to be an exciting time. With tensions rising between the colonists and the British Crown, there was plenty to see and do in the city. Monroe, like many others, was caught up in the patriotic fervor.

James Monroe came to college already distrustful of the English Crown. Both his father and grandfather had participated in the Westmoreland Resolves, also known as the Stamp Act Resolution, in 1765. The Resolves advocated the colonies to break away from England. For Monroe, his family's political activities introduced him to the ways of civil disobedience.

In 1775, the royal governor, fearing for his and his family's life, fled the capital. In June 1775, spurred on by the battles of Concord and Lexington, Monroe and some of his fellow classmates helped loot the arsenal at the Governor's Palace, making off with 200 muskets and 300 swords, which they promptly gave to the Williamsburg militia. In 1776, after being in school for barely two years, Monroe, like many of his classmates, left school to join ranks with the American patriots to fight against the British.

Military Experience

In the spring of 1776, Monroe enlisted in the Third Virginia Regiment as a lieutenant. After a few months of training in Virginia, the Third Infantry moved to New York to join American forces under General George Washington, then stationed near Manhattan. Monroe saw plenty of fighting, participating in the battles of Harlem Heights and White Plains, and was part of the retreating forces that left New Jersey for Pennsylvania.

It was at the Battle of Trenton that Monroe earned a reputation for bravery and courage under fire. On a snowy Christmas night in 1776, Washington and his army crossed the frozen Delaware River for a surprise attack on the British at dawn. Leading the way with Washington was the Third Infantry of Virginia and James Monroe. As the Americans approached the enemy camp, Hessian soldiers saw them and attempted to turn the American soldiers back. With Monroe leading his soldiers in a cavalry charge, the Americans successfully captured Trenton and Monroe and his men successfully captured an enemy cannon. The battle was a critical victory for the American patriots and inspired one of the most famous historical paintings, *Washington Crossing the Delaware*, in which Monroe is depicted holding the American flag.

As a result of his bravery, Monroe was promoted to the rank of captain. He participated in a number of other crucial battles during the war including the Battles of Brandywine, Germantown, and Monmouth. He was promoted once again, to the rank of major and served as an aide to General William Alexander.

In the end, Monroe preferred to be on the front lines rather than working as a staff aide. In 1779, he resigned his commission in the Continental army and returned to Virginia, where he was appointed colonel in the Virginia service. Monroe also had hopes of raising his own regiment and then returning to the war. However, unable to recruit any soldiers, Monroe was left at odds. It was during this period that Monroe made the acquaintance of the then-governor of Virginia, Thomas Jefferson. The meeting was a turning point for Monroe and the beginning of a lifelong friendship with Jefferson, who was fifteen years older. Jefferson found Monroe to be a thoughtful and inquisitive man who was drawn to many of the same interests as Jefferson himself, including politics. Jefferson also realized that Monroe possessed a deep love for his country and a willingness to be of service to the new nation. In 1780, Jefferson sent Monroe to North Carolina to report on troop movements of the British army.

FACT

Monroe's actions at the Battle of Trenton almost cost him his life. Leading his troops into battle, Monroe was shot through the shoulder. Had he not received immediate medical attention, he most likely would have bled to death. Recovery from the wound took nearly a month.

Law and Politics

After the war, Monroe decided to resume his law studies, this time with Thomas Jefferson acting as his mentor. Politics also beckoned the young Monroe and in 1782, the same year Monroe was admitted to the Virginia bar, he was elected to the Virginia Assembly, representing King George County, where he also had begun to practice law. Monroe's political ascent was quick; he was chosen to serve on the Council of State, which advised the governor, and his talents were quickly noted by the more established political leaders in Virginia. The following year, Monroe was selected as part of the Virginia delegation to the Continental Congress in New York City, along with his mentor and friend Thomas Jefferson. Jefferson's stay was short; he left in July 1784 for Paris where he was to serve as the American minister to France. He left behind for his young friend a collection of books and his French cook. But Jefferson's most prized gift to Monroe was a letter of introduction to another Virginia politician, James Madison. As a delegate, Monroe was instrumental in issues such as expanding the power of Congress, organizing some type of government structure for the newly expanded western frontier country, and protecting American navigation rights on the Mississippi River.

Marriage and Family

While in New York, Monroe also found time to meet and court the young Elizabeth Kortright, the daughter of a prominent merchant who had lost much of his wealth during the Revolution. On February 16, 1786, the couple wed in New York City. After a brief honeymoon on Long Island, the Monroes returned to New York, where they lived with the Kortwrights until the congressional session adjourned. Monroe and his new wife then left New York to move to Fredericksburg, Virginia, where he opened a law office. The couple would eventually have three children: two daughters and a son.

The youngest child of James and Elizabeth Monroe, Maria Hester Monroe, married her second cousin, Samuel L. Gouverneur on March 8, 1820. Her wedding ceremony was the very first ever performed in the White House.

As a successful lawyer and politician, James Monroe was also able to fulfill a lifelong dream of owning a large plantation and becoming a landowner. For twenty-four years Monroe and his family lived at Highland, an Albemarle County plantation not far from his friend Thomas Jefferson's Monticello. Monroe envisioned his home to be a working farm and he experimented with planting a number of different crops such as timber, tobacco, and grain. He even tried to cultivate grapes for wine, but found the endeavor costly and frustrating.

Despite his efforts, Monroe's plantation was never very profitable. Even though he owned land and slaves and even speculated in land dealings, his political career kept him away from Highland and he was unable to oversee the daily running of the plantation. This meant that his slaves were often treated harshly and the plantation struggled to be productive. It did not help that Monroe enjoyed a lavish lifestyle, which often meant he had to sell off land in order to pay his debts.

The Politics of Nation Building

In 1788, Monroe was elected as a delegate to the Virginia convention called to ratify the new American Constitution. During the convention, Monroe displayed his independent streak when he voted against ratifying the Constitution, despite the fact that he was a strong political ally of James Madison who is considered one of the authors of the document. Monroe believed that a strong bill of rights needed to be added that guaranteed protection for the nation's citizens. He also opposed the direct election of senators and the president.

Despite his opposition to the Constitution, Monroe remained good friends with James Madison and with Thomas Jefferson for the rest of his life. Together the three would continue to support Federalist policies, particularly those supported by John Adams and Alexander Hamilton.

Even as the Virginia delegation approved the Constitution, Monroe did not protest, but pledged to do his best in helping the new government. The following year after the convention in 1790, Monroe challenged James Madison for a seat in the House of Representatives but lost the election by 300 votes. Instead, Monroe found himself appointed to a seat in the Senate in 1790.

Minister to France and Britain

Beginning in 1794, Monroe undertook a series of important government positions that helped the new United States abroad. That year, President Washington appointed Monroe as minister to France; Monroe was then dispatched to Paris. For the next two years, Monroe found himself in the middle of a highly charged atmosphere as the French Revolution broke out.

Monroe's first responsibility during the crisis was to maintain the American policy of strict neutrality toward Britain and France, who historically were enemies.

When Thomas Paine, the author of *Common Sense* and *The Crisis*, was imprisoned for his refusal to support the execution of the French King Louis XVI, Monroe won his release. Monroe also offered Paine a place to live and for a time Paine lived with Monroe and his family at the American minister's residence in Paris.

Monroe's task was made even harder when the French learned that the United States had signed a new treaty—the Jay Treaty—with Great Britain. When asked by the French government to provide details of the treaty, Monroe was unwilling to do so, stating that the treaty in no way affected relations between the Americans and the French. The relations between the two countries deteriorated to such a degree that Monroe was called back to America where he was heavily criticized by the Federalists for the diplomatic crisis with France.

On Saturday April 30, 1803, Robert Livingston, James Monroe, and Barbé Marbois signed an agreement that became known as the Louisiana Purchase. The agreement was for the biggest real estate deal in American history, with the United States purchasing 828,000 square miles of Louisiana territory for 60 million Francs (approximately $15 million). The purchase doubled the size of the existing United States. Eventually fourteen states would be carved out of the Louisiana Territory.

Monroe returned to Virginia to practice law and attend to his plantations. In 1799, he was called back into politics again when he was elected governor. During his time in office, Monroe pushed for public education as well as campaigning on behalf of his friend Thomas Jefferson, who was seeking the presidency. After winning the election of 1800, Jefferson did not forget his friend. In 1803, Monroe traveled overseas to Paris again, this time as a special envoy to help negotiate terms for the Louisiana Purchase.

After returning from France, Monroe was appointed as the American minister to Great Britain from 1803 to 1807; for a brief time in 1805, Monroe also worked as a special envoy to Spain.

Monroe's time in Great Britain was almost as contentious as his time in Paris. One of the biggest issues between the two countries was the practice of impressments. Monroe tried to negotiate a treaty in which the British would honor a ban on the practice.

What were impressments?
Impressments were the British practice of seizing seamen on their own merchant ships and from other countries and forcing them to serve in the British navy. After the American Revolution, the British navy took up the practice of stopping American ships and impressing American sailors into the British navy. This was one of many other actions that eventually led to the War of 1812.

Monroe returned to the United States in 1808 and was soon put on the ticket by Republicans to oppose his friend James Madison for the Democratic-Republican presidential nomination. Although Monroe allowed himself to be nominated, he never considered his challenge to Madison seriously; Madison carried the election. Monroe returned to the political arena again in January 1811, when he was elected to another term as governor of Virginia. However his term was short-lived, for his old friend President Madison appointed him as his secretary of state.

Secretary of State, Secretary of War, and Presidency

Monroe's biggest challenge again was negotiating the tricky labyrinth of world affairs, particularly American relations with Britain and France. The two European powers were once more at war with each other; the hostilities were beginning to impact American shipping and trade. It was Monroe's duty to convince the two countries to recognize and respect American commercial interests, as the United States was a neutral country. Monroe was particularly interested in maintaining good relations with the British, even as they continued with their practice of seizing American sailors and forcing them to serve in the British navy.

The United States declared war on Britain in June 1812; by December Madison's secretary of war resigned, and Monroe took over the office on a temporary basis, serving from December 1812 to February 1813, and again from August 1814 until March 1815. In August 1814, when British troops landed at the Potomac River, Monroe led a scouting party to report on their advance and then sent word to Madison warning that the British were marching toward Washington, D.C. With the British bearing down on the capital, Monroe stayed in the city to help citizens evacuate. By the time the war ended, James Monroe would become the first and only person to serve in two cabinet positions at the same time: secretary of state and secretary of war.

"The Era of Good Feelings"

Monroe's popularity rose after the war, due to his service in Madison's cabinet and his actions during the War of 1812. By 1816, Monroe was so well-positioned to win the nomination for the Democratic-Republican Party that he did and then went on to win the presidency, becoming the fifth president of the United States. He would also be the third president in a row and the last hailing from the state of Virginia, following the presidencies of his friends Thomas Jefferson and James Madison.

The period under which Monroe governed as president is known as "The Era of Good Feelings," so-called because it was a time in which all things seemed to be well. There was no threat of war and no economic crisis. Relations with other nations were peaceful and the United States was enjoying a period of great economic prosperity. To build trust in the country, Monroe made two national tours where he was greeted by cheering throngs of people. His popularity was so great he easily won a second term as president in 1816.

Monroe was known as a mean of conservative bearing and this also was reflected in his style of dress. He still favored the old style knee breeches, white stockings, and buckled shoes, despite the changing fashion of men wearing long pants, and powdered his hair in the style of eighteenth-century gentlemen. His White House also exhibited a conservative taste, with the rooms furnished with the elegant furniture brought back from his time in Europe.

Monroe Doctrine

Of all Monroe's contributions to his nation, by far the most enduring has been the legacy of the Monroe Doctrine. In a speech made to Congress on December 2, 1823, Monroe announced that the Americas, North and South, should be free from future European colonization and free from European interference in political affairs. Monroe also stated that it was the intention of the United States to remain neutral in European affairs both in peacetime and war. Further, any interference on the part of any European power with countries in North or South America would be construed as hostile acts toward the United States. Monroe's speech effectively set into motion the isolationism that America practiced well into the twentieth century.

During his last term in office, Monroe also made other important foreign policy decisions that benefited the United States, including the acquisition of Florida from Spain and the removal of defense forces along the Canadian border, making it one of the few undefended borders in the world. Also by recognizing the new governments formed in many Latin American countries, Monroe effectively set in place the hope of good relations with Latin America.

Later Life

After his term of office ended, Monroe retired once again to Virginia and settled on Monroe Hill, which had served as the family farm. Monroe had sold the property in 1817 to the University of Virginia, but the institution allowed Monroe to continue living there. He would go on to serve on the Board of Visitors with Thomas Jefferson and James Madison.

Monroe, like many of the Founding Fathers suffered from financial insecurity and was deeply in debt. Not only did he have to sell Monroe Hill, but also Highland Plantation, now called Ash Lawn-Highland. The property is owned today by Monroe's alma mater, the College of William and Mary, which has opened it to the public.

Monroe and his wife lived in Oak Hill, Virginia, until Elizabeth's death on September 23, 1830. Monroe moved to New York City to live with his daughter and on July 4, 1831 he died from heart failure and tuberculosis. He was the third president to die on July 4, five years after the deaths of John Adams and Thomas Jefferson. He was originally buried in New York City's Marble Cemetery, but in 1858 his body was taken back to his beloved Virginia where he was re-interred in the President's Circle at Hollywood Cemetery in Richmond.

Legacy

It was said of James Monroe that he was so honest that if you turned his soul inside out, you would not find a spot on it. Monroe's steadfast dedication to his country and his thoughtful manner helped mold the young United States into a nation that steered clear of European entanglements and instead began concentrating on its own economic and geographic growth. His diplomatic efforts as a cabinet member and later as president helped to strengthen that office as well as demonstrating the power of the Oval Office in domestic affairs.

Monroe may not have commanded the larger-than-life status of other members of the Virginia Dynasty. He was not a natural leader like Washington, nor was he possessed of the Renaissance-like man qualities that marked Jefferson. Monroe's interest—his passion—was politics. He was possessed of a keen and deliberate mind that allowed him to look at problems from all sides, inviting solutions from all who debated with him. His greatest achievement lay in those abilities that allowed him to guide a still-young nation through a challenging time in relative peace and harmony.

CHAPTER 26

The Legacy of the Founding Fathers

The men who undertook the revolution against Great Britain were unusually prudent and cautious. In their minds, they had not rebelled for "light and transient causes." Rather, important ideas about government, power, and human nature supported their decision to sever relations with the British Empire and assert their identity as an independent people destined to forge an independent nation.

The Ideology of Revolution

Central to the Founding Fathers' ideology of revolution was a new concept of government. Believing that human beings were fallible, selfish, and corrupt, the Founding Fathers thought that government was necessary to protect individuals from the evil inherent in human nature. Corruptible people also ran the government, and so it, too, required safeguards against the abuse of power.

For most Americans, the English system of constitutional government provided the best means ever devised to maintain the ordered liberty they cherished. By distributing power among the three components of society—the monarchy, the aristocracy, and the commons—the English political system ensured that no individual or group could exercise unrestrained authority. Yet by the 1760s, many Americans were becoming convinced that the king and his ministers were corrupt, and had come to wield tyrannical power over government and society. To counter this circumstance, the Founding Fathers sought to create a new form of government that would not itself become a threat to liberty. By 1776, the colonists' understanding of this tyrannical British conspiracy against liberty was complete. They responded with unrestrained enthusiasm to the passionate appeal of Thomas Paine's *Common Sense* to take their stand:

> *Every spot of the old world is overrun with oppression. Freedom hath been hunted round the globe. Asia and Africa have long expelled her. Europe regards her like a stranger, and England hath given her warning to depart. O! receive the fugitive, and prepare in time an asylum for mankind.*

Paine helped to convince the colonists that they were fighting not only in defense of their own rights, but that they were also engaged in a struggle to save liberty itself.

The Founding Fathers in Today's Political Landscape

It is always tempting to speculate about the reactions of the Founding Fathers to the outcome of their aspirations and labors. What would they think of modern America? Three aspects of contemporary American life would almost certainly draw their immediate attention and concern. The first is the prominence of war and the military. The second is the presence of the national government in the affairs of towns, cities, states, and the lives of individual citizens. The third is the number of Americans who are only loosely attached to groups of any kind, and who eschew the values of family, kinship, and community, who assert their individuality and embrace the cash nexus to the virtual exclusion of all other associations.

A cash nexus refers to the idea that in a capitalist society all values are reduced to the sum of their cash value.

The members of the founding generation who might steal back from beyond the grave to survey the results of their handiwork would find much to disappoint, confuse, anger, and frighten them. They had, for example, feared the existence and influence of large standing (i.e. permanent) armies on the life of the nation. Armies were expensive and dangerous. What doubtless would astonish them the most is that their precious republic had become an imperial power far greater than Great Britain, against which they had rebelled in the eighteenth century. The Founding Fathers would doubtless swoon when they learned that between 1914 and 2011, the United States had participated in a seemingly endless series of wars waged in the most remote parts of the globe.

The Founding Fathers and Today's World

Although the original intentions of the Founding Fathers continue to excite disagreement and debate, it seems safe to say that they designed the Constitution of the United States for a people more interested in governing itself than in policing the rest of the world. At the time of its birth, the new nation had the priceless advantage of two great oceans to separate it from the turbulence of Europe and Asia. The Founding Fathers relied on that advantage to draft the most non-military constitution in history. A permanent state of war was the last thing that they wanted. They would have regarded it as a serious threat to both the stability and the liberty of the United States. And though they protected the citizens' right to bear arms, the Founding Fathers would have been appalled to learn that in the United States an epidemic of violence had prompted civilians to arm themselves for their own protection.

Any of the Founding Fathers who returned to observe the contemporary United States would also be staggered by the extent of the interference from the national government in the everyday lives of its citizens. They shared an abiding distrust and fear of power and a hatred of tyranny, which, in their time, they identified with the government of George III as well as with the despotic regimes of France, Prussia, and Russia.

Thus, it would dismay the Founding Fathers to discover that the republic they had crafted between 1775 and 1791 had become the largest bureaucratic state in the world. They would not be much comforted that it is also the most benign and most solicitous bureaucracy in history. They would see that American citizens, who enjoy the gifts of life, health, education, and welfare that the bureaucracy provides, also despise it—or at least say that they do. As a result, each incoming president dutifully vows to reduce its size and the unfathomable debt that it generates. These promises notwithstanding, each president also departs office having increased the size of the federal bureaucracy, the national debt, and the budget deficit.

The Founding Fathers would no doubt be stunned and perhaps even outraged by the suffocating and labyrinthine complexity of a federal bureaucracy that rarely hesitates to intrude into the most intimate aspects of life. They had witnessed such oppression from afar, and, in framing a new government, had sought to avoid it at all costs. They understood where such political oppression invariably led. To a man, the Founding Fathers believed that political centralization ended with the rise of selfishness, corruption, and irresponsibility in public life.

Although they hailed liberty as among the greatest human attributes, the Founding Fathers found it inconceivable that individuals be granted boundless freedom simply for the indulgence and satisfaction of private whims and desires. They knew the calamity that the autonomous self could release on the rest of humanity when liberated from a sense of responsibility to fellow human beings. There was no force on earth powerful enough to restrain the destructive passions of such individuals.

Eminently political men, the Founding Fathers nonetheless mistrusted politics, political ambition, and power. Washington, Jefferson, Adams, Hamilton, Madison, Henry, and their contemporaries did not intend the political, social, and economic arrangements that they fashioned to rob their contemporaries or their descendants of the most precious of human endowments: the cultivated mind and the moral imagination. They understood that liberty, although the natural right of all men, could yet be lost through neglect and folly. They consoled themselves with the belief that societies and civilizations were not governed by inexorable, unalterable laws against which the human mind and moral imagination were impotent. All social, political, and economic problems, however intractable, were at least in theory subject to human correction.

It was just such a revolution of ideas that prompted Americans of the eighteenth century to reject British rule and create an independent nation. John Adams recognized as much when he wrote during the last years of his life that "the Revolution was effected before the war commenced. The Revolution was in the minds and hearts of the people." Adams, of course, exaggerated. Few Americans were willing to consider complete independence from Great Britain until after the fighting had begun. But Adams was certainly correct to argue that even before 1775, a fundamental transformation had already occurred in the way in which Americans viewed the world and themselves, prompting them to take up arms in defense of the liberty that was their birthright.

APPENDIX A

Historic Sites of the Founding Fathers

John Adams: Adams Historical Park

135 Adams Street
Quincy, MA 02169
www.nps.gov/adam/index.htm

John Dickinson: Poplar Hall Plantation

340 Kitts Hummock Road
Dover, DE 19901
http://history.delaware.gov/museums/jdp/jdp_main.shtml

Benjamin Franklin House

36 Craven Street
London WC2N 5NF
www.benjaminfranklinhouse.org

Alexander Hamilton: Hamilton Grange

St. Nicholas Park
New York, NY 10005
www.nps.gov/hagr/index.htm

Benjamin Harrison: Berkeley Plantation

12602 Harrison Landing Road
Charles City, Virginia 23030
Charles City, VA 23030
www.berkeleyplantation.com

Patrick Henry: Red Hill

1250 Red Hill Rd
Brookneal, VA 24528-3302
www.redhill.org

Patrick Henry: Scotchtown

16120 Chiswell Lane
Beaverdam, VA 23015
www.apva.org/scotchtown

John Jay Homestead

400 Jay Street
Katonah, NY 10536
www.johnjayhomestead.org

Thomas Jefferson: Monticello

931 Thomas Jefferson Parkway
Charlottesville, VA 22902
www.monticello.org

Rufus King Park

Fl 7, 150-03 Jamaica Ave
Jamaica, NY 11432-6101
www.nycgovparks.org/parks/Q023

Lee Family of Virginia: Stratford Hall

483 Great House Road
Stratford, VA 22558
www.stratfordhall.org

Francis Lee House

52 Pleasant Street
Vincentown, NJ 08088
www.historicsouthamptonnj.org/html/francis_lee_house.html

James Madison: Montpelier

11407 Constitution Highway
Montpelier Station, VA 22957
www.montpelier.org

John Marshall House

818 East Marshall Street
Richmond, VA 23219
www.preservationvirginia.org/marshall/house

James Monroe: Ash Lawn–Highland

1000 James Monroe Parkway
Charlottesville, VA 22902
www.ashlawnhighland.org

James Monroe Museum and Memorial Library

908 Charles Street
Fredericksburg, VA 22401-5801
www.umw.edu/jamesmonroemuseum

Governeur Morris Museum

30 Church Street
Governeur, NY 13642
www.gouverneurmuseum.org

Charles Cotesworth Pinckney National Historic Site

1254 Long Point Road
Mount Pleasant, SC 29466
www.nps.gov/chpi/index.htm

George Washington: Mount Vernon

3200 Mount Vernon Memorial Highway
Mount Vernon, VA 22309
www.mountvernon.org

Independence Hall National Historical Park

143 S. Third Street
Philadelphia, PA 19106
www.nps.gov/inde/index.htm

APPENDIX B

Roll Call of the Founding Fathers

The Signers of the Declaration of Independence

Massachusetts

John Hancock
Samuel Adams
John Adams
Robert Treat Paine
Elbridge Gerry

New Hampshire

Josiah Bartlett
William Whipple
Matthew Thornton

Rhode Island

Stephen Hopkins
William Ellery

Connecticut

Roger Sherman
Samuel Huntington
William Williams
Oliver Wolcott

New York

William Floyd
Philip Livingston
Francis Lewis
Lewis Morris

New Jersey

Richard Stockton
John Witherspoon
Francis Hopkinson
John Hart
Abraham Clark

Pennsylvania

Robert Morris
Benjamin Rush
Benjamin Franklin
John Morton
George Clymer
James Smith
George Taylor
James Wilson
George Ross

Delaware

Caesar Rodney
George Read
Thomas M'Kean

Maryland

Samuel Chase
William Paca
Thomas Stone
Charles Carrol

Virginia

George Wythe
Richard Henry Lee
Thomas Jefferson
Benjamin Harrison
Thomas Nelson Jr.
Francis Lightfoot Lee
Carter Braxton

North Carolina

William Hooper
Joseph Hewes
John Penn

South Carolina

Edward Rutledge
Thomas Heyward Jr.
Thomas Lynch, Jr.
Arthur Middleton

Georgia

Button Gwinnett
Lyman Hall
George Walton

The Signers of the Articles of Confederation

New Hampshire

Josiah Bartlett
John Wentworth Jr.

Massachusetts

John Hancock
Samuel Adams
Elbridge Gerry
Francis Dana
James Lovell
Samuel Holten

Rhode Island

William Ellery
Henry Marchant
John Collins

Connecticut

Roger Sherman
Samuel Huntington
Oliver Wolcott
Titus Hosmer
Andrew Adams

New York

James Duane
Francis Lewis
William Duer
Gouverneur Morris

New Jersey

John Witherspoon
Nathaniel Scudder

Pennsylvania

Robert Morris
Daniel Roberdeau
Jonathan Bayard Smith
William Clingan
Joseph Reed

Delaware

Thomas McKean
John Dickinson
Nicholas Van Dyke

Maryland

John Hanson
Daniel Carroll

Virginia

Richard Henry Lee
John Banister
Thomas Adams
John Harvie
Francis Lightfoot Lee

North Carolina

John Penn
Cornelius Harnett
John Williams

South Carolina

Henry Laurens
William Henry Drayton
John Mathews
Richard Hutson
Thomas Heyward Jr.

Georgia

John Walton
Edward Telfair
Edward Langworthy

The Signers of the U. S. Constitution

New Hampshire

John Langdon
Nicholas Gilman

Massachusetts

Rufus King
Nathaniel Gorham

Connecticut

Roger Sherman
William Samuel Johnson

New York

Alexander Hamilton

New Jersey

William Livingston
David Brearley
William Paterson
Jonathan Dayton

Pennsylvania

Benjamin Franklin
Thomas Mifflin
Robert Morris
George Clymer
Thomas Fitzsimons
Jared Ingersoll
Gouverneur Morris
James Wilson

Delaware

George Read
Gunning Bedford Jr.
John Dickinson
Richard Bassett
Jacob Broom

Maryland

James McHenry
Daniel Carroll
Dan of St. Thomas Jenifer

Virginia

John Blair
James Madison Jr.
George Washington

North Carolina

William Blount
Richard Dobbs Spaight
Hugh Williamson

South Carolina

John Rutledge
Charles Cotesworth Pinckney
Charles Pinckney
Pierce Butler

Georgia

William Few
Abraham Baldwin

Other Founding Fathers

Samuel Adams
Patrick Henry
John Jay
Robert Livingston
Thomas Paine
Edmund Randolph
Charles Thomson

APPENDIX C

Bibliography

Adams, Gretchen A. *"Deeds of Desperate Valor": The First Rhode Island Regiment. http://revolution.h-net.msu.edu/essays/adams2.html*

Appleby, Joyce. *Thomas Jefferson*. New York: Times Books, 2003.

Bailyn, Bernard. *To Begin the World Anew. The Genius and Ambiguities of the American Founders*. New York: Alfred A. Knopf, 2003.

Beeman, Richard R. *Patrick Henry: A Biography*. New York: McGraw-Hill, 1974.

Bernstein, Richard B. *Are We to Be a Nation? The Making of the Constitution*. Cambridge, MA.: Harvard University Press, 1987.

______. *The Founding Fathers Reconsidered*. New York: Oxford University Press, 2009.

Bradford, M.E. *Founding Fathers: Brief Lives of the Framers of the United States Constitution*. University Press of Kansas, 1994.

Bramen, Lisa. "Swilling the Planters with Bumbo: When Booze Bought Elections," Smithsonian.com, October 20, 2010. *http://blogs.smithsonianmag.com/food/2010/10/swilling-the-planters-with-bumbo-when-booze-bought-elections/*

Brodsky, Alyn. *Benjamin Rush: Patriot and Physician*. New York: Truman Talley Books/St. Martin's Press, 2004.

Brookhiser, Richard. *Gentleman Revolutionary. Gouverneur Morris-The Rake Who Wrote the Constitution*. New York: Free Press, 2003.

Brookhiser, Richard. *What Would the Founding Fathers Do? Our Questions, Their Answers*. New York: Basic Books, 2006.

Brown, Abram English. *John Hancock, His Book*. Boston: Lee and Shepard Publishers, 1898.

Brown, Richard D. "The Founding Fathers of 1776 and 1787: A Collective View," *William and Mary Quarterly*, 3rd Ser., Vol. 33, No. 3 (Jul., 1976), pp. 465–480.

Burns, James McGregor and Dunn, Susan. *George Washington*. New York: Times Books, Henry Holt and Company, 2004.

Chernow, Ron. *Alexander Hamilton*. New York: Penguin Books, 2004.

Crawford, Alan Pell. *Twilight at Monticello: The Final Years of Thomas Jefferson*. New York: Random House, 2008

Ellis, Joseph J. *Founding Brothers: The Revolutionary Generation*. New York: Alfred A. Knopf, 2000.

______. *American Sphinx: The Character of Thomas Jefferson*. New York: Vintage Books. 1998.

______. *American Creation. Triumphs and Tragedies at the Founding of the Republic*. New York: Alfred A. Knopf, 2007.

Finkelstein, Robert Z. *Merchant, Revolutionary, and Statesman: A Re-Appraisal of John Hancock, 1737–1793*. Ph.D. dissertation, University of Massachusetts Amherst, 1981.

Givens, Ron. "Jefferson Tribute to Independence Refusenik Found." *American History* April 2010, p. 9.

Goodrich, Rev. Charles A. *Lives of the Signers to the Declaration of Independence*. New York: William Reed & Co., 1856.

Hale, Mary Ann B. *John Adams and Alexander Hamilton: A Clash of Styles*. M.A. Thesis, University of Missouri, Kansas City, 2003.

Jacobson, David L. *John Dickinson and the Revolution in Pennsylvania, 1764–1776*. Berkeley: University of California Press, 1965.

Jones, Sarah L., *Francis Lightfoot Lee: Forgotten Revolutionary*. Yale University, Class of 2006. *www.menokin.org/pdf/history/FLL Intro.pdf*

King Manor Museum *www.kingmanor.org*

King, Charles R., ed. *The Life and Correspondence of Rufus King*, Vol. I: 1755–1794. New York: G.P. Putnam's Sons, 1894.

McCullough, David. *John Adams*. New York: Simon and Schuster, 2001.

McDonald, Forrest. *The Presidency of Thomas Jefferson*. Lawrence: University Press of Kansas, 1976.

McGaughy, J. Kent. *A Faction of One: Richard Henry Lee of Virginia*. Ph.D. Dissertation, University of Houston, 1997.

Mayer, Henry. *Son of Thunder: Patrick Henry and the American Republic*. New York: Grove Press, 2001.

The Menokin Foundation *www.menokin.org/history.htm*

Messett, Kevin. *Robert Morris http://pabook.libraries.psu.edu/palitmap/bios/Morris_Robert.html*

Morris, Richard B. *Seven Who Shaped Our Destiny: The Founding Fathers as Revolutionaries*. New York: Harper & Row, 1973.

Robert Morris: America's Founding Capitalist *www.npr.org/2010/12/20/132051519/-robert-morris-america-s-founding-capitalist*

Murphy, Hazel Veronica, "Charles Cotesworth Pinckney: A Biography." MA Thesis, University of Chicago, 1928.

Nuxoll, Elizabeth M. *The Bank of North America and Robert Morris's Management of the Nation's First Fiscal Crisis*, Papers of Robert Morris, Queens College. *www.h-net.org/~business/bhcweb/publications/BEHprint/v013/p0159-p0170.pdf*

Peters, William. *A More Perfect Union. The Making of the United States Constitution*. New York: Crown Publishers, Inc., 1987.

Proctor, Donald J. "John Hancock: New Soundings on an Old Barrel," *Journal of American History*, Vol. 64 No. 3 (December 1977): 652–677.

Rakove, Jack. "The patriot who refused to sign the declaration of independence: John Dickinson believed it was foolhardy to brave the storm of war in a skiff made of paper." *American History* August 2010, pp. 58+.

Rush, Benjamin. *The Autobiography of Benjamin Rush: His "Travels Through Life" Together with his Commonplace Book for 1789–1813*, New York: Greenwood Press, 1970.

Selesky, Harold E., ed. *Encyclopedia of the American Revolution: Library of Military History*. Detroit: Charles Scribner's Sons, 2006.

Simon, James F. *What Kind of Nation: Thomas Jefferson, John Marshall, and the Epic Struggle to Create a United States*. New York: Simon & Schuster, 2002.

Smith, Jean Edward, *John Marshall: Definer Of A Nation*. New York: Henry Holt and Company, 1996.

Stille, Charles J. *The Life and Times of John Dickinson*. Philadelphia: Historical Society of Pennsylvania, 1891.

Stratford Hall *www.stratfordhall.org*

"Thomas Paine." *Encyclopedia of the American Revolution: Library of Military History*, Harold E. Selesky. Detroit: Charles Scribner's Sons, 2006. *Gale Biography In Context*, Web. 19 Dec. 2010.

Virginia, Mary Elizabeth. *Richard Henry Lee of Virginia: A Biography*. Ph.D. Dissertation, State University of New York-Buffalo, 1992.

Wernick, Robert. "Chief Justice Marshall takes the law in hand: upsetting presidents and setting precedents, he helped forge a nation." *Smithsonian*, November 1998: 156+.

White, G. Edward. "Reassessing John Marshall," *William and Mary Quarterly* 2001 58(3): 673–693.

Wood, Gordon S. *The Americanization of Benjamin Franklin*. New York: The Penguin Press, 2004.

———. *Revolutionary Characters: What Made the Founders Different*, New York: Penguin Press, 2006.

———. "1801: Adams appoints Marshall: critical decisions by the Chief Justice saved the Supreme Court's independence—and made possible its wide-ranging role today." *American Heritage*, Winter 2010: 40+.

Index